Beyond Liberation Theology

Beyond Liberation Theology: A Polemic

Ivan Petrella

scm press

British Library Cataloguing in Publication data

A catalogue record for this book is available
from the British Library

978 0 334 04134 4

First published in 2008 by SCM Press
13–17 Long Lane,
London EC1A 9PN

www.scm-canterburypress.co.uk

SCM Press is a division of
SCM-Canterbury Press Ltd

Typeset by Regent Typesetting, London
Printed and bound in Great Britain by
William Clowes Ltd, Beccles, Suffolk

Contents

Acknowledgements

Many people contributed to this book in one way or another. Many thanks to: Thia Cooper who read every word; Jeannine Hill Fletcher, Grace Kao, Michelle Gonzalez Maldonado, Irene Oh and Savita Vega for their comments on parts of the manuscript; Stephen Sapp and David Kling for their support; Dexter 'Dr D' Callender for lunch and much more; Maruja; my folks always, el Tincho too; Javi, one and a half years old, for being the only one to recognize me on TV; Karele now a mother of two, Luqui (the real courage is the courage to abandon the PhD, a courage he didn't have), el Gordo; Xavier (dead or crippled) Pardo; Kristin 'meow' Dennis, Barbara Laing for making SCM such a wonderful press to work with and for making this book and the *Reclaiming Liberation Theology* series possible; and Karina and Marcelo Chechik for letting me use their 'Journey to the Promised Land' on the cover.

Series Editors' Preface

Liberation theologies are the most important theological movement of our time. In the twentieth century their influence shook the Third and First Worlds, grass-root organizations and the affluent Western academy, as well as the lives of priests and laypeople persecuted and murdered for living out their understanding of the Christian message. In the twenty-first their insights and goals remain – unfortunately – as valid as ever.

Liberation theologies are born from the struggles of the poor and the oppressed, struggles that were translated into an epistemological break with the whole of the Western theological tradition; that is, they are not one theological school among others in the canon. Instead, they sought and seek a new understanding of theology itself. The basis of that new understanding is the attempt to do theology from the perspective of the oppressed majority of humankind. Here lies the epistemological break: liberation theologians – whether Latin American, black, womanist, African, feminist, queer, etc. – realize that theology has traditionally been done from a standpoint of privilege. Western theology is the product of a minority of humankind living in a state of affluent exception and enjoying gender, sexual, and racial dominance. Oppression and poverty remain the norm for the majority of the world's population. By grounding themselves in the perspective of the oppressed, therefore, liberation theologies come as close as possible to being the first truly global theologies.

This series recovers the heart and soul of liberation theology by focusing on authors who ground their work in the perspective of the majority of the world's poor. This need not mean that the authors are solely located in the Third World; it is widely recognized that the First World/Third World distinction is today social as well as geographical. What matters is not the location of one's physical space but the perspective from which theology is done. *Reclaiming Liberation Theology* is the first to present the writings of a new generation of thinkers grounded in the liberationist tradition to the wider public. As such, this is the venue for the most radical, innovative, and important theological work produced today.

Liberation theologies were born with the promise of being theologies that would not rest with talking about liberation and instead would actually further liberation. Let us hope that they will one day no longer be necessary.

Marcella Althaus-Reid
Ivan Petrella

Introduction

In August 1975 the 'Theology in the Americas' conference was held in Detroit. It was an exceptional gathering that brought together major figures of the American theological landscape – by which I mean the Americas as a whole – including, among others, Gustavo Gutiérrez and James Cone, Hugo Assmann and Rosemary Radford Ruether, Juan Luis Segundo and Deotis Roberts, Enrique Dussel and Gregory Baum. To read the proceedings is to be transported to a different time, a time giddy in the hope that the theological transformation brought about by liberation theology would also change society.[1] Passion, urgency, at times anger, emerges from discussions framed around the question 'What would constitute a "theology in the Americas"?'[2] While this question, and the many answers posed, obviously deeply mattered to liberation theology's founding figures, whether Latin American, black, feminist, Chicano, native American or white, it is no longer asked. The purpose of this book is to ask it again.

To ask this question, however, I must counter dominant trends in both scholarship on liberation theology and the current theologies themselves: scholarship focuses on individual liberation theologies while the liberation theologies themselves concentrate on the particular community from which each arises. Neither, therefore, fosters a dialogue between and across the various present-day liberation theologies.[3] In reflecting upon 'Theology in the Americas,' Robert McAfee

---

1 Other notable participants included Avery Dulles, Monika Hellwig, José Miranda, Frederick Herzog, José Miguez Bonino, Leonardo Boff, Beatriz Melano Couch, Beverly Harrison, Robert McAfee Brown and Phillip Berryman. For the proceedings, see Sergio Torres and John Eagleson (eds), *Theology in the Americas*, Maryknoll, NY: Orbis Books, 1976 and Cornel West, Caridad Guidote, and Margaret Coakley (eds), *Theology in the Americas: Detroit II Conference Papers*, Maryknoll, NY: Orbis Books, 1982.

2 Robert McAfee Brown, 'A Preface and a Conclusion', in Sergio Torres and John Eagleson (eds), *Theology in the Americas*, Maryknoll, NY: Orbis Books, 1976, p. xviii.

3 For an example of Black/Hispanic dialogue which serves as an exception, see Anthony Pinn and Benjamín Valentín (eds), *The Ties That Bind: African American and Hispanic American/Latino/a Theologies in Dialogue*, New York: Continuum, 2001. This book, however, seeks to expand the dialogue further; indeed, as will become clear, past theology itself.

Brown stressed that it must be a combination of particularity and global vision. On the one hand, he wrote, blacks are going to have to develop their theology together, while women were going to have to develop their feminist theology together, and so on. On the other hand, however, Brown suggested that the many contexts must be related to one another since none exists in isolation: 'Each struggle for liberation is finally related to all other struggles for liberation; differing initial agendas may help to establish self-identity and self-worth, but all agendas, if authentic, will gradually converge.'[4] The tendency toward particularity emerges, of course, from liberation theology's stress on the contextual nature of the theological enterprise. My approach too will be contextual, no one can escape context, but it will be contextual of American liberation theology as a whole; that is, I will think across particular liberation theologies to reveal the overarching context within which a liberation theologian of any stripe must work. In the process I surely overlook many important differences, collapse many perspectives, and silence many voices, but I do so to reveal what I see as the central framework that must unite liberation theologies as they face the future.

I understand this book, in its entirety, as a necessary preface to future liberation theology. It shows what American liberation theologians – liberation theologians in the Americas – must recognize, about the state of the world and their discourse, to do theology properly in the early half of the twenty-first century. The argument develops in the following fashion: Chapter 1 presents the global socio-economic context within which a liberation theologian works. This context is yours independently of whether you live in the First or Third Worlds; it is inescapable. The defining mark of the current global context is the spread of zones of social abandonment, or 'Vita', where those for whom the reigning social order finds no use are left to die. The chapter has three parts. In the first, I show that at the heart of Vita lies idolatry; our modern world is not secular, it is idolatrous; in the second, I show that the institutions that govern the global order are the incarnations of the idolatrous logic at Vita's root; finally, in the third, I paint a portrait of the world as a zone of social abandonment, the world as Vita. The chapter also presents the type of analysis that should become commonplace within liberation theology. Readers familiar with liberation theology will notice that the display of the mechanisms by which idolatry rules is made much more concrete through my analysis of the World Trade Organization (WTO) and the agreements through which

---

4 McAfee Brown, 'A Preface and a Conclusion', p. xix.

the parameters of global economic governance are set. For the critique of idolatry to be effective it must be as specific as possible, otherwise it remains at the level of vague denunciations and dismissed as such.

Chapter 2 presents the national socio-economic context within which US liberation theologians – black, Hispanic/Latino(a) and womanist – work. I argue that the national and global contexts are essentially the same; the wealthiest and most powerful nation in the world is no stranger to Vita. Quite the contrary, zones of social abandonment spread in the USA as well. This chapter opens an argument that is currently taboo within US theologies; indeed, within the bulk of US political discourse in general, that it is in fact possible to rank types of oppression and that in such a ranking class emerges as primary. Let me stress, I strongly believe that oppressions based on race, gender, and sexuality are important. But I equally strongly believe that poor blacks suffer more than middle-class blacks, that poor women suffer more than middle-class women and so forth. And that liberation theology cannot be a liberation theology unless issues of class are at the forefront. As such, I recover the primacy of class for liberationist discourse.

Chapter 3 examines the American theological context within which a liberation theologian works. I argue that liberation theologians throughout the Americas share the same theological context, an inability to deal successfully with their material context. A liberation theologian works within a theological context in which there is a proliferation of liberation theologies of different stripes, yet they are all incapable of dealing with the spread of zones of social abandonment. Their incapacity, moreover, stems from their lack of attention to issues of economics and class. Here I reveal and dissect what I call the 'debilitating conditions' – monochromatism, amnesia, gigantism and naiveté – that reduce liberation theology to a theology for the middle class. Unless this situation is remedied, Cornel West's warning to black theology's pale vision of liberation applies across the board:

> It roughly equates liberation with American middle class status, leaving the unequal distribution of wealth relatively untouched . . . Liberation would consist of including Black people within the mainstream of liberal capitalist America. If this is the social vision of Black theologians, they should drop the meretricious and flamboyant term 'liberation' and adopt the more accurate and sober word 'inclusion'.[5]

---

5 Cornel West, 'Black Theology and Marxist Thought', in James Cone and Gayraud

The final chapter opens with the frustrated musings of prominent liberation theologians. Indeed, to find dissatisfaction with liberation theology's present state you need not turn to outside critics; they can be found within the guild. In response, I argue that liberation theology must recover the rebellious spirit of its youth and once again rebel. This time, however, it must rebel against itself. Not one merely to criticize, I mark the path of rebellion with a series of signposts that contest the established and paralysing pieties that plague liberationist discourse. To walk this road, I believe, is to move beyond liberation theology as it currently stands.

Wilmore (eds), *Black Theology: A Documentary History, Vol. I 1966–1979*, Maryknoll, NY: Orbis Books, 1993, p. 413.

The Global Material Context
of the Liberation Theologian:
The Poverty of the Majority

I visited a little Catholic community center in Windhoek, Namibia, in February. It was a place where people living with AIDS could network, find a support group, have a meal, try to earn some money through an income generating project. What was the project in this instance? The sister running the center took me out back to show me. A group of men were making miniature papier mache coffins for infants, and as they affixed the silver handles, they said to me with a mixture of pride and anguish: 'We can't keep up with the demand.'

Stephen Lewis, UN envoy to Africa[1]

The history of modern thought is a storehouse of images, metaphors and stories that seek to describe and explain the abject state of our world. What best captures the miserable material context within which a liberation theologian must work? Karl Barth's *The Epistle to the Romans*, for example, includes a beautiful reflection on the knowledge acquired when Adam and Eve ate the forbidden fruit from the fateful tree. The tree governed the knowledge of the infinite difference between us and God, 'men ought not to know that they are merely – men . . . So long as ignorance prevailed, the Lord walked freely in the garden in the cool of the day, as though in the equality of friendship.'[2] Barth reads Michelangelo's 'Creation of Eve' as a reflection on the consequences of the knowledge born of our first betrayal:

in the fullness of her charm and beauty she rises slowly, posing herself in the fatal attitude of – worship. Notice the Creator's warning

---

1 Cited in Paul Davis and Meredith Fort, 'The Battle Against Global Aids', *Sickness and Wealth: The Corporate Assault on Global Health*, Sickness and Wealth, Cambridge, MA: South End Press, 2004, p. 146.

2 Karl Barth, *The Epistle to the Romans*, trans. Edwyn C. Hoskyns, Oxford: Oxford University Press, 1968, p. 247.

arm and careworn, saddened eyes, as He replies to Eve's gesture of adoration . . . When men stretch out their hands and touch the link which binds them to God, when they touch the tree *in the midst of the garden*, which ought not to be touched, they are by this presumptuous contact separated from Him . . . With open eyes they see that they are separated from God and – naked.[3]

Insofar as we worship God, we are separated from God and thus unable to be truly at peace with ourselves. The root of religion lies in the separation that makes God an object to be worshipped; indeed, the incarnation can be understood as God's attempt, through Christ, once again to share our humanity and walk with us as an equal, as friend, rather than objectified Lord. Here the expulsion and separation from God is the root of our ills.

The expulsion from the garden, however, 'Cursed be the ground because of you/By toil shall you eat of it/All the days of your life', separated us not only from God, but also from nature, and ultimately from each other.[4] When the initial unity between humanity and nature is broken, we no longer recognize ourselves as part of nature. Humanity now faces nature as an entity which must be struggled against to survive. In the process, however, we too become things to be organized and controlled for the most efficient manipulation of nature. Control over nature cannot be disentangled from control over persons.

Georges Bataille makes this the starting point for his understanding of sacrifice, the ritual destruction of what is useful, as a rebellion against a world in which everything is judged by its utility. For him,

> the first labor established the world of *things*, to which the profane world of the Ancients generally corresponds. Once the world of things was posited, man himself became one of the things of the world, at least for the time in which he labored. It is this degradation that man has always tried to escape. In his strange myths, in his cruel rites, man is *in search of a lost intimacy* from the first.[5]

Similarly, Martin Heidegger saw the essence of technology as the process by which subjects are turned into objects: 'agriculture is now motorized food industry – in essence the same as the manufacturing of corpses in gas chambers and extermination camps, the same as the blockading and starving of nations, the same as the manufacture of

---

3 Barth, *Romans*, pp. 247–8.
4 Genesis 3.17
5 Georges Bataille, *The Accursed Share*, Vol. 1, New York: Zone Books, 1991, p. 57.

hydrogen bombs.'[6] In this light, the Heideggerian call for a return to our dwelling or abode is a call to escape our fate as commodities and human resources.

For Max Weber, the melancholy fate of our time is threefold: disenchantment, the inability to measure up to workday existence, and the turn to material goods as compensation for the *pianissimo* of our lives within capitalism.[7] We are not the Puritans of the Protestant ethic, 'the Puritan wanted to work in a calling; we are forced to do so . . . In Baxter's view the care for external goods should only lie on the shoulders of the "saint like a light cloak, which can be thrown aside at any moment." But fate decreed that the cloak should become an iron cage.'[8] Weber's iron cage is perhaps the most famous metaphor used to describe our status as objects in the contemporary world. But it is not the only one.

Equally unsettling is Michel Foucault's vision of a disciplinary society based on Jeremy Bentham's design for a prison, the Panopticon. The Panopticon is designed as a circular building with a surveillance tower in the middle. Inmates are housed in individual cells, isolated from everything but the tower. The tower sees everything, the inmates see nothing. The design thus functions as a round-the-clock surveillance machine ensuring that no prisoner can ever see the 'inspector' who conducts surveillance from the privileged central location within the radial configuration. The prisoner could never know when he was being watched – mental uncertainty that in itself would prove to be a crucial instrument of discipline. For Foucault, the Panopticon is a metaphor for a wider society that through institutions such as schools, hospitals, factories, and of course prisons, as well as disciplines such as the social sciences, moulds individuals that can function in a social order that needs them to be objects for production. The iron cage, therefore, is no longer necessary within a society organized around panopticism: 'it is not that the beautiful totality of the individual is amputated, repressed, altered by our social order, it is rather that the individual is carefully fabricated in it, according to a whole technique of forces and bodies.'[9] We are shaped into, as Foucault puts it, docile bodies.

---

6 Cited in Richard Bernstein, *The New Constellation: The Ethical-Political Horizons of Modernity/Postmodernity*, Cambridge, MA: MIT Press, 1992, p. 130.

7 See Max Weber, *The Protestant Ethic and the Spirit of Capitalism*, trans. Talcott Parsons, foreword by R. H. Tawney, New York: Scribner's, 1958, p. 181. *Pianissimo*, a musical term that means to play very softly, is used by Weber in 'Science as Vocation', in H. H. Gerth and C. Wright Mills (eds and trans), *From Max Weber: Essays in Sociology*, New York: Oxford University Press, 1958, p. 155.

8 Weber, *Protestant Ethic*, p. 181.

9 Michel Foucault, *Discipline and Punishment: The Birth of the Prison*, trans. Alan Sheridan, New York: Vintage-Random House, 1979, p. 217.

These are just a few examples of the images that haunt recent think-ing. For all these giants of modern thought the culprit of our world's abject state is a seemingly inexorable drive toward the objectification of God, nature, and ourselves. None of these metaphors, however, truly captures the current state of our world. They bemoan our objectifica-tion and ache with nostalgia for a time before we were objects. But they don't fully recognize objectification's ultimate outcome – unjust, premature, death. I suspect this is no coincidence. Located both intel-lectually and geographically in the rich world, these thinkers come from a context of affluence; the suffering they speak to is real and painful, yet rarely life threatening. To witness the link between objec-tification and death you need to turn to the reality of the Third/Two-Thirds World.[10] And so the image I'll use here, fittingly, comes from a witness, an anthropologist.[11]

The image is Vita, a zone of social abandonment. Vita is both a place and a practice. As a place in Southern Brazil near Porto Alegre, Vita is 'situated on a hill of absolute misery, overcrowded, with tents, a wooden chapel, and an inadequate kitchen, and no hot water or bath-room facilities'.[12] Vita is an infirmary and recovery centre,

---

10 Achille Mbembe, for example, writing from the context of Africa, is well aware of the connection between death and objectification. In the context of colonization, objec-tification is taken to the extreme: 'The colonized does not exist as a self; the colonized *is*, but in the same way as a rock *is* – that is, as nothing more . . . The colonized belongs to the universe of immediate things – useful things when needed, things that can be molded and are mortal, futile and superfluous things, if need be.' In the African context, objectification always flirts with death: 'What distinguishes our age from previous ages, the breach over which there is apparently no going back, the absolute split our times breaks up the spirit and splits it into many, is again contingent, dispersed, and powerless existence: existence that is contingent, dispersed and powerless but reveals itself in the guise of arbitrariness and the absolute power to give death any time, anywhere, by any means, and for any reason . . . and thereby permits power to be exercised as a right to kill and invests Africa with deaths at once at the heart of every age and above time.' The existence of the colonized is recognized insofar as they are useful or being killed. Out-side these spheres of objectification and death, their lives have no meaning. See Achille Mbembe, *On the Postcolony*, Berkeley: University of California Press, 2001, pp. 187 and 13 respectively.

Let me add that I'm aware of the criticisms that the notion of a 'Third World' has received. But I find the fact that it highlights a position of inferiority useful. At the same time, the term Two-Thirds World is useful because it stresses that those in a position of inferiority happen to be the majority of the world's population.

11 In what follows I draw from João Biehl, *Vita: Life in a Zone of Social Abandon-ment*, Berkeley: University of California Press, 2005 and 'Vita: Life in a Zone of Social Abandonment', *Social Text* 19.3, Fall 2001, pp. 131–48. I find the article more compel-ling than the book.

12 Biehl, *Vita*, p. 35 and Biehl, 'Vita', p. 132.

the infirmary was separated from the recovery area by a gate, policed by volunteers who made sure that the sickest would not freely move around the hill. The sickest of Vita wandered around the dust of their lot, rolled on the ground, crouched over and under their beds – when they had beds. Each one was alone, most were silent . . . Scratching bugs and scabs away, spitting, coughing, only a few even looked at us in the infirmary. There was no apparent aggression. Still, we thought, they must plan to leave. But when some do manage to escape, they beg, humiliated, to return. There is no other place for them to go.[13]

With no place to go, the centre itself is surrounded by a slum known as the 'village' built, shack by shack, by those who have passed through the recovery centre. Vita grows outward, 'it's the deposit of life's left-overs', a repository of 'unclaimed lives in terminal desolation'.[14] As a zone of social abandonment, it's the place where those who have no one and nothing wait for death – 'a place in the world for populations of "ex-humans"'.[15]

As a practice, Vita carries the objectification of human beings to the extreme. Vita was born when a former street kid and drug dealer, Ze das Drogas, converted to Pentecostalism and had a vision in which he was commanded to create a refuge where those like him could make their lives anew. Soon, however, 'an increasing number of homeless, mentally ill, and dying persons began to be dumped there by the police, by psychiatric and general hospitals, by families and neighbors'.[16] The practice of dumping human beings, in the same way that you can dump trash, lies behind Vita's existence as a place. To be dumped like trash is to be socially dead; society declares you dead before your biological death. Insofar as you are socially dead yet biologically alive, you've overextended your lease on life. Your future is dead, yet you live on. Society, therefore, creates and sustains this zone of social abandon-ment: 'Family, city, and state institutions were complicit with that precarious existence, and they kept bringing diseased, criminal, and abandoned bodies to die in Vita.'[17] It is the practice of 'socially author-ized death, mundane and unaccounted for' in which society rejects its weakest and most helpless members.[18] Despite the fact that Vita itself

13 Biehl, 'Vita', p. 133.
14 Biehl, 'Vita', pp. 131 and 133.
15 Biehl, 'Vita', p. 142.
16 Biehl, 'Vita', p. 131.
17 Biehl, 'Vita', p. 132.
18 Biehl, Vita, p. 38 and 'Vita', p. 134.

is located at the outer edge of society, its practice of dumping those who are socially dead is not an aberration, but part of the normal working of society itself. Dying at Vita is 'constituted in the interaction of modern human institutions. These institutions and Vita are in fact symbiotic: they make death's job easier.'[19]

This chapter develops from the suggestion that Vita as a place is a metaphor for the globe as a whole, and, more importantly, Vita as a practice is a metaphor for all the ways the global order leaves the poorest to die. As the tango 'Las cuarenta' put it, 'y se que con mucha plata, uno vale mucho mas'.[20] I will suggest that the global material context within which a liberation theologian works is today best understood as a zone of social abandonment, while the organizing practice or logic behind that material context is the creation of zones of social abandonment. The chapter will be divided in three parts: first, I explicate the logic behind the creation of zones of social abandonment. I suggest that at the heart of Vita, and in fact, at the heart of objectification, lies the liberationist understanding of idolatry. Idolatry lies at the heart of the process of objectification and is the master key to understanding why melancholy images populate modern thought. Second, I show that the institutions that govern the global order are the incarnations of the idolatrous logic at Vita's root. Finally, I present the tragic upshot – the world as a zone of social abandonment.

The Logic That Rules: Idolatry and Vita

The basis of Vita, the place, is Vita, the practice – an idolatrous logic which makes the market the ultimate judge of the value of every human life. This claim is key to the way I understand liberation theology throughout the work, so let me take some time to explain. My analysis is grounded in liberation philosophy and liberation theology's conviction that the reproduction of human life is a universal philosophical and theological precondition for any normative judgement.[21] Both

---

19 Biehl, 'Vita', p. 134.

20 'Las cuarenta', 1937. 'I know that with money, one is worth much more.' Lyrics by Francisco Gorrindo, music by Roberto Grela.

21 While central to liberation theology and liberation philosophy as a whole, this notion is most developed in Franz Hinkelammert, Enrique Dussel and, more recently, Jung Mo Sung's work. For a sampling of Hinkelammert, see José Duque and German Gutiérrez, *Itinerarios de la Razon Crítica: Homenaje a Franz Hinkelammert en Sus 70 Años*, San José: DEI, 2001; Franz Hinkelammert, *El Grito del Sujeto*, San José, Costa Rica: DEI, 1998; *Cultura de la Esperanza y Sociedad sin Exclusión*, San José, Costa Rica: DEI, 1995; *Crítica a la Razon Utópica*, San José: DEI, 1990; *Las Armas Ideologicas de la Muerte; el Discernimiento de los Fetiches: Capitalismo y Cristianismo,*

schools of thought, arguably the most important philosophical and theological movements to emerge from the Third/Two-Thirds World, arise from a context in which life is negotiable and precarious. At the heart of their thinking thus lies the defence of the value of human life, which is understood to be non-negotiable. Although this work deals with liberation theology, I'll begin by saying a few words about liberation philosophy and so provide the reader with a wider sense of the traditions that shape my thinking.

For liberation philosophy, life itself isn't a goal, but rather underlies the possibility of having goals. Life, as Dussel explains, exists within strict limits and demands specific contents:

> if the planet's temperature rises, we die of heat; if we can't drink because of desertification – like is happening in sub-Saharan Africa – we die of thirst; if we can't feed ourselves, we die of hunger . . . Human Life sets limits, requires a normative order, has its own demands. It also sets contents: life needs food, housing, security, liberty, sovereignty, cultural identity and values, spiritual plenitude.[22]

A person lives his or her life within a context that cannot be violated without danger of death. Goals, therefore, are determined from within the context of needs that human life demands for its survival and development. The reproduction of life isn't an ethical norm; life, in fact, precedes all such norms.

In developing this idea, liberation philosophy sets itself against two North Atlantic ethical systems – communitarianism and discourse

Centroamerica: EDUCA, 1977; in English see Franz Hinkelammert, 'Liberation Theology in the Economic and Social Context of Latin America: Economy and Theology, or the Irrationality of the Rationalized', in David Batstone, Eduardo Mendieta, Lois Ann Lorenzten, and Dwight N. Hopkins (eds), *Liberation Theologies, Postmodernity, and the Americas*, New York: Routledge, 1997, pp. 25–52 and *The Ideological Weapons of Death: A Theological Critique of Capitalism*, Maryknoll, NY: Orbis Books, 1986. For Dussel see, Enrique Dussel, *Etica de la Liberación en la Edad de la Globalización y de la Exclusión*, Madrid: Editorial Trotta, 1998; *The Underside of Modernity: Apel, Ricouer, Rorty, Taylor, and the Philosophy of Liberation*, New York: Humanity Books, 1998; *The Invention of the Americas: Eclipse of the 'Other' and the Myth of Modernity*, New York: Continuum, 1995; *Historia de la Filosofía y la Filosofía de la Liberación*, Bogota, Colombia: Editorial Nueva America, 1994. For Sung consult, Jung Mo Sung, *Deseo, Mercado y Religion*, Santander: Editorial Sal Terrae, 1999; *Neoliberalismo y Pobreza*, San José, Costa Rica: DEI, 1993; *La Idolatría del Capital y la Muerte de los Pobres*, San José, Costa Rica: DEI, 1991. Also relevant, Hugo Assmann, *La Idolatría del Mercado*, San José, Costa Rica: DEI, 1997 and *Economía y Religión*, San José, Costa Rica: DEI, 1994.

22 Dussel, *Etica de la Liberación*, p. 129; translation my own.

ethics.[23] Take, for example, communitarianism.[24] Communitarians oppose liberal ethical theories that believe it's possible to come up with norms that are independent of time and place.[25] Instead, they believe that there are multiple ethical traditions, based on different cultures, that are worthy of dignity and respect. Norms, however, are relative to particular traditions, and the traditions themselves are incommensurable – one cannot be translated into another. As a result it's not possible to have a rational debate between traditions, so debates remain internal to those traditions. To support these claims communitarians recover the history of culturally situated ethical traditions and through this process aim to correct ethical perspectives that blindly

---

23 By North Atlantic I mean Western European and United Statesian. I prefer 'United Statesian' to 'North American'. As Justo Gonzalez writes, 'Even the name "America" raises the question: What preposterous conceit allows the inhabitants of a single country to take for themselves the name of an entire hemisphere? What does this say about the country's view of other nations who share the hemisphere with it?' Justo Gonzalez, *Mañana: Christian Theology from a Hispanic Perspective*, Nashville: Abingdon Press, 1990, p. 37. I did not coin the term itself, but have been unable to recover the reference.

24 For communitarianism's most influential texts see Alasdair MacIntyre's, *Whose Justice? Whose Rationality?*, Notre Dame, Indiana: University of Notre Dame Press, 1988 and *After Virtue: A Study in Moral Theory*, Notre Dame, Indiana: University of Notre Dame Press, 1981; Charles Taylor's, *The Ethics of Authenticity*, Cambridge, MA: Harvard University Press, 1992 and *Sources of the Self: The Making of Modern Identity*, Cambridge, MA: Harvard University Press, 1989; as well as Michael Walzer, *Spheres of Justice: A Defense of Pluralism and Equality*, New York, NY: Basic Books, 1983.

25 As such, liberal ethical systems ignore the point made by Marx's critique of Feuerbach in his 'Contribution to the Critique of Hegel's *Philosophy of Right*: Introduction', – 'man is not an abstract being, squatting outside the world. Man is the human world, the state, society.' Robert Tucker (ed.), *The Marx-Engels Reader*, New York, NY: W.W. Norton & Company, 1978, p. 53. The most famous attempt to base ethics on an 'abstract being' remains John Rawls, *A Theory of Justice*, Cambridge, MA: Harvard University Press, 1971. In this classic, Rawls imagines a 'veil of ignorance' behind which a person is ignorant of his/her gender, race, nationality, class status, etc. Norms derived from within the veil are believed to be just. In particular, Rawls imagines two such norms, the principle of equal liberty and the difference principle. In the former, each person has an equal right to the most extensive liberties compatible with similar liberties for all; in the latter, social and economic inequalities should be arranged so that they are to the greatest benefit of the least advantaged persons. In my mind, Dussel's critique of the difference principle hits the nail on the head. Rawls fails to explain why, if the first principle stresses political equality, the difference principle assumes economic and social inequality. The difference principle implicitly assumes that some people are workers, while others are owners of capital; that is, Rawls takes as universal what is in reality a historical relationship – that of labour and capital – that is particular to a capitalist market economy. In this case, therefore, the veil failed. See Dussel, *Etica de la Liberación*, pp. 174–80 and endnotes 67 and 80 on pages 220 and 221. In his later work Rawls moves away from his attempt to ground ethics through the original position and 'political liberalism' applies only to modern Western liberal democracies, not to abstract man. Rawls essentially becomes a communitarian. See most notably John Rawls, *Political Liberalism*, New York, NY: Columbia University Press, 2005.

universalize a Eurocentric ethos. In practice, however, communitarian thought remains hostage to Aristotle and Hegel; their espousal of cultural difference fails to see beyond the dominant Eurocentric history of philosophy which moves from Greece to Europe then to be joined also by the United States.[26] In addition, while communitarians focus on history, the concrete good given in a culture, and different spheres of justice, at no point do they recognize that all these elements, even in different cultures, are based upon the common reality which is physical human life itself. Their focus is on cultural reproduction which, while central to all human life, must still be based on the reproduction of the material needs necessary to physical existence.

Discourse ethics agrees with communitarianism that there can be no consensus on conceptions of the good as opposed to the right.[27] Unlike communitarianism, however, a discourse ethics claims that in the very act of communication lie implicit formal conditions that are the basis for an ethics of right. Within communicative action – geared toward mutual understanding – there exist unavoidable presuppositions of dialogue; for example, one assumes that a person is being truthful, that a person can talk freely, that they are in no way coerced, that there is unrestricted access to the conversation, and that the force of the better argument is to be acknowledged. To deny these conditions is to deny the dialogue; they can't be denied without a performative contradiction. The sceptic cannot deny the conditions because in the very act of arguing he or she assumes their existence; language itself requires these validity claims. Discourse ethics, therefore, finds in language the basis for determining the conditions for valid dialogue. It's when those conditions are given that norms for an ethic of the good

26 This understanding of the history of philosophy is brilliantly dismantled in Dussel, *Etica de la Liberación*, pp. 19–90.

27 Habermas and Apel are the main referents. For a sampling of Habermas, see Jürgen Habermas, *Between Facts and Norms*, Cambridge, MA: Massachusetts Institute of Technology Press, 1996; *The Philosophical Discourse of Modernity: Twelve Lectures*, trans. Frederick Lawrence, Studies in Contemporary German Social Thought, Cambridge, Massachusetts: MIT Press, 1987; *Reason and the Rationalization of Society*, Boston: Beacon Press, 1984, vol. 1 of *Theory of Communicative Action*, trans. Thomas McCarthy; *Lifeworld and System: A Critique of Functionalist Reason*, Boston: Beacon Press, 1987, vol. 2 of *The Theory of Communicative Action*, trans. Thomas McCarthy. For a sampling of Apel see Karl-Otto Apel, *Selected Essays: Ethics and the Theory of Rationality*, New Jersey: Humanities Press, 1996; *Selected Essays: Towards a Transcendental Semiotics*, New Jersey: Humanities Press, 1994; *Understanding and Explanation: A Transcendental-Pragmatic Perspective*, trans. Georgia Warnke, Studies in Contemporary German Social Thought, Cambridge, Massachusetts: MIT Press, 1984; *Towards a Transformation of Philosophy*, trans. Glyn Adey and David Frisby, The International Library of Phenomenology and Moral Sciences, London: Routledge & Kegan Paul, 1980.

can be determined by all interested participants. From the perspective of liberation philosophy, however, the limitations of a discourse ethics emerge when suicide is considered.[28] Imagine that all the conditions for discourse are perfectly given, and the decision arrived at is mass suicide. While meeting all the formal requirements, this decision would eliminate the formal criteria that make discourse valid, as well as, of course, the possibility of discourse itself, and thus would be irrational. At its outer limit, therefore, discourse ethics must assume liberation philosophy's understanding of life as the starting point for all else: 'Liberation philosophy thinks that the "absolute *pragmatic* condition of all argumentation" (therefore of all communication communities) is the *factum* of reason that the "subject be alive" (a *dead* subject can hardly argue).'[29] Life, like discourse ethics' understanding of communicative action, is universal, as well as foundational to the act of communication itself. Yet it resembles the communitarian understanding of the good in dictating contents such as freedom from hunger, thirst, lack of shelter, which cut across cultures and thus are not incommensurable demands.

I now turn to theology. Liberation philosophy's focus on the reproduction of human life as the precondition for all normative claims finds its parallel in liberation theology's understanding of God as a God of life – not an abstract ethereal 'life' but material human life in the flesh.[30] As Matthew stresses in the Gospel: 'for I was hungry and you gave me food, I was thirsty and you gave me something to drink, I was a stranger and you welcomed me, I was naked and you gave me clothing, I was sick and you took care of me, I was in prison and you visited me.'[31] And

---

28 The discussion of suicide in relation to discourse ethics is taken from Duque and Gutiérrez, *Itinerarios*, pp. 110–14.

29 Dussel, *Underside of Modernity*, p. 59.

30 The following draws from Sung, *Idolatría del Capital*, pp. 31–3.

31 Matthew 25.35–46. This remains one of the most powerful passages within the Christian canon and is worth quoting at greater length. 'Then the king will say to those at his right hand, "Come, you that are blessed by my Father, inherit the kingdom prepared for you from the foundation of the world; for I was hungry and you gave me food, I was thirsty and you gave me something to drink, I was a stranger and you welcomed me, I was naked and you gave me clothing, I was sick and you took care of me, I was in prison and you visited me." Then the righteous will answer him, "Lord, when was it that we saw you hungry and gave you food, or thirsty and gave you something to drink? And when was it that we saw you a stranger and welcomed you, or naked and gave you clothing? And when was it that we saw you sick or in prison and visited you?" And the king will answer them, "Truly I tell you, just as you did it to one of the least of these who are members of my family, you did it to me." Then he will say to those at his left hand, "You that are accursed, depart from me into the eternal fire prepared for the devil and his angels; for I was hungry and you gave me no food, I was thirsty and you gave me nothing to drink, I was a stranger and you did not welcome me, naked and you did not give me clothing, sick

as St Irenaeus puts it: '*Gloria Dei vivens homo*.'[32] From God's focus on bodily life, liberation theology derives a unified anthropology and a unified understanding of history. Liberationists see a key difference between a Semitic biblical anthropology that focuses on the bodily nature of persons and a Greek anthropology that sees body and soul as two separate entities in conflict with each other. Thus, for the Greeks, escaping the body was a goal, while in Egypt the body was worshipped and preserved after death. Noting this distinction, liberationists reread the Pauline epistles to argue that for Paul 'body' and 'soul' don't refer to two separate entities but rather are correctly viewed as tendencies within a human being that needs to be understood as a whole. The resurrection, therefore, does not substitute the body but rather gives it life.[33] For Paul, all human existence is bodily; Christ resurrects in his body because there is no life without one.[34] According to Hinkelammert, this is the true scandal of the Christian message: 'The scandal consists of Paul declaring, through the resurrection of the body, the eternity of bodily life in the Greek world for whom eternity is that of ideas and the soul.'[35] The preferential option for the poor is thus based on God's own focus upon those who lack the means to sustain bodily life. Finally, the ideas of a God of life and a unitary anthropology correspond to a unitary vision of history, since to speak of a God of life is also to speak of the concrete conditions for human life within this history. For liberation theology there is no distinction between creation and salvation; history is one.[36] As Gutierrez himself writes, 'the history of salvation is the very heart of human history.'[37]

Liberation theology's God of life stands in opposition to the idols of

---

and in prison and you did not visit me." Then they also will answer, "Lord, when was it that we saw you hungry or thirsty or a stranger or naked or sick or in prison, and did not take care of you?" Then he will answer them, "Truly I tell you, just as you did not do it to one of the least of these, you did not do it to me."' (NRSV)

32 'God's glory is the human being alive.' Cited in Sung, *Idolatría del Capital*, p. 31.

33 See Romans 8.11, 'If the Spirit of him who raised Jesus from the dead dwells in you, he who raised Christ from the dead will give life to your mortal bodies also through his Spirit that dwells in you.' See also Romans 8.23, 'and not only the creation, but we ourselves, who have the first fruits of the Spirit, groan inwardly while we wait for adoption, the redemption of our bodies.' (NRSV)

34 This anthropology is best examined in Enrique Dussel, *El Humanismo Semita*, Buenos Aires: Eudeba, 1969. Sung's discussion takes place in *Idolatría del Capital*, p. 32.

35 Hinkelammert, *Armas Ideológicas*, p. 100.

36 Sung cites the following from Gutiérrez: 'Creation is presented in the Bible, not as a stage previous to salvation, but as part of the salvific process.' Gustavo Gutiérrez, *A Theology of Liberation: History, Politics and Salvation*, trans. and ed. Sister Caridad Inda and John Eagleson, Maryknoll, New York: Orbis, 1973, p. 154.

37 Gutiérrez, *Theology of Liberation*, p. 153.

death.[38] An idol is a god to whom lives are sacrificed. Are there idols today? I answer, yes. The most infamous example of the idolatry behind the creation of zones of social abandonment lies in a memo written by Larry Summers while he was the World Bank's Chief Economist and Vice-President for Development Economics.[39] In the memo, Summers presents the economic logic behind the dumping of polluting industries in the poorest parts of the globe. There are three parts to the argument, lets look at each in turn: He argues,

> the measurements of the cost of health impairing pollution depends on the foregone earnings from increased morbidity and mortality. From this point of view a given amount of health impairing pollution should be done in the country with the lowest wages. I think the economic logic behind dumping a load of toxic waste in the lowest wage country is impeccable and we should face up to that.[40]

The reasoning is simple. If one were to place toxic waste in a rich country it would lead to the illness and death of wealthy people with high life-expectancy. A citizen of the United States or Europe contributes $20,000 per year in gross national product while an inhabitant of one of the lowest-wage countries contributes a paltry $360 per year. If both are 40 years old, the wealthier of the two can be expected to work for at least 25 more years during which he will contribute a total of $500,000 to the global economy. The poor person at 40, on the other hand, will likely work for only 15 more years to muster a mere $5,400. In economic terms, the lives of the wealthy are far more important to the workings of the global economy than the lives of the poor: 'thus it is indeed economically logical that illness and death should occur in places where the foregone earnings will be the least.'[41]

---

38 See Pablo Richard *et al.*, *The Idols of Death and the God of Life*, Maryknoll, New York: Orbis Books, 1983.

39 Summers then left the bank to become the undersecretary of the Treasury for the Clinton administration. He later became president of Harvard University, and now has recently resigned over a series of scandals. I quote the memo from William Tabb, *Unequal Partners: A Primer on Globalization*, New York: The New Press, 2002, pp. 48–9 but take the analysis from the excellent Susan George and Fabrizio Sabelli, *Faith and Credit: The World Bank's Secular Empire*, Boulder, CO: Westview, 1994, chapter 5.

40 Tabb, *Unequal Partners*, p. 48.

41 Sabelli and George also note that if the rich person 'sustained health damage due to toxic waste, s/he would also be more likely to possess the cultural know how and financial capacity to sue the companies that dumped it. This could cost them dearly in legal damages, thereby reducing their profits.' The poor person, however, 'is unlikely to worry the company much in case of toxic disaster, as the victims of Union Carbide's plant

Summers continues:

the costs of pollution are likely to be non-linear as the initial incre-
ments of pollution probably have very low cost. I've always thought
that under-populated countries in Africa are vastly UNDER-
polluted; their air quality is probably vastly inefficiently low compared to Los Angeles or Mexico City. Only the lamentable facts
that so much pollution is generated by non-tradable industries and
that the unit costs of solid waste are so high prevent world welfare
enhancing trade in air pollution and waste.[42]

In under-populated countries, where people aren't concentrated in
small places (as they are in Europe, for example) it will take a longer
time for the additional pollution to have any noticeable effect; thus
his claim that air pollution in under-populated countries is 'vastly
inefficiently low'.
He concludes:

the demand for a clean environment for aesthetic and health reasons
is likely to have very high income elasticity. The concern over an
agent that causes a one in a million change in the odds of prostate cancer is obviously going to be much higher in a country where
people survive to get prostate cancer than in a country where under
5 mortality is 200 per thousand. Also, much of the concern over
industrial atmosphere discharge is about visibility impairing partic-
ulates. These discharges have very little direct health impact. Clearly
trade in goods that embody aesthetic pollution concerns could be
welfare enhancing.[43]

---

in Bhopal can readily testify.' George and Sabelli, *Faith and Credit*, p. 99. For Zygmunt
Bauman: 'The production of "human waste", or more correctly wasted humans (the "excessive" and "redundant", that is the population of those who either could not or were
not wished to be recognized or allowed to stay), is an inevitable outcome of modernization, and an inescapable accompaniment of modernity. It is an inescapable side-effect of
order-building (each order casts some part of the extant population as "out of place",
"unfit", or "undesirable") and of *economic progress* (that cannot proceed without degrading and devaluing the previously effective modes of "making a living" and therefore
cannot but deprive their practitioners of their livelihood).' Zygmunt Bauman, *Wasted
Lives: Modernity and Its Outcasts*, Cambridge: Polity Press, 2004, p. 5. Let me stress
that I don't subscribe to the belief that modernization or modernity *inevitably* leads to
the production of human waste. The bulk of this chapter, as you'll see, is devoted to
describing the concrete mechanisms that produce waste. The mechanisms are concrete,
they can be changed – there is nothing in the essence of 'modernization' that leads to
human waste.
42 Tabb, *Unequal Partners*, pp. 48–9.
43 Tabb, *Unequal Partners*, p. 49.

Here Summers makes two main points: on the one hand, the more money you have the more you can worry about pollution; and, on the other hand, the more money you have the more you actually should worry about pollution. Men in poor countries can worry less about getting prostate cancer for the simple fact that they will probably not live long enough to get the disease in the first place. Men in rich countries, however, live longer, and are therefore at greater risk of contracting the disease, a risk that is even greater if they're exposed to toxins found in pollution. In poor countries the demand for pure air is just not as high as it is in rich countries, and neither is the cash to be able to buy clean air if it were an option.[44]

Now remember Vita. How is it that people come to be defined as trash, as something to be dumped? Implicit is a ranking of lives, some lives are worth more than others:

> The *abandonados* in Vita are the carriers and witnesses of the ways in which the social destinies of the poorest and sickest are ordered . . . Those occupying the upper strata of society not only live longer;

---

44 George and Sabelli, *Faith and Credit*, p. 100. A piece from *The New York Times*, 'Global Sludge Ends in Tragedy for Ivory Coast', provides an example of Summers' reasoning in practice. The paper reports: 'It was his infant son's cries, gasping and insistent, that first woke Salif Oudrawogol one night last month. The smell hit him moments later, wafting into the family's hut, a noxious mélange reminiscent of rotten eggs, garlic and petroleum. Mr. Oudrawogol went outside to investigate. Beside the family's compound, near his manioc and corn fields, he saw a stinking slick of black sludge. "The smell was so bad we were afraid," Mr. Oudrawogol said. "It burned our noses and eyes." Over the next few days, the skin of his 6-month-old son, Salam, bloomed with blisters, which burst into weeping sores all over his body. The whole family suffered headaches, nosebleeds and stomach aches. How that slick, a highly toxic cocktail of petrochemical waste and caustic soda, ended up in Mr. Oudrawogol's backyard in a suburb north of Abidjan is a dark tale of globalization. It came from a Greek-owned tanker flying a Panamanian flag and leased by the London branch of a Swiss trading corporation whose fiscal headquarters are in the Netherlands. Safe disposal in Europe would have cost about $300,000, or perhaps twice that, counting the cost of delays. But because of decisions and actions made not only here but also in Europe, it was dumped on the doorstep of some of the world's poorest people. So far eight people have died, dozens have been hospitalized and 85,000 have sought medical attention, paralysing the fragile health care system in a country divided and impoverished by civil war, and the crisis has forced a government shakeup. "In 30 years of doing this kind of work I have never seen anything like this," said Jean-Loup Quéru, an engineer with a French cleanup company brought in by the Ivorian government to remove the waste. "This kind of industrial waste, dumped in this urban setting, in the middle of the city, never." . . . Africa has long been a dumping ground for all sorts of things the developed world has no use for. "This is the underbelly of globalization," said Jim Puckett, an activist at the Basel Action Network, an environmental group that fights toxic waste dumping. "Environmental regulations in the north have made disposing of waste expensive, so corporations look south."' Lydia Polgreen and Marlise Simons, *The New York Times*, 2 October 2006.

their right to live longer is bureaucratically decreed or biomedically ensured through the mechanisms of the market.[45]

Within Vita, as it is with Summers, the market is the judge of the value of a human life: 'if one is no longer useful, one is worth nothing.'[46] As Ze, Vita's founder, puts it: 'Society lets them rot because they don't give anything in return anymore.'[47] The ability to play a part in the market is required for recognition as a member of society. Even within the desolation of a zone of social abandonment, the focus on market worthiness as a prerequisite for a place in society does not disappear. The goal of recovery, therefore, is to 'help them be placed in the market; it is there that they belong'.[48] Yet incapable of producing anything but 'bodily infections, parasites, and silent suffering' its inhabitants are useless.[49] As such, zones of social abandonment are the places 'where living beings go when they are no longer considered people'.[50] Indeed, Vita itself *means life in a dead language*;[51] that is, a language that exists but no longer has any use – just like the people that inhabit its wasteland.

At the heart of Vita, therefore, lies the very same logic exemplified by Summers. Little does it matter that José Lutzenberger, Brazil's secretary of the environment at the time, wrote to Summers: 'Your reasoning is perfectly logical but totally insane ... Your thoughts provide a concrete example of the unbelievable alienation, reductionist thinking, social ruthlessness and the arrogant ignorance of many conventional "economists" concerning the nature of the world we live in.'[52] The more you can consume or produce, the greater your value. Market logic trumps human life. Within this logic, human beings are reduced to objects of greater or lesser worth. Nature, in fact, also falls prey to this logic. An international forestry consultant can analyse the rain forest as follows: 'The important question is how much of this biomass represents trees and parts of trees of preferred species that can be profitably marketed ... by today's utilization standards, most of the trees, in these humid tropical forests, are from an industrial material standpoints, clearly weeds.'[53] Unless it can be marketed, a tree has no

---

45 Biehl, 'Vita', p. 136.
46 Biehl, 'Vita', p. 135.
47 Biehl, *Vita*, p. 41 and 'Vita', p. 135.
48 Biehl, *Vita*, p. 59 and 'Vita', p. 144.
49 Biehl, 'Vita', p. 145.
50 Biehl, *Vita*, p. 2.
51 Biehl, 'Vita', p. 132, italics in original.
52 Cited in Tabb, *Unequal Partners*, p. 49
53 James Bethel, 'Sometimes the Word is "Weed"', *Forest Management* 1984 (June

worth. From this standpoint, Vita is populated with human weeds; having no value in the economic sphere they are to be discarded. The basis of Vita is thus idolatry; zones of social abandonment are spurred by an idolatrous logic in which the value of life is determined by the ability to contribute to the market as a producer or a consumer. It's this logic that reduces us to objects to be organized according to the parameters of the reigning economic order. When worth is measured according to this logic the poor are inevitably sacrificed, and that sacrifice, moreover, is scandalously justified as legitimate.[54]

Incarnating Idolatry: Vita and Institutions

In August of 2000, in an address to the Inter-American Development Bank, Canada's Minister of Foreign Trade aptly expressed the dominant understanding of globalization: 'Globalization, quite simply, is part of the natural evolutionary process. It goes hand in hand with the progress of humanity, something which history tells us no one can stand in the way of.'[55] From this perspective, globalization is an inevi-

---

1984), pp. 17–22, cited in Vandana Shiva, *Monocultures of the Mind: Perspectives on Biodiversity and Biotechnology*, New York: Zed Books, 1993, p. 24.

54 Summers takes idolatry's sacrificial logic to its ultimate conclusion, but there are other examples which, while less extreme, point at the ranking of human life implicit in the global order. Naomi Klein notes: 'Since September 11, I've been thinking about that incident, about how we in the media participate in a process that confirms and reconfirms the idea that death and murder are tragic, extraordinary and intolerable in some places and banal, ordinary, unavoidable, even expected in others ... Are we, in the media, neutral observers of this deadly mathematics? No. Sadly, it is we who do much of the counting. It is we who have the power to choose whose lives are presented in Technicolor, and whose in shades of grey. It is we who decide when to cry "tragedy" and when to shrug "ordinary"; when to celebrate heroes and when to let the bloodless statistics tell the story; who gets to be an anonymous victim – like the Africans killed in the U.S. embassy bombings in 1998 – and who gets to have a story, a family, a life – like the firefighters in New York. On September 11, watching TV replays of the buildings exploding over and over again in New York and Washington, I couldn't help thinking about all the times media coverage has protected us from similar horrors elsewhere. During the Gulf War, for instance, we didn't see real buildings exploding or people fleeing, we saw a sterile Space Invader battlefield, a bomb's-eye view of concrete targets – there and then none. Who was in those abstract polygons? We never found out ... The global "we" – as defined by London and New York – now reaches into places that are clearly not included in its narrow parameters, into homes and bars where local losses are not treated as global losses, where those local losses are somehow diminished relative to the grandness, the globalness of our projected plan.' Naomi Klein, *Fences and Windows: Dispatches From the Front Lines of the Globalization Debate*, New York, NY: Picador USA, 2002, pp. 165–7.

55 Cited in Klein, *Fences and Windows*, p. 130.

table and value-free process, the necessary unfolding of history itself. Of course, only the foolish will stand in history's way; to do so is to risk the fate of Schweitzer's Christ:

> Soon after that comes Jesus, and in the knowledge that He is the coming Son of Man lays hold of the wheel of the world to set it moving on that last revolution . . . It refuses to turn, and He throws Himself upon it. Then it does turn; and crushes Him . . . The wheel rolls onward, and the mangled body of the one immeasurably great Man, who was strong enough to think of Himself as the spiritual ruler of mankind and to bend history to His purpose, is hanging upon it still.[56]

Globalization, however, is not an automatic process inherent to natural capitalist dynamics, which is often how liberation theologians – whether Latin American, black, Hispanic/Latino(a) and feminist – have looked at the process.[57] The truth is that globalization is far from neutral; globalization is Vita, the spread of zones of social abandonment, resulting from the simple fact that Summers's idolatrous logic is incarnated in the institutions that govern the global economy – the International Monetary Fund (IMF), the World Bank, and the World Trade Organization (WTO). Not surprisingly, these institutions set rules of interaction between nations that heavily favour the richest countries and in particular the United States. As Henry Kissinger bluntly confesses, 'the basic challenge is that what is called globalization is really another name for the dominant role of the United States.'[58] Liberation

---

56 Albert Schweitzer, *The Quest of the Historical Jesus: A Critical Study of Its Progress from Reimarus to Wrede*, ed. James M. Robinson, trans. W. B. D. Montgomery, New York: Macmillan, 1968, pp. 370–1.

57 In fact, the pro-globalization discourse on the political right and the anti-globalization discourse on the theological left often share the same view of globalization as driven by inevitable technological necessity – the difference being that the former sees it as positive while the latter sees it as negative. For an examination of the ways Latin American liberation theology has understood capitalism and globalization see chapter 4 of Ivan Petrella, *The Future of Liberation Theology: An Argument and Manifesto*, London: SCM Press, 2006, first published as a hardcover by Ashgate in 2004. I'll be citing from the SCM paperback hereon.

58 Henry Kissinger cited in Celia Iriart, Howard Waitzkin, and Emerson Merhy, 'HMO's Abroad: Managed Care in Latin America', in Meredith Fort, Mary Anne Mercer, and Oscar Gish (eds), *Sickness and Wealth: The Corporate Assault on Global Health*, Cambridge, MA: South End Press, 2004, p. 69. Not much has changed. According to a 1948 US State Department policy planning study, 'the US has about 50 percent of the world's wealth but only 6.3 of its population. This situation cannot fail to be the object of envy and resentment. Our real task . . . is to devise a pattern of relationships which will permit us to maintain this position of disparity without positive detriment to

theologians have typically focused on the World Bank and the IMF – I'll focus on the WTO.[59] By this I don't mean to minimize the impact of the first as an export financing operation for North Atlantic corporations or that of the second as a debt collector for international financial institutions. But the World Bank and IMF step in at times of crisis to ensure that they are resolved without detriment to the developed world and its business interests. While all three work together, it's the WTO that is dictating rules for global economic activity that ensure that the logic of profit over life operates as the global norm.

The WTO is based on a vision of harmonized international standards for economic production and global business. Akio Morita, founder of Sony Corporation, summarized the vision in an open letter to the 1993 G-7 Summit in Tokyo where he challenged them to find

> the means of lowering all economic barriers between North America, Europe, and Japan – trade, investment, legal, and so forth – in order to begin creating the nucleus for a new world economic order that would include a harmonized world business system with agreed upon rules and procedures that transcend national boundaries.[60]

While the stated goal is to 'harmonize' international standards, the end effect is to deprive the governments of the poor nations of the power to dictate their own economic future. For my purposes, there-

---

our national security.' George Kennan, *State Department Policy Planning Study #23*, Washington, DC: US Department of State, 1948; cited in Stephen Bezruchka and Mary Anne Mercer, 'The Lethal Divide: How Economic Inequality Affects Health', in Meredith Fort, Mary Anne Mercer, and Oscar Gish (eds), *Sickness and Wealth: The Corporate Assault on Global Health*, Cambridge, MA: South End Press, 2004, p. 12. George Kennan, of course, was the mastermind behind the cold war policy of *detente* and is probably the most famous US diplomat of the twentieth century.

59 For two general introductions to the WTO see Amrita Narlikar, *The World Trade Organization: A Very Short Introduction*, New York, NY: Oxford University Press, 2005 and Kent Jones, *Who's Afraid of the WTO?*, New York, NY: Oxford University Press, 2004. Also useful to get a wider sense of disagreements in perspective are Jacques H. J. Bourgeois, *Trade Law Experienced: Pottering About in the GATT and WTO*, London: Cameron May, 2005; Gary P. Sampson, *The WTO and Sustainable Development*, New York, NY: United Nations University Press, 2005; Homi Katrak and Roger Strange (eds), *The WTO and Developing Countries*, New York, NY: Palgrave Macmillan, 2004; and Fatoumata Jawara and Aileen Kwa, *Behind the Scenes at the WTO: The Real World of International Trade Negotiations*, New York, NY: Zed Books, 2003.

60 Akio Morita, 'Toward a New World Economic Order', *Atlantic Monthly*, June 1993, p. 88, cited in David C. Korten, *When Corporations Rule the World*, San Francisco, CA and Bloomfield, CO: Berrett-Koehler Publishers, Inc. and Kumarian Press, 2001, p. 124. This is an excellent book, and pages 124–26 provide a summary of the vision in question.

fore, what warrants examination is not the fact that despite the WTO's focus on trade liberalization, Europe and the United States subsidize agriculture at the rate of one billion dollars a day, leading to annual welfare losses of $40 billion a year to the poorest of the poor.[61] What's most important is not that Europe and the United States practise tariff escalation so that tariffs are higher on processed raw materials to keep agricultural producers from moving into industrial processing based on their comparative advantage.[62] What warrants examination is not that North Atlantic subsidies on agriculture flood the market of cheap commodities, driving down the price of the only products that poor countries produce, or that North Atlantic tariffs are highest on labour-intensive goods such as textiles in which the developing world has a comparative advantage. Here no one fails to see the injustice; the hypocrisy is obvious and overt. The danger of focusing on these examples, then, lies in that they can then be presented as exceptions to what is otherwise a fair framework for governing global economic relations. What warrants examination is not the exceptional but rather that which is deemed normal. Otherwise one fails to see the hidden and thus more insidious ways in which the WTO is creating an order where the crisis of the Third/Two-Thirds World will no longer be an exceptional circumstance – it'll be the law of the land. Indeed, the WTO provides a legal gloss over a global economic order that deprives the Third World of the policy space necessary to escape poverty and masks the interests of the richest countries and their corporations as the interest of all.[63] There are three main WTO agreements that need to be looked at to support this claim: the 'Trade-Related Aspects of Intellectual Property Rights Agreement' (TRIPS), the 'Trade-Related Investment Measures Agreement' (TRIMS), and the 'General Agree-

---

61 For the numbers see Narlikar, World Trade Organization, p. 70. Let's be blunt: 'In Mali, where the per capita income is $270 annually, cotton is a critical raw commodity to export for economic sustainability of the people. The native people grow corn and millet to eat and produce unprocessed cotton to export. With a level playing field in trade, Mali could develop a stable economy to match its democratic system. However, the trade rules are tilted to create more poverty, not more wealth in Mali. The U.S. government subsidized its own farmers to grow cotton. Without having to compete with these American subsidies, the income for cotton producers in Mali would go up 30%. The government in Mali can't afford to subsidize its own cotton production.' Robert Isaak, *The Globalization Gap: How the Rich Get Richer and the Poor Get Left Further Behind*, New York: Prentice Hall, 2005, p. 185.

62 Tabb, *Unequal Partners*, p. 94.

63 See the essays in Kevin P. Gallagher (ed.), *Putting Development First: The Importance of Policy Space in the WTO and International Financial Institutions*, New York, NY: Zed Books, 2005. This is the best book on the topic.

ment on Trade in Services' (GATS).[64] In their wake, zones of social abandonment spread.

TRIPS

TRIPS sanctions with legality the existing inequality in knowledge development between the North and South, in which the former produces knowledge that the latter consumes. Broadly stated, TRIPS covers the protection of patents, copyrights, trademarks, industrial designs, and data secrets. On paper, the agreement merely obliges WTO members to install uniform standards for the protection of intellectual property and provides an enforcement and dispute resolution mechanism. In practice, however, 'TRIPS raises the price of patentable knowledge to consumers and so raises the flow of rents from South to North. According to World Bank estimates, US companies would pocket an additional net $19 billion a year in royalties from full application of TRIPS.'[65]

TRIPS sets a minimum period of 20-year patent protection ensuring a monopoly over a patented drug. No generic alternative can come to the market for that period. Freed from competition, a company is able to price the drug as high as it desires.[66] TRIPS extends the scope of patent protection to both products and processes. In the former, patents provide for the protection of the product, while in the latter patents provide protection in terms of the method of manufacture and the technology used for manufacture. A process system by itself would promote a competitive environment as well as provide a check on prices. Together, however, a product and process system makes it possible to apply for patent rights over a product, and once the 20 years expire, to apply for further protection for processes. TRIPS, moreover, requires patenting regardless of whether the products are imported or produced locally. A company can thus supply foreign markets under the patent monopoly by exporting the finished product. The result is that there

---

64 I draw the basic details of each agreement from Robert Wade, 'What Strategies Are Viable for Developing Countries Today? The World Trade Organization and the Shrinking of "Development Space"', in Kevin P. Gallagher (ed.), *Putting Development First: The Importance of Policy Space in the WTO and International Financial Institutions*, New York, NY: Zed Books, 2005, pp. 80–101.

65 Wade, 'What Strategies', p. 82.

66 *The New York Times* reports that 'in 2003, for example, Abbott Laboratories raised the price of Norvir, an AIDS drug introduced in 1996, from $54 to $265 a month. AIDS groups protested, but Abbott refused to rescind the increase.' *The New York Times*, 12 March 2006.

is no incentive for a company to transfer technology or make foreign direct investment by producing the product in a developing country. The rules of the game are thus rules for those nations, usually in the First World, that already have the infrastructure to develop products and patents, while the Third/Two-Thirds World is left out. [67]

The stakes at play within TRIPS are momentous and most visible when dealing with the pharmaceutical and biotechnology industries. In 2002, for example, the World Health Organization estimated that six million people with HIV/AIDS would clinically qualify for antiretroviral therapy. In the same year, however, only an estimated 60,000 were actually receiving therapy.[68] TRIPS, the pharmaceutical industry, and the governments of the wealthy nations all act together to ensure that only those who can pay the price of drugs are able to live with AIDS. In South Africa, for example, AIDS is a pandemic: 'the South African economy is predicted to be 17% smaller in ten years than it would be without AIDS. By 2010, there are expected to be 2 million AIDS orphans in South Africa.'[69] In an attempt to deal with the crisis the South African government passed the Medicine Act in 1996, which was designed to make essential medicines more accessible through compulsory licensing and parallel importing.[70] In response, the United States government argued that the Medicine Act violated TRIPS, imposed trade sanctions and placed South Africa on the '301 Watch List' of countries under scrutiny for their trading practices. Only intense activist pressure on Al Gore, who was then campaigning for President, led the United States government to back down.[71]

---

67 TRIPS, moreover, provides mechanisms by which developed countries can enforce their rights but no mechanisms by which developing countries may do so. If developing countries don't meet their obligations they can be taken to the WTO's dispute settlement mechanism (DSM). If developed countries don't meet their obligation, which is to make sure their firms provide technology to developing countries, there is no legal recourse. In fact, a developing country has never taken a developed country to DSM because the costs of mounting a case are high, the United States and the European Union could threaten reprisals, and the obligations of developed countries with regard to technology transfer and everything else are vague.

68 Davis and Fort, 'Battle Against Global Aids', p. 147.

69 Tabb, *Unequal Partners*, p. 107.

70 Compulsory licensing allows governments to grant licences permitting a company to manufacture a patented product without the authorization of the patent holder in cases of public health emergencies, while providing compensation to the patent owner. Parallel importing, on the other hand, is the practice of buying drugs from a third party in another country, rather than from the manufacturer, making the most of the fact that pharmaceutical companies often charge lower prices in one country than another. Davis and Fort, 'Battle Against Global Aids', pp. 49–50.

71 For accounts see Davis and Fort, 'Battle Against Global Aids', pp. 150–52 and Tabb, *Unequal Partners*, pp. 107–10.

Nevertheless, 39 multinational drug companies filed lawsuits against President Mandela in 1998, further tying up the law in South African courts.

South Africa is not the only country to come under attack for seeking to make antiretroviral drugs more accessible. Brazil provides free distribution of antiretroviral drugs through its public health system, cutting the number of AIDS-related deaths by 50% in five years.[72] In the process, the Brazilian government has favoured the local production of drugs to cut costs. Brazil spends an average of $4,716 per AIDS patient per year while the same treatment costs approximately $12,000 per year in the United States.[73] When the drugs are not produced locally, Brazil has used the threat of compulsory licensing to force drug companies to lower the costs.[74] In February of 2001, for example, Brazil stated that it was considering breaking patents for drugs by Roche and Merck if they didn't reduce their prices. In response, the USA claimed that compulsory licensing was in conflict with TRIPS and challenged Brazil in the WTO court. In April of 2001, however, the 57th session of the UN Human Rights Commission approved a Brazilian resolution that established the increased accessibility to medical drugs during pandemics a basic human right. In June, the United States withdrew its complaint from the WTO. Finally, the fourth ministerial conference of the WTO, under intense pressure from the developing world and NGOs, released the Doha Declaration, giving countries the right to issue compulsory licences in national health emergencies.

A remedial document such as Doha, however, can't change the asymmetries that underlie TRIPS. When patents are threatened, governments step in to ensure their companies' profit. The reality is that developing countries have been reluctant to use compulsory licensing or parallel importing for fear of trade sanctions by developed countries or of being taken to WTO court.[75] While late in 2001, Canada overrode Bayer's patent for the anthrax-treating drug Cipro. Health Canada stated: 'Canadians expect and demand that their government

---

72 Tabb, *Unequal Partners*, p. 110.

73 Tabb, *Unequal Partners*, p. 110.

74 I take the following from Jane Galvão, 'Access to Antiretroviral Drugs in Brazil', *The Lancet*. Published online 5 November 2002; http://image.thelancet.com/extras/01art9038web.pdf

75 On this see Narlikar, *World Trade Organization*, pp. 95–8. The cost of going to WTO court is often beyond the means of a developing nation. A developing country, moreover, has yet to issue a compulsory licence. The United States, on the other hand, has issued compulsory licences on goods ranging from infrared goggles for military usage to special seating for tow truck operators. Davis and Fort, 'Battle Against Global Aids', p. 149.

will take all steps necessary to protect their health and safety.'[76] Unlike AIDS in South Africa or Brazil, however, Canada had yet to face a single diagnosed case of anthrax. The United States quickly followed suit by threatening to buy generic substitutes to force price concessions from Bayer, asserting the very same rights denied to countries crippled by AIDS.[77] Must I stress that patents in medicine make profit the overriding mechanism by which a drug is evaluated? Pharmaceutical companies based in the United States, Europe or Japan today barely produce, let alone research, drugs against malaria or tuberculosis, which ravage the Third World yet are extremely rare in the industrialized nations.[78] Drug companies argue that patents are needed to recoup the money spent on research and development of new drugs. Studies have shown, however, that US drug companies often spend more on marketing, advertising and administration than they do on R&D. In this model, medicine is only for those who can pay, and is judged as valuable insofar as it can be paid for by the wealthy. James Orbinski, international president of Doctors Without Borders, puts it thus: 'He who can't pay, dies.'[79]

It's not just medicine that is being patented out of reach of the majority of the world's population – it's also seeds and the communal knowledge of traditional societies. Seeds are the beginning of the food chain, and as such the source of all life. As the prophet Isaiah states, 'all flesh is grass.'[80] Traditionally, by planting each year's crop, farmers repro-

---

76 The Canada and anthrax case, as well as the quotation from Health Canada, is taken from Klein, *Fences and Windows*, p. 82. See also Tabb, *Unequal Partners*, p. 113.

77 Tabb, *Unequal Partners*, p. 113.

78 See Tabb, *Unequal Partners*, p. 114 and Paul Farmer, *Pathologies of Power: Health, Human Rights, and the New War on the Poor*, Berkeley: University of California Press, 2003, pp. 316–19. In addition, studies demonstrate that of the 1,035 new drugs approved by the US Food and Drug administration between 1989 and 2000 only 15 per cent were innovative drugs. The others were modified versions of new drugs with low research and development costs. In the specific case of AIDS, many antiretrovirals were developed by publicly funded laboratories and tested with public funds. One more case: when a Ghanaian pharmaceutical distributor purchased an Indian-made generic version of Glaxo-Wellcome's Combivir, Glaxo threatened retribution for violation of its patent. Combivir costs $7,000 while Cipla Ltd, in India, offers a finished generic version for $275. India's Health Minister reacted to the pharmaceutical offer to provide cheaper drugs to Africa with the following comment: 'If they can offer an 80% discount, there was something wrong with the price they started with.' Farmer, *Pathologies of Power*, p. 200.

79 Cited in Tabb, *Unequal Partners*, p. 114.

80 Isaiah 40.6; cited in Jack Ralph Kloppenburg, *First the Seed: The Political Economy of Plant Biotechnology, 1492–2000*, New York, NY: Cambridge University Press, 1988, p. 1. On agriculture and seeds see also Vandana Shiva, *Tomorrow's Biodiversity*, New York, NY: Thames & Hudson, 2000; *Protect or Plunder? Understanding Intellectual Property Rights*, New York: Zed Books, 2001; *Monocultures of the Mind*; Shiva

duce the seeds necessary for their livelihood. Plants produce their own seeds that can be replanted, and if a farmer purchases seeds, those left over can be planted the following year. This simple pattern, however, is under attack. Through genetic engineering, seeds are increasingly hybrid products developed in and patented by North Atlantic laboratories. As such, they fall under TRIPS regulatory capacity. The end effect, one consciously undertaken as a goal by corporations, is to bring all farmers into the seed market every year.[81] Monsanto, for example, controls 91% of world-wide genetically modified (GM) soybean planted, 97% of all GM maize, and 63.5% of all GM cotton. In addition, Monsanto controls 31% of the global seed market in beans, 38% of the global market in cucumbers, as well as similar percentages of many other vegetables.[82] And more land is planted with their Roundup Ready soybeans than any other genetically engineered variety. That seed, however, only grows when sprayed by Monsanto's Roundup herbicide. As such, it requires farmers to purchase the inputs from Monsanto that will actually make the seed grow. The seed is fully a corporate product. Take also the patent awarded to the Delta and Pine Land Company, the largest cotton seed company in the world, in collaboration with the United States Department of Agriculture – Patent Number 5,723,765, Control of Plant Gene Expression.[83] This patent allows for the creation of sterile seeds by programming a plant to kill its own embryos. If the plant is saved at harvest for future crops the seeds produced by these plants will not grow; 'pea pods, tomatoes, peppers, heads of wheat and ears of corn will essentially become seed morgues.'[84] Small wonder that some have dubbed this patent 'terminator technology'. Indeed, given the fact that the global food supply is increasingly concentrated in a few corporate hands, this window into

---

usually bases herself on Kloppenburg's excellent book. Also useful are the essays in Brian Tokar (ed.), *Redesigning Life? The Worldwide Challenge to Genetic Engineering*, New York, NY: Zed Books, 2001.

81 Kloppenburg quotes Dr Hans Leenders, secretary of the International Seed Trade Federation in 1986: 'In most countries the farmer may do on his own farm whatever he chooses . . . Plant reproductive material has increasingly become a technical product in which money has been invested. Even though it has been a tradition in most countries that a farmer can save seed from his own crop, it is under the changing circumstances not equitable that farmers can use this seed and grow a commercial crop out of it without payment of a royalty.' Kloppenburg, *First the Seed*, p. 266.

82 http://www.etcgroup.org/documents/Comm90GlobalSeed.pdf

83 See Martha L. Crouch, 'From Golden Rice to Terminator Technology: Agricultural Biotechnology Will Not Feed the World or Save the Environment', in Brian Tokar (ed.), *Redesigning Life? The Worldwide Challenge to Genetic Engineering*, New York, NY: Zed Books, 2001, pp. 31–5 and Shiva, *Protect or Plunder?*, pp. 80–5.

84 Shiva, *Protect or Plunder?*, p. 81.

their world is unsettling to say the least (not to speak of the increased cost of seeds that price out poor farmers throughout the world).

Behind the patenting of seeds lies the appropriation and privatization of Third World resources and knowledge by First World corporations. The seeds and plant germplasm with which US and European companies develop their genetically modified hybrids are not original to the wealthy parts of the globe – they are taken.[85] Within TRIPS, the various plant germplasms used to modify seeds and plant varieties are seen as a product of nature and thus deemed the common heritage of humankind. Once the germplasm is modified in a North Atlantic laboratory, it's returned, that is, sold back to the Third World: 'Plant genetic resources leave the periphery as the common – and costless – heritage of mankind, and return as a commodity – private property with exchange value.'[86] Expropriation is legalized by denying the Third World's contribution to the development of seeds. The reasoning works as follows: TRIPS patents seeds that have been modified by human hands. Insofar as the genetic material from the Third World is a natural product, unmodified by human hands, it can't be patented and is a product of free access. And 'it is no exaggeration to say that the plant genetic resources received as free goods from the Third World have been worth untold *billions* of dollars to the advanced capitalist nations.'[87]

---

85 In fact, the world's less developed regions have contributed the plant genetic material for 95.7 per cent of global food crop production. Latin America and the West Central Asiatic themselves contributed 65.6 per cent, the Mediterranean accounts for a mere 1.4 per cent and none of the world's 20 most important food crops is indigenous to the United States or Canada. The conquest of the Americas by Spain began not only the pillaging of gold and silver, but also the appropriation of seeds that were to become staples of the European diet. In colonial times plant and seed transfers quickly took on political and economic import: 'Elaborate measures were taken by the Dutch, English, and French to keep useful materials out of competitors' hands. The Dutch, for example, destroyed all nutmeg and clove trees in the Moluccas except those on three islands where they located their plantations. The French made export of indigo seeds from Antigua a capital offense.' Kloppenburg, *First the Seed*, p. 154. For the above percentages see p. 181.

86 Kloppenburg, *First the Seed*, p. 169. On the same page he cites a monograph celebrating Ferry-Morse Seed Company's 100th anniversary: 'For the watermelon, America owes a real debt of gratitude to Africa. Ferry-Morse is helping in part to repay the debt by supplying North African and Eastern Mediterranean countries with thousands of pounds of watermelon seeds each year.' Of course, these seeds were not free.

87 Kloppenburg, *First the Seed*, p. 169; italics in original. He gives a few examples: 'A Turkish land race of wheat supplied American varieties with genes for resistance to stripe rust, a contribution estimated to have been worth $50 million per year. The Indian selection that provided sorghum with resistance to greenbug has resulted in $12 million in yearly benefits to American agriculture. An Ethiopian gene protects the American barley crop from yellow dwarf disease to the amount of $150 million per annum . . . the

These plants are *not* simply products of nature. This is a pillaging of resources as well as cultural and intellectual piracy. Numerous studies outline the contributions traditional societies have made, and continue to make, to plant breeding.[88] Plant genetic resources are deemed valueless only because TRIPS denies the work and knowledge of Third World society's market value. The case of *neem*, a tree used in India for centuries as medicine and pesticide, provides an example of both resource and cultural piracy.[89] For centuries the practices of Indian peasants and doctors in relation to neem were ignored by colonial powers. Growing opposition to chemical pesticides in the developed world, however, gained *neem* the attention of North Atlantic corporations. Soon afterwards the multinational chemical corporation W. R. Grace & Co. took out patents on *neem* and purchased almost all of the seed previously available to farmers and indigenous health practitioners; a resource once cheaply available disappeared. Grace justified its patents by claiming that their modern extraction processes are a genuine innovation. Such a claim, though, stemmed from an ignorance of local Indian practice; the patented methods are merely extensions of traditional processes used for thousands of years for making *neem*-based products. Proof lies in the fact that a coalition of NGOs challenged the patent and won.[90] Given the organizational obstacles and sheer size of resources involved, however, most acts of biopiracy stand unchallenged. Notice also that a US patent can only be invalidated by claims of prior use if there is evidence of use in a form recognizable by North Atlantic courts and patent examiners:

> accessible documentation or prior patents are needed to invalidate
> a claim. If indigenous, traditional knowledge is largely expressed in

---

value to the American tomato industry of genes from Peru that permitted an increase in the soluble solid content of the fruit is $5 million per annum. And new soybean varieties developed by University of Illinois plant breeders using germplasm from Korea may save American agriculture an estimated $100–500 million in yearly processing costs. Kloppenburg, *First the Seed*, pp. 167–9.

88 See Kloppenburg, *First the Seed*, p. 185.

89 On neem I draw from Shiva, *Protect or Plunder?*, pp. 57–61; *Tomorrow's Biodiversity* and Vandana Shiva, 'Biopiracy: The Theft of Knowledge and Resources', in Tokar (ed.), *Redesigning Life?*, pp. 40–4 and David Magnus, 'Intellectual Property and Agricultural Biotechnology: Bioprospecting or Biopiracy?' in David Magnus, Arthur Caplan, and Glenn McGee (eds), *Who Owns Life?*, Amherst, NY: Prometheus Books, 2002, pp. 265–76. This chapter is a good introduction to the issue of biopiracy.

90 To be more specific, the Research Foundation for Science, Technology and Ecology, the International Foundation of Organic Agriculture Movements and the European Greens challenged the neem patent in the European Patent Office on grounds of piracy and won.

customs, habits, and oral traditions, they will not be recognized in the patent system . . . This results in systematically favoring nations with well-established IP systems similar to the ones in the United States, and it favors nations that have strong written rather than oral traditions.[91]

That the system is stacked against Third/Two-Thirds World countries should come as no surprise; multinational corporations are the real authors of TRIPS. In 1995 Pfizer wrote:

In conjunction with more than a dozen companies from all the relevant sections of US business, Pfizer and IBM co-founded the Intellectual Property Committee or IPC. The US trade representative was impressed and suggested that we increase our effectiveness internationally by joining forces with UNICE, the principal pan-European business group, and its counterpart in Japan, Keidanren . . . our combined strength enabled us to establish a global private sector network which lay the groundwork for what became 'TRIPS'.[92]

---

91 Magnus, 'Intellectual Property', p. 273.

92 Cited in Beth Burrows, 'Patents, Ethics and Spin', in Tokar (ed.), *Redesigning Life?*, p. 250. The original was published in *The Economist*, 27 May 1995, p. 26. Ultimately, behind the patenting of life-saving drugs, and the appropriation of seeds and knowledge, lies the patenting of life. As Jack Krol, former DuPont chairman, once stated: 'In the 20th century, chemical companies made most of their products with non-living systems. In the next century, we will make many of them with living systems.' A series of controversial legal decisions in US courts paved the way for this goal. In 1980 the US Supreme Court ruled in the landmark case of *Diamond vs Chakrabarty* that genetically modified microorganisms are patentable; in 1985 the US Patent and Trademark Office ruled that plants qualified under industrial patent laws, and in 1987 the US Patent and Trademark Office ruled that animals were also patentable. The upshot can be found in *John Moore vs the Regents of the University of California*. While under treatment for hair cell leukaemia, Moore's doctor noticed that his blood cells produced a blood protein that showed promise as an anti-cancer agent. The doctor took out a patent on Moore's cell line without his knowledge or consent. Upon finding out Moore sued the doctor, the university and the pharmaceutical company which had a licence for his cell line. The case was resolved in 1990 when the California Supreme Court denied Moore's claim to ownership of cells removed from his body. The reason? To do so would obstacalize scientific research. Krol is cited in Hope Shand, 'Gene Giants: Understanding the "Life Industry"', in Tokar (ed.), *Redesigning Life?*, p. 222. On the Chakrabarty case see Kimberly A. Wilson, 'Exclusive Patents, Enclosure and the Patenting of Life', in Tokar (ed.), *Redesigning Life?*, pp. 290–6 and A. M. Chakrabarty, 'Patenting of Life-Forms: From a Concept to Reality', in David Magnus, Arthur Caplan, and Glenn McGee (eds), *Who Owns Life?*, Amherst, NY: Prometheus Books, 2002, pp. 17–24. On Moore see Burrows, 'Patents, Ethics and Spin', pp. 245–7. Moore is also discussed in 'Taking the Least of You', in *The New York Times Magazine*, 16 April 2006.

TRIMS

TRIMS requires that governments give foreign firms national treatment in the area of production and trade of goods. It thus eliminates tariffs and subsidies geared toward the creation of a local industrial base and restricts the use of tools – such as local content requirements, technology transfer, local employment, joint venturing, and performance requirements – through which governments have sought to steer local benefits from foreign direct investment. As with TRIPS, the consequences are momentous. Follow the sequence: since tariffs and subsidies are illegal the government of a developing country is deprived of the ability to nurse infant industries; that is, it's no longer able to help foster a national industrial base. It must by necessity look externally to foreign direct investment from multinational corporations. But what can it offer? Why would a multinational want to set up shop in a developing country? The only thing a developing country can offer is low wages. Unfortunately, every other developing country is in the same boat, so low wages are not enough to entice foreign investment. Developing countries thus engage in a race to the bottom, offering tax exemptions, waivers of industry regulation, guarantees against expropriation, lax social, environmental and labour regulations, even lower wages and a military willing to crush social unrest. The poverty and degradation of the population becomes the allure and selling point.

The spread of export processing zones (EPZs) is the direct consequence of this logic.[93] There are an estimated one thousand such zones throughout the world employing approximately 27 million workers, approximately 80% of whom are single women between the ages of 18 and 25. Naomi Klein describes her visit to Cavite, an EPZ in the town of Rosario in the Philippines: 'the economic zone is designed as a fantasyland for foreign investors. Golf courses, executive clubs and private schools have been built on the outskirts of Rosario to ease the discomforts of Third World life.'[94] The contrasts are glaring:

> In Cavite . . . the workers are uniformed, the grass manicured . . . There are cute signs all around the grounds instructing workers to 'Keep Our Zone Clean' and 'Promote Peace and Progress of the Philippines'. But walk out the gate and the bubble bursts . . . The

---

93 What follows draws from Naomi Klein, *No Logo*, New York, NY: Picador USA, 2000, pp. 202–29 and Jim Yong Kim, Joyce Millen, Alec Irwin, and John Gershman (eds), *Dying for Growth: Global Inequality and the Health of the Poor*, Boston, MA: Common Courage Press, 2000, pp. 188–204.

94 Klein, *No Logo*, p. 206.

roads are a mess, running water is scarce and garbage is overflow-ing.[95]

Workers either live in bunkers within Cavite or in the slums that grow outside its door. The rented piece of land upon which Cavite stands, moreover, exists as a separate country, a denationalized piece of territory:

> the Cavite zone . . . is under the sole jurisdiction of the Philippines' federal Department of Trade and Industry; the local police and municipal government have no right even to cross the threshold. The layers of blockades serve a dual purpose: to keep the hordes away from the costly goods being manufactured inside the zone, but also, and perhaps more important, to shield the country from what is going on inside the zone.[96]

What is going on inside these zones?[97] Workers are primarily migrants living far from home with little connection to the place where the zones are located. The work itself is short-term and often not renewed. Wages are low, sometimes below the nation's minimum-wage laws. Hours are long. Workers suffer varied types of abuse. Drinking water is often unavailable and ventilation is poor. Mandatory produc-tion quotas beyond achievable limits force employees to work overtime without compensation. Women are often beaten, sexually harassed and abused by their employers. Girls may be forced to take birth con-trol pills or injections to avoid costly pregnancies. Pregnancy tests are mandatory and pregnant workers are fired. Even forced abortions have been reported. When 7,000 workers from Sri Lanka's Colombo EPZ marched peacefully to deliver a complaint to their Prime Minister they were attacked with truncheons and fired upon by the police. In the Mexican *maquiladoras* – the assembly plants in the free-trade zone

---

95 Klein, *No Logo*, p. 208.

96 Klein, *No Logo*, p. 207.

97 In the words of a 15-year-old seamstress in a Guatemala City EPZ: 'The starting bell for work rings at 6:15 and I can feel pretty tired the first hour but I have to work fast anyway – we have quotas. When the bell finally rings at 6:30pm [over 12 hours later], you are ready to go home – but it is not always possible. If there is more work, the owners tell you they need people to stay for the night shift. If not enough people say yes, the supervi-sor sits in front of the doors and no one can leave. They let you rest for a few minutes, and work starts again at 7:00pm. When the bell rings at 3am, they pass out cardboard from old boxes. I look for my friends, and we put our cardboard boxes next to each other and sleep under the tables. Then you go back to work whether you are tired or not.' Cited in Kim, Millen, Irwin, and Gershman, *Dying for Growth*, p. 189.

on the Mexican side of the US border – workers have been denied the right to form independent labour unions. While in the midst of a two-month labour strike Ford Motor Company unilaterally nullified its union contract, fired 3,400 of its workers, and cut wages by 45%. When the workers rallied around dissident labour leaders and tried to form a union outside the state-sponsored labour apparatus, gunmen hired by the official government-dominated union shot workers at random in the factory.[98]

As Naomi Klein notes, the rationale behind EPZs is simple: '*of course* companies must pay taxes and strictly abide by national laws, but just in this one case, on this specific piece of land, for just a little while, an exception will be made – for the case of future prosperity.'[99] In the past, the strategy has worked and countries have climbed up the wage ladder, most notably in the case of the East Asian tigers.[100] But it worked when there were far fewer EPZs and before TRIMS outlawed the mechanisms by which the Asian tigers created linkages that ensured the transfer of technology and knowledge. Today, if a country fails to lower its labour and environmental regulations, it faces the risk of being bid out of the global economy. When a country lowers its regulations, however, workers are left unprotected from abuse and lack job security. The greater the competition to attract foreign firms the greater the incentives. Cameroon, for example, offers foreign investors a 100% tax exemption for ten years and free repatriation of profits; in its EPZ, multinational corporations can fire workers at will without compensation and are exempt from the nation's minimum wage laws.[101] The exploitation of the worker, environment and nation

---

98 Kim, Millen, Irwin, and Gershman, *Dying for Growth*, p. 190.

99 Klein, *No Logo*, p. 207.

100 The best examinations of the rise of the East Asian 'tigers' remain Alice Amsden, *The Rise of the 'Rest': Challenges to the West from Late-Industrializing Economies*, Oxford: Oxford University Press, 2001 and Robert Wade, *Governing the Market: Economic Theory and the Role of Government in East Asian Industrialization*, Princeton, NJ: Princeton University Press, 1990.

101 One should note that 'it is often assumed that people in poor countries choose to migrate to urban centers and work in free processing zones in order to improve their living standards and increase their degree of personal freedom. However, workers in many regions migrate because they have little choice: either they have been forced off their land by (often transnational) agribusiness, or they were pushed to abandon their farms when their crops could no longer compete in markets flooded with cheaper foreign goods. The question of volition is important because foreign employers tend to argue that their workers are not being forced to work in the factories and that workers would leave if they did not want to be there. The idea that remuneration from their work in the factories has improved their living standards or personal freedom needs to be assessed in light of conditions previous to TNC [transnational corporation] penetration.' Kim, Millen, Irwin, and Gershman, *Dying for Growth*, p. 466.

as a whole is not the exception; it's intrinsic to the EPZ as a path to development. It's not surprising, therefore, that multinational corporations seem to avoid investing in democracies; workers in democracies are harder to exploit. In 1989, democracies accounted for more than half of all US imports from the Third World; today, with more democracies to choose from they constitute merely one-third. It makes sense: 'lower wages, bans on labor unions, and relaxed environmental laws give authoritarian regimes an edge in attracting foreign investment . . . as more of the world's countries adopt democracy, more American businesses appear to prefer dictatorships.'[102]

GATS

GATS extends WTO rules in trade in goods to trade in services such as banking, education, trash collection, health delivery, water supply and sanitation. Under GATS, like TRIMS, a government must treat firms from all WTO members equally; you cannot discriminate between local and foreign providers, even if the former is a community non-profit and the latter is a giant corporation. Foreign multinationals cannot be required to use local suppliers, managers or staff, and there is no limit on the number of service suppliers or where they operate. At stake in GATS is the commodification of basic services and the social contract between government and people – in which the former provides affordable public services to the latter. For example, over a billion people lack access to safe drinking water and over two billion lack adequate sanitation. Water, however, can be considered a commodity to be sold or it can be considered a basic social right. Within GATS, water is a commodity best delivered by the private sector. As US trade representative Mickey Kantor once stressed, 'when water is traded as a good, all provisions of the agreement governing trade in goods apply'.[103]

The most famous case of water commodification remains the privatization of the water supply in Cochabamba, Bolivia. In 2002 the *San Francisco Chronicle* reported that: 'In a Goliath-versus-David face-off, Bechtel Group of San Francisco, the largest private company in the Bay Area, is taking legal action against the government of Bolivia, one

---

102 Manfred Steger, *Globalism: The New Market Ideology*, Lanham, MD: Rowman & Littlefield, 2002, pp. 76–7. He is drawing from a study in the *Chicago Tribune*, 'Democracies are Paying the Price', 19 November 1999.

103 Cited in Vandana Shiva, *Water Wars: Privatization, Pollution, and Profit*, Cambridge, MA: South End Press, 2002.

of the poorest countries in the hemisphere.'[104] Bechtel, one of the most powerful corporations in the world – with $14.3 billion in revenue in 2000 – was suing Bolivia, whose national budget is only $2.7 billion, for $50 million in damages. In 1998 the IMF approved a $138 million loan for Bolivia to help the country control inflation and bolster economic growth. In compliance with IMF-drafted 'structural reforms' for the nation, Bolivia agreed to sell off 'all remaining public enterprises', including national oil refineries and Cochabamba's local water agency, SEMAPA. After closed-door negotiations, the Bolivian government signed a $2.5 billion contract to hand over Cochabamba's municipal water system to Aguas del Tunari, a multinational consortium of private investors, dominated by the Bechtel Corporation. Within weeks, in a city where the average monthly wage is $67, in a country in which 65% of the 8 million population is mired in poverty, city water rates rose by more than 50% and in some cases even higher. The water price hikes were met with angry public protest. Cochabamba, a city of about 500,000 people, was shut down by general strikes three times. In an effort to protect the Bechtel contract, the Bolivian government declared a state of martial law and began arresting protest leaders at their homes in the middle of the night. Protests originating in Cochabamba's central plaza spread to La Paz, other cities and outlying rural communities. Thousands clashed with riot police and an unarmed 17-year-old boy was shot and killed by Bolivian Army personnel. At least 175 others were injured. In April 2000, Bechtel was forced to leave the country and the water company was returned to public ownership. Asked to comment, former World Bank President James Wolfensohn stressed that 'the biggest problem with water is the waste of water through lack of charging'.[105]

The case provides an example of how the IMF, the World Bank and the WTO work together in creating an idolatrous order that sacrifices the poor for the sake of corporate interest.[106] First, the IMF makes the

---

104 http://www.sfgate.com/cgi-bin/article.cgi?file=/chronicle/archive/2002/02/02/MN41536.DTL; a good timeline of the issue can be found at http://www.pbs.org/frontlineworld/stories/bolivia/timeline.html

105 http://www.pbs.org/frontlineworld/stories/bolivia/timeline.html

106 For a fascinating first-person account see John Perkins, *Confessions of an Economic Hit Man*, San Francisco, CA: Berrett-Koehler Publishers, 2004. His task: 'First, I was to justify huge international loans that would funnel money back to MAIN [his employer, allegedly an economic think tank] and other U.S. companies (such as Bechtel, Halliburton, Stone & Webster, Brown & Root) through massive engineering and construction projects. Second, I would work to bankrupt the countries that received the loans (after they had paid MAIN and the other U.S. contractors, of course) so that they would be forever beholden to their creditors, and so they would present easy targets when we needed favors, including military bases, UN votes, or access to oil and other natural resources' (p. 15).

opening up of basic services to multinationals a prerequisite of any new loans. Services now account for 70% of gross domestic product (GDP) and employment in the North Atlantic countries. To continue to expand, these countries and their multinationals need access to the service industry of the developing world. The IMF, through its loan conditionality, grants them such access. Second, the World Bank steps in to enforce the contract. In November 2001, Bechtel and its associates filed their case with the International Center for Settlement of Investment Disputes (ICSID) at the World Bank. The ICSID process bars the public and media from being present at its proceedings or disclosing who testifies. The company, moreover, filed the case with ICSID under a bilateral investment treaty between the Netherlands and Bolivia. Although Bechtel is a US corporation, its subsidiary established a presence in the Netherlands in order to make use of the treaty. The lawsuit was dropped in January of 2006 after protesters closed down Bechtel's San Francisco headquarters twice, company officials were bombarded by critical e-mails, and citizen groups from 43 nations endorsed a legal petition to the World Bank demanding that the case be opened to public participation. Finally, the WTO created the conditions so that this exceptional case becomes the norm.

As I've already noted, the WTO operates a state-to-state dispute settlement process which can overturn the decisions of national governments. In 1999, for example, the WTO, after a US complaint, overturned the European Union's ban on the sale of meat from cattle treated with artificial hormones despite the fact the ban had widespread popular support. In the case of a developing country, moreover, even the threat of going to court can lead to a shift of health policies. In 1988, Guatemala adopted the WHO-UNICEF Infant Formula Marketing Code into laws forbidding infant formula companies from using advertising labels that made their products appear to be healthier than breast milk. Gerber Products refused to comply and launched a campaign to eliminate the law. In 1995, Gerber gained US support to challenge the law in a WTO tribunal, and the threat of trade sanctions was enough to have the government exempt imported baby food products from Guatemala's infant health laws.[107] New treaties such as the North American Free Trade Area (NAFTA) and the Free Trade Area of the Americas (FTAA) represent an even more extreme transfer of power from states to multinational corporations. In these treaties,

---

107 I get both these examples from Ellen Shaffer and Joseph Brenner, 'Trade and Health Care: Corporatizing Vital Human Services', in Meredith Fort, Mary Anne Mercer, and Oscar Gish (eds), *Sickness and Wealth: The Corporate Assault on Global Health*, Cambridge, MA: South End Press, 2004, p. 82.

private foreign investors can directly sue governments if a regulation is seen as tantamount to expropriation of present and future profits.[108] The Metclad Corporation, for example, took the Mexican state of San Luis de Potosi to a NAFTA court for not allowing the installation of a toxic waste site, arguing that the declaration of the site as an ecological zone violated provisions of the treaty. The secret tribunal required the Mexican government to pay Metclad $16.7 million in damages.[109] Sun Belt Water is seeking $14 billion in damages from Canada because British Columbia banned the export of bulk water, thus impeding their entry into water-export trade in that region.[110] Jack Lindsey, CEO of Sun Belt, put it thus: 'Because of Nafta, we are now stake holders in the national water policy of Canada.'[111] And a WTO negotiator bluntly admitted, 'without the enormous pressure generated by the American financial services sector . . . there would have been no GATS service agreement.'[112] As with TRIPS, surprise at the end effect of these agreements is only for the misinformed.

Idolatry Realized: the World as Vita

The implementation of TRIPS, TRIMS and GATS require human sacrifices. These agreements are expressions of the idolatrous logic that rules our world, in which the value of a human life is measured by its ability to consume and produce. Since an idol is a false god, its logic is

108 Kevin P. Gallagher, 'Globalization and the Nation-State: Reasserting Policy Autonomy for Development', in Gallagher (ed.), *Putting Development First: The Importance of Policy Space in the WTO and International Financial Institutions*, New York, NY: Zed Books, 2005, p. 11.

109 Shaffer and Brenner, 'Trade and Health Care', p. 88.

110 Shaffer and Brenner, 'Trade and Health Care', p. 88. This case is still awaiting resolution. Environmental regulations get in the way of corporate ambition in the United States as well. In 1997, the US Environmental Protection Agency weakened its Clean Air Act regulations to comply with a WTO ruling barring US limits on contaminants in imported foreign gasoline. Venezuela claimed that the limits, which affected California and eight other states, acted as an unfair trade barrier. The WTO also ruled against the US ban on shrimp imports from nations whose fishing fleets do not use devices to keep endangered sea turtles out of the nets. Finally, Congress has weakened the Marine Mammal Protection Act to comply with a 1992 WTO ruling against the US 'dolphin-safe' tuna certification geared toward tuna that isn't caught using mile-long nets blamed for snaring and killing thousands of dolphins per year.

111 Cited in Shiva, *Water Wars*, p. 97.

112 'The pressure came especially from the US coalition of Service Industries, the European Services Forum, and the UK's Liberalization of Trade in Services Group.' Wade, 'What Strategies Are Viable for Developing Countries Today?', p. 98. The WTO negotiator is cited on the same page.

based on a lie that takes lives. But let me be specific: in the case of the WTO, the lie is that strong intellectual property rights and free trade in goods and services will benefit all. This flies in the face of the economic history of the North Atlantic nations. The WTO freezes a country's endowments and preferences to the present and ignores the fact that in a modern economy comparative advantage is created. In depriving nations of the capacity for creation, these agreements condemn the majority of the globe to poverty. The truth is that every single one of the rich countries grew wealthy through lax intellectual property rights and protected industries. England was protectionist as it tried to catch up with the Netherlands; Germany was protectionist as it tried to catch up with England; the USA was protectionist as it tried to catch up with England and Germany; Japan was protectionist until the 1970s while Korea and Taiwan were protectionist till the 1990s.[113] All the developed countries used interventionist industrial, trade and technology policies aimed at developing their economic base. All of them tried to control the transfer of technology to potential competitors.[114] The British Empire, for example, passed a series of laws preventing the export of new machines, their plans or models. Skilled workers were not allowed to leave England lest they transfer their knowledge to a competitor.[115] The USA did not become a champion of free trade until its rise to sole industrial prominence after World War Two.[116] In fact, famed economic historian Paul Bairoch once described the USA as 'the

---

113 For an overview of this history see Wade, 'What Strategies Are Viable', Ha-Joon Chang, 'Kicking Away the Ladder: "Good Policies" and "Good Institutions" in Historical Perspective', in Gallagher (ed.), *Putting Development First*, pp. 102–25; Ha-Joon Chang and Duncan Green, *The Northern WTO Agenda on Investment: Do As We Say, Not As We Did*, Geneva: South Center and CAFOD, 2003; Ha-Joon Chang, *Kicking Away the Ladder: Development Strategy in Historical Perspective*, London: Anthem Press, 2002; Liah Greenfeld, *The Spirit of Capitalism: Nationalism and Economic Growth*, Cambridge, MA: Harvard University Press, 2001; Alice Amsden, *The Rise of 'The Rest': Challenges to the West from Late-Industrial Economies*, Oxford: Oxford University Press, 2003; and Paul Bairoch, *Economics and World History: Myths and Paradoxes*, Chicago, IL: University of Chicago Press, 1993.

114 See Chang, *Kicking Away the Ladder*; for a summary of the book consult Chang, 'Kicking Away the Ladder'.

115 Shiva notes the more brutal methods as well: 'The British Empire was built through the destruction of manufacturing capacities in the colonies and the prevention of the emergence of such capacity. "Free trade" during the era of the "technological superiority" of England was based on the thumbs of master weavers in Bengal being cut off, the forced cultivation of indigo by the peasants of Bihar, the slave trade from Africa to supply free labour to cotton plantations in the US and the extermination of the indigenous people of North America.' Shiva, *Protect or Plunder?*, pp. 34–5.

116 Chang, 'Kicking Away the Ladder', p. 108.

mother country and bastion of modern protectionism'.[117] Claims that the global economic order instituted by the IMF, the World Bank and the WTO are of benefit to all should be read in light of Friedrich List's take on the behaviour of countries at the forefront of economic development:

> It is a very clever common device that when anyone has attained the summit of greatness, he kicks away the ladder by which he has climbed up, in order to deprive others of the means of climbing up after him . . . Any nation which by means of protective duties and restrictions on navigation has raised her manufacturing power and her navigation to such a degree of development that no other nation can sustain free competition with her, can do nothing wiser than to throw away the ladders of her greatness, to preach to other nations the benefits of free trade, and to declare in pertinent tones that she has hitherto wandered in the paths of error, and has now for the first time succeeded in discovering the truth.[118]

Given the idolatry at the very basis of the world's ruling institutions, it's not surprising that 50 years of development have led to a world where more and more people are poor.[119] The data are stark and well known, so I will be brief and provide just some representative samples. One quarter of the world's population lives with less than one dollar a day, while half live with less than two dollars a day.[120] The 20% of

---

117 Cited in Chang, 'Kicking Away the Ladder', p. 108; from Bairoch, *Economics and World History*, p. 30.

118 Both Wade and Chang make this same point and quote List. See Wade, 'What Strategies Are Viable', p. 91 and Chang, 'Kicking Away the Ladder', p. 107. They're citing from Friedrich List, *The National System of Political Economy*, New York, NY: Augustus Kelley, 1966, p. 368. In the nineteenth century Ulysses S. Grant shrewdly noted that 'for centuries England has relied on protection . . . there is no doubt that it is to this system that it owes its present strength. After two centuries, England has found it convenient to adopt free trade because it thinks that protection can no longer offer it anything. Very well then, Gentlemen, my knowledge of our country leads me to believe that within 200 years, when America has gotten out of protection all that it can offer, it too will adopt free trade.' Cited in Chang, 'Kicking Away the Ladder', pp. 108–9.

119 For an overarching critique of development as a discourse see Arturo Escobar, *Encountering Development: The Making and Unmaking of the Third World*, Princeton, NJ: Princeton University Press, 1995. For two good overviews of approaches to development see Richard Peet and Elaine Hartwick, *Theories of Development*, New York: The Guilford Press, 1999 and Ray Kiely, *Sociology and Development: The Impasse and Beyond*, London: UCL Press, 1995.

120 The data that follows is compiled from the following sources: Jeremy Seabrook, *The No-Nonsense Guide to World Poverty*, New York, NY: Verso, 2003; Wayne Ellwood, *The No-Nonsense Guide to Globalization*, New York, NY: Verso, 2003;

the world's population that resides in the affluent Northern hemisphere receives 60% of the world's income, engages in 80% of the world's trade, four-fifths of the world's health spending and consumes 86% of the world's goods. They also consume 45% of the world's meat and fish, 58% of its energy, 84% of all paper, 85% of all water, and they own 87% of all the world's vehicles.

The world's 497 billionaires in 2001 registered a combined wealth of $1.54 trillion, well over the combined gross national products of all the nations of sub-Saharan Africa ($929.3 billion) or those of the oil-rich regions of the Middle East and North Africa ($1.34 trillion). It's also greater than the combined incomes of the poorest half of humanity. The GDP (Gross Domestic Product) of the poorest 48 nations (that is, a quarter of the world's countries) is less than the wealth of the world's three richest people – Bill Gates, the Walton Family and the Sultan of Brunei – combined. In 2004, the total wealth of the top 8.3 million people around the world rose 8.2% to $30.8 trillion, giving them control of nearly a quarter of the world's financial assets. So about 0.13% of the world's population controlled 25% of the world's assets in 2004. Indeed, in 1960, the poorest 20% of the world's population received 2.3% of global income. Today, they receive 1.1%.

The developing world now spends $13 on debt repayment for every $1 it receives in grants. In the 1990s developing countries paid more in debt service than they received in new loans, transferring $77 billion from the poor to the rich. In Africa as a whole, governments pay their foreign creditors four times what they spend on health and education for their citizens. In Brazil over 75% of all government revenue goes to debt servicing, while 35% goes to social services expenditure. In Guatemala, 58% goes to debt servicing, and 38% to social services. In Nicaragua, where three out of four people live below the poverty line, debt repayments exceed the total social sector budget; in Bolivia, where only 16% of the population has access to safe water, debt payments are three times as high as spending to reduce poverty. Robert Isaak notes: 'Not surprisingly, the retained earnings of the World Bank go up each year – from $19 billion in 2000 to $27 billion in 2003, with net income growing from $1,489 billion in 2001 to $5,344 billion in 2003.'[121]

Of the 2.2 billion children in the world, one billion – every second child – lives in poverty. One in three of the 1.9 billion children in the

---

Paul Farmer, *Pathologies of Power*, Berkeley: University of California Press, 2003; Bob Sutcliffe, *100 Ways of Seeing an Unequal World*, New York: Zed Books, 2001; Kim, Millen, Irwin, and Gershman, *Dying for Growth*, and http://www.globalissues.org/TradeRelated/Facts.asp. This, by the way, is a fantastic webpage.

121 Isaak, *The Globalization Gap*, p. 25.

developing world lack adequate shelter, one in five lack access to safe water and one in seven lack access to health services. Of the annual average 10 million child deaths under the age of five, 97% occur in developing countries of avoidable causes – this equals the entire child population of France or Italy. Each year 2.2 million children die for lack of immunization and 15 million children have been orphaned due to HIV/AIDS, equalling the total child population of Germany or the United Kingdom. Finally, of the 31,000 children under the age of five that die each day, 210,000 children per week – 50% – die of hunger despite the fact that food supply has doubled in the past decades, exceeding the rate of population growth.

Finally, recorded growth in world trade has bypassed rather than integrated the developing world into the world economy.[122] Similarly, the developing world's share of foreign direct investment has dwindled.[123] Today, the top fifth of the world's population enjoys 82% of the export trade and 68% of foreign direct investment – the bottom fifth, barely more than 1%. Far from an expansion of economic opportunity, globalization is marked by 'an accelerated withdrawing, a *shrinking* of the global map, rather than an *expanding* phenomenon, and one which expels ever more people from the interactive circle of global capitalism'.[124] Developing countries and their inhabitants are being squeezed out of the global order. Remember the Enclosure Acts? They were passed in eighteenth-century England to allow the emerging capitalist class to expropriate land that was owned by no one and thus of common use. Marx saw them as a key move in the development of capitalism. They pushed peasants off the land, took away their means of subsistence and thus gave them no choice but to work in emerging capitalist factories; the Enclosure Acts gave birth to the proletariat.

---

122 Share of developing country participation in world trade increased by a mere 3.6 per cent from 1953 to the end of the 1990s. That increase, however, includes Hong Kong, Korea, Taiwan, and Singapore – the Asian Tigers – which account for 33 per cent of the developing world's share of trade while representing only 1.5 per cent of its population. In 1995, once you exclude the Asian Tigers, the developing world's share of global trade was only 18.3 per cent, down from the 1950 share of 25.9 per cent, calculated again excluding the Asian Tigers. Latin America's share of world trade in 1995 was 4.8 per cent, down from 10 per cent in 1950.

123 Up to 1960, the developing nations received half the world's total direct investment flows. By 1988–9 that percentage was down to 16.5 per cent, with over half going to different parts of Asia. The 1990s saw a turnaround with the developing world receiving 38 per cent of FDI by 1997, yet fully one third of this investment is concentrated in China's eight coastal provinces and in Beijing. In fact, in the first half of the 1990s, 86 per cent of all FDI went to 30 per cent of the world's population.

124 See Ankie Hoogvelt, *Globalization and the Postcolonial World: The New Political Economy of Development*, Baltimore: Johns Hopkins University Press, 1997, p. 70.

The world as a zone of social abandonment is today built through a modern-day Enclosure Act in which people are denied the basic require-ments that make life viable.[125] In this new enclosure, in the world as a zone of social abandonment, where humankind is denied water, food, shelter, medication, and life itself, death is the norm, and exploitation often a luxury.

Vita, Revisited

In the face of Vita, the melancholy images that populate modern thought seem almost trite. Given the spread of zones of social aban-donment, a fate that echoes Weber's lament for 'specialists without spirit or sensualists without heart', or a future as one of Foucault's docile bodies, is better than most.[126] Perhaps the best image to describe Vita from a theorist located both intellectually and physically in the First World is Giorgio Agamben's notion of 'bare life'. Agamben devel-ops this idea in relation to the Nazi concentration camps: 'Insofar as its inhabitants were stripped of every political status and reduced to bare life, the camp was also the most absolute biopolitical space ever to have been realized, in which power confronts nothing but pure life, without any mediation.'[127] Vita also creates bare life, at the edge of execution. Vita is a camp in which the majority of humankind is trapped and in which the determination of which lives are unworthy of being lived is made every day. The Jews in the camp had a visible persecutor whereas the global inhabitants of Vita are even denied an executioner in human form. No arm guides this death sentence; it happens automatically and by default.

Liberation theology, however, saw more deeply into our objectifica-tion than all of North Atlantic thought, as it realized that at the root of objectification lies idolatry and that the wages of idolatry is death. For this reason, liberation theology's main challenge, famously expressed by Gustavo Gutiérrez, comes not from the sceptic but from the non-person or the non-human – the human being who isn't recognized as such by the prevailing social order.[128] Such is the liberationist transla-tion of bare life. Let me stress that the term 'non-human' is not a meta-

---

125 See Karl Marx, *Capital*, introd. by Ernest Mandel, trans. Ben Fowkes, vol. 1, The Marx Library, New York: Vintage-Random House, 1977, chapter 27.

126 Weber, *The Protestant Ethic*, p. 182.

127 Giorgio Agamben, *Homo Sacer: Sovereign Power and Bare Life*, Stanford, CA: Stanford University Press, 1998, p. 171.

128 See Gustavo Gutiérrez, *Teología Desde el Reverso de la Historia*, Lima, Peru: Ed. CEP, 1977, for an extended discussion of this theme.

phor. It would take $6 billion of additional yearly investment to ensure basic education in all developing countries; $8 billion a year are spent on cosmetics in the United States. It would take $9 billion to insure clean water and sanitation for all; $11 billion are spent on ice cream in Europe. It would take $13 billion to guarantee basic health and nutrition for every person in the developing world; $17 billion are spent on pet food in Europe and the United States combined. It would take approximately an additional $40 billion to achieve universal access to basic social services; 0.1% of the world's income, a rounding error, would cover the bill for basic education, health, nutrition, clean water and sanitation for every single person on the planet.[129] Gutiérrez's choice of the term 'non-human' is not a rhetorical flourish intended to provoke; it is a literal description of Vita's terrible reality. The people the above data refer to are quite literally lacking personhood; they are quite literally non-human, in the basic sense that their needs do not count at all for the way the world's resources are distributed. This is the global material context a liberation theologian today faces. To quote Sancho Panza: 'Dos linajes hay solos en el mundo, como decía mi abuela, que son el tener y el no tener.'[130]

---

129 For this data see *Human Development Report 1998*, United Nations Development Programme, 1998, especially chapter 1.

130 'There are only two lineages in the world, as my grandmother used to say, the haves and have nots.' Miguel de Cervantes Saavedra, *El Ingenioso Hidalgo Don Quijote de la Mancha*, Madrid: Aguilar S.A., 1993, from memory.

2

The Material Context of the
US Liberation Theologian:
Poverty in the Midst of Plenty

With the fresh eyes that an outsider sometimes can bring to a situation most of us take for granted, Susan asked Rushika: 'Where are the bodies? If forty million Americans don't have health insurance, there must be a lot of bodies. I would think that American cities would look like Delhi or Calcutta, where trucks collect corpses from the streets each morning. Where is America hiding its uninsured sick and dying citizens?'[1]

There are two sides to Miami. One side includes the University of Miami, where I work, and surrounding Coral Gables. The University of Miami is one of the most expensive private schools in the nation and in the student parking lot I get to marvel at the latest Jaguars, BMWs, Mercedes and Hummers. On an especially good day, I'll even see a Ferrari. Coral Gables, where the University's main campus is located, was initially planned on 1,600 acres of citrus and avocado groves. Today it is a residential community of large houses and even larger mansions, many built in the 1920s and 30s in a beautiful Spanish Mediterranean colonial style. Thanks to Miami's tropical climate nature explodes and the landscaping is lush; flowers in vivid pink and deep purple line entrances and boulevards, trees sprout out of trees with vines so high and thick you half expect monkeys to swing by. Green parrots and lanky white ibises fly overhead while tiny lizards, gray except for a surprising burst of orange that balloons from their throat, scramble underfoot.

This side of Miami also includes downtown Brickell, Miami's business hub, where the skyline is cut by gleaming skyscrapers housing the firms that make Miami the financial capital of the Americas. Lawyers and bankers spend their day adding to the accounts of the wealthiest

---

1 Susan Starr Sered and Rushika Fernandopulle, *Uninsured in America: Life and Death in the Land of Opportunity*, Berkeley: University of California Press, 2005, p. 1.

of Latin Americans; in the evening they take their designer suits to the happy hour at the Mandarin Oriental Hotel on Brickell Key. There you can unwind at M-Bar by relaxing on one of the luxurious couches, drinking one of the 250 martini choices and enjoying the panoramic views of downtown Miami and glittering Biscayne Bay. Order sushi under the Japanese lanterns or walk across the infinity pool outside to the Mandarin's 20,000 square-foot, private white-sand beach to lie under a canopy on an exotic white cushioned bed. When a beach butler comes by offering Bulgari-scented towelettes to cool you off on an especially hot evening order a few more drinks. Relax; you might even see some dolphins playfully jumping out on the bay.

Most famously, this side of Miami includes South Beach, where the phrase 'playground of the rich and famous' is not a cliché but a fact. Crossing the Macarthur Causeway from Brickell to South Beach you will see the multi-million dollar mansions of Star and Palm Island on your left, basketball star Shaquille O'Neal lives in one, cruise ships as long as skyscrapers are tall preparing to depart for the Caribbean on your right, as well as Fisher Island, a private island accessible by ferry only if you're a resident or have a guest pass, and the United States' wealthiest zip code. Rock stars, fashion designers, actors, directors, and athletes come to South Beach for its blue skies, turquoise waters, 10-mile-long beaches, gleaming Art Deco hotels, fancy restaurants, high fashion and trend-setting nightclubs. Locals, tourists and celebrities cruise around on scooters and go people-watching on Lincoln Road or Ocean Drive where long-legged models pose for magazine covers with the ocean as a backdrop. Others might lounge on one of the beds pool-side at the Delano Hotel sipping caipirinhas and snacking on the bar's frozen grapes. You can have lunch at the Blue Door restaurant, whose chef Claude Troisgros is flown in weekly from Brazil. At nightfall the pool becomes a champagne party as shoes are removed, evening dresses hiked up and dancing in its shallow side reigns. In South Beach you won't look twice at a Hummer or the latest Mercedes Benz – they are all over the place – as Maseratis, Bentleys and Lamborghinis line sidewalks as if they were everyday commuting cars. But keep your eyes open, because in addition to resident superstars such as Gloria Estefan and Ricky Martin, you could run into Elton John taking in a sunset, Sting at a bar, Sophia Loren behind big sunglasses and Oprah Winfrey at a gourmet market. There are good reasons why *Vogue* baptized South Beach 'America's Riviera'.

Scratch underneath the glitzy and glamorous surface, however, and you'll find Miami's other side. *The New York Times* reports on Umoja, a shantytown in downtown Miami which I've visited often:

With 16 huts cobbled together from plywood, discarded closet doors and cardboard, Umoja is a shantytown in the shadow of the biggest construction boom Miami has seen since the 1920s . . . Most of the 40 residents said they had been sleeping on the streets before moving into Umoja's colorful shacks. The eyesore has become a warm community, with a resident poet entertaining regularly, and has won over some neighbors, including those who now bring by homemade sweet potato pies, despite previous complaints about trash and noise. The city commissioner who represents the area, Michelle Spence-Jones, had tried to shut the settlement down with an ordinance to require a permit for gatherings on public land. But after several visits to Umoja, she withdrew the ordinance and instead promised to arrange for trash pickup at the site three times a week. Ms. Spence-Jones stopped short, however, at the group's request for a mailbox. 'That sends a whole other message', she said.[2]

If instead of taking a right from Brickell on to the Macarthur Causeway toward South Beach glitter you take a left, just one block forth you are in a different world. Instead of glass towers you'll see boarded up warehouses; rather than smelling tropical flowers you will catch the stench of trash-filled lots; rather than enjoying the sight of parrots and ibises you will be looking out for rats and roaming packs of dogs; instead of running into models and celebrities you will run into the unemployed and the destitute – I once counted 20 homeless men huddled in cardboard boxes just three blocks from Miami's new

2 More from the article: 'The shantytown is based on a 1998 court ruling in which a federal district court judge said Miami could not criminalize homeless people for conducting "life-sustaining acts" including eating, sleeping, lighting a fire and building temporary structures on public land if local shelters were filled . . . With apartment vacancy rates at 1.7 per cent, down from 4.7 per cent three years ago, and rents rapidly rising amid gentrification of poor neighborhoods, a report in October by the Miami-Dade County planning department estimated that the area would need 294,200 new housing units by 2025, 42 per cent of them for "very low- or low-income households." A separate 2006 study by Florida International University found that half the families in West Liberty City could not afford a studio apartment in the area. Sam Gil, a spokesman for Camillus House, one of Miami's oldest homeless shelters, said that the local homeless population had decreased to about 5,000 from its peak of 7,000 in the 1980s, but that the county had just 1,350 emergency shelter beds. Michael Stoop, executive director of the National Coalition for the Homeless, said shantytowns like Umoja were "indicative that shelters are not the solution, and that homeless folks want to have themselves treated in a more dignified way". The shacks, many covered with blue tarps, are ringed by a row of earthen plots where residents grow cabbage, collard greens, kale and papaya. A portable toilet, stacks of firewood, and the kitchen and pantry are lined up along one side, and an improvised shower sits in the back.' *The New York Times*, 'An Experiment and a Protest in Shantytown for the Homeless', 16 January 2007.

$500 million Carnival Center for the Performing Arts. Despite Coral Gables' Spanish luxury, Brickell's investment banks and South Beach's celebrity machine, Miami is always in the running for, and often wins, the right to be named the poorest city in the United States.[3]

While median household income in the United States is $46,326, median household income in Miami-Dade county stands at $35,966 and out of the 100 largest cities in the country, Miami ranks last at $24,031. With 28.3% of its residents living in poverty – defined as less than $9,570 per individual or $19,500 for a family of four – the city has the third-highest poverty rate in the nation. It is widely acknowledged, however, that if all undocumented residents were included in census data Miami would easily earn the distinction of poorest city in the nation. *The Miami Herald* reports on the rise of hunger in the Miami area:

> The canned peaches have dwindled and candied yams have all but disappeared, replaced by empty crates piled high inside the Stop Hunger Inc. warehouse nestled at Northeast 120th Street and 14th Avenue in North Miami. On some mornings, the line extends out to the parking lot, so 77-year-old Shirley Williams arrives early, about 8 a.m., and pushes her wheelchair out of the sweltering heat. 'At my age, you can't afford to get lost in the crowd,' Williams joked on a recent Tuesday. Farther north, hundreds pack the tiny two-story building at Broward County's Cooperative Feeding Program, where staff members have had to add a second meal to daily feedings. The crowds – and the increasing demand for food – reflect a growing number of people across the state pushed into severe poverty, with income levels at or below half of the federal poverty line . . . In the meantime, volunteers at South Florida food banks see more and more new faces while their supply diminishes. 'We don't know half the people who come in here now. And our food shelves are constantly empty,' said Marti Forman, head of the Cooperative Feeding Program in Broward. The pantry has increased meals 24 per cent from 2004 to 2005, Forman said. At Stop Hunger, meal distributions have doubled to half a million meals a month in the last five years. The center also distributes food to 82 neighboring churches. 'We see more and more people . . . but our supplies have been cut

---

3 The Miami data that follows is drawn from a Brookings Institute study that can be found in pdf format at http://www.brookings.edu/es/urban/livingcities/miami.htm. See also the federal census data at http://www.fedstats.gov/qf/states/12/1245000.html, and the *Miami New Times* special issues at http://www.miaminewtimes.com/issues/2002-09-26/special.html, http://www.miaminewtimes.com/issues/2002-10-03/special.html.

considerably,' said Malcolm Gabriel, Stop Hunger's executive director for programs. 'There's just a growing sense of desperation.' At
the warehouse, Santiago Torres waited until most people left before
picking up his own supplies. 'I'm embarrassed,' the 33-year old cus-
todian said with a sigh. 'I've never done this before . . . but I can't let
my kids starve.'[4]

In Miami, income differentials vary widely by race and ethnicity.
Whites earn on average $49,000, Latinos $22,000 and blacks $17,000
per year. This poverty is marked by low levels of education. Nation-
ally, approximately 84% of adults aged 25 and over have a high-school
diploma; in Miami a mere 53% have graduated from high school while
only 16% of the adult population has a college degree. Like income,
educational attainment is also coloured by race and ethnicity. Of
Miami whites, 46% have earned college degrees, while only 13% of
Latinos and 6% of blacks have done so. Given this data, it is perhaps
not surprising that Miami has the highest percentage of adults that
do not participate in the labour force at almost 50% and more than
one in four Miami children live in households with no adult workers.
Thus over half of Miami families with children live below or near the
poverty line; indeed, child poverty rate in Miami is the highest in the
nation at 38.5%.[5]

---

4 The piece reports that severe poverty 'increased from 859,888 in 2000 to 943,670
in 2005, a 9.7 percent rise, according to new census data. Over those years, Broward's
number of severely poor grew from 77,942 to 82,327; Palm Beach County's increased
from 57,855 to 63,327. Miami-Dade County had a slight decrease, from 161,301 to
158,593. However, Miami-Dade's 6.8 percent deep-poverty rate was among the highest
in the state. The numbers suggest that the region's rising cost of living is not just squeez-
ing the middle class and the working poor, but pushing the poorest further under the
radar. "We hear of professional people leaving Miami because of the high cost of living
all the time," said Daniella Levine, executive director of the Human Services Coalition.
"But for the very poor, there's not a lot of options." It's happening despite a record-low
unemployment rate, 3.5 percent. "There's a great deal of construction going on which has
created tons of jobs," said Barry E. Johnson, president of the Greater Miami Chamber of
Commerce. Construction is expected to create about 1,400 jobs a year for the next eight
years, said Rick Beasley, executive director of the South Florida Workforce. The problem:
Those jobs are not available to most unskilled workers. "The construction jobs are there,
but we're suffering a shortage in labor skills," Beasley said. "We need to be more focused
on offering job-training initiatives." Experts argue that government-sponsored social
programs that include required job training, early-education intervention and better
mental-health services are the most effective remedy for extreme poverty. "We would
have to become more European," said Bruce Nissen, director of research for the Institute
on Social and Economic Policy at Florida International University.' *The Miami Herald*,
'Extreme Poverty on the Rise in the State', 25 February 2007.
5 The Brookings Institute notes that 'Only half of the City of Miami's working residents are employed within the city . . . Today, moreover, a majority of commutes in the

Within this widespread poverty, the city of Miami also includes pockets of even more extreme need. Just a few miles north of the Macarthur Causeway, Little Haiti has a poverty rate of 46% and an unemployment rate of 50%. Wynwood, which now houses a few art galleries and is promoted in glossy magazines as Miami's little Soho, has a median household income of only $20,500. The prize for the poorest zip code in the United States, however, goes to Overtown. Overtown stands just a couple of blocks from the multimillion dollar condominiums – with names such as Nirvana, Jade, Icon, Skyline, Marina Blue – that sprouted during Miami's recent real-estate boom.[6] Walk these

---

Miami metro area begin and end in the suburbs, and city residents are driving to work in greater numbers. Miami's black residents, in particular, may be especially disconnected from the growing suburban job market, as more than 40 percent do not have access to an automobile.' http://www.brookings.edu/es/urban/livingcities/miami.htm.

6 A boom which has come to an end. In a piece titled 'The Dark Side of the Boom' *The Miami Herald* reports on the human consequences of the downturn: 'The once spotless apartment is a gutted shell now, a place where junkies shoot up and urine saturates the carpet beneath layers of fast-food wrappers, tangled window blinds and broken glass. Five months ago, it was the tiny but pin-neat home of Martha Pomare and her two boys. Now, the only trace of the former occupants is the white paint on the walls. When the residents of the Cameo Apartments, 1825 NE Fourth Ave., were forced out in June by development plans, they found themselves on the dark side of Miami's condo-building boom, which gobbled up affordable housing in favor of glitzy new high-rises. But the Cameo still stands. Nothing new has been built there. Vagrants and addicts have moved in, and the building has been stripped of salvageable metal down to the light sockets . . . All around the dilapidated Cameo, new condo towers are nearing completion. But Miami's overheated real-estate market has cooled, and projects that haven't broken ground face increasingly difficult conditions. The future of those projects – Portico included – remains in question . . . Many planned projects have stalled, he said. In many cases, those projects already had cleared out rental apartments and knocked the buildings down . . . For the former residents of the Cameo, it will be a relief when the building finally comes down. It stands as a reminder of the afternoon they found notices on their doors giving them less than three weeks to move. A new condo was taking the building's place . . . The tenants, who had no leases, received their deposits back and ultimately were allowed to stay in their $500-a-month apartments for up to six weeks without paying rent. Dominguez said his company, which bought the Cameo in 2004, allowed renters to stay in the apartments for two years without raising their rents while the Portico project was being planned . . . But the search for new homes was still a mad scramble. Some ended up paying more than they could afford for new rentals in the tighter market. Others doubled up with roommates or left the state . . . Inside the Cameo, the newest residents are sleeping off last night's high. Nearly every apartment has been vandalized. In one, green garbage bags filled with trash are piled in the middle of the living room. In another, a wall is smeared with feces. Larry, stretched out on a lounge chair in a second-floor apartment, keeps headphones on to drown out the construction racket. He has lived in the complex "a couple months," he said. He's 52, from Boston originally, and works three nights a week, for $7 an hour, parking cars downtown. Is it dangerous to live in a room with near-strangers, no windows and no privacy? He shrugs. "I sleep in the closet," he said. "Three walls, and you just have to watch the doorway." Martha Pomare, the former tenant who lived a few doors from the apartment where Larry now sleeps, says that learning what has

blocks and you will experience a shift in reality so quick and extreme it's unsettling. The 12,000 residents who live in Overtown's 1.8 square miles have a median household income of just $14,000 and a poverty rate of over 50%. Fear runs rampant – for security reasons Domino's Pizza refuses to deliver to Overtown. Miami has two sides; they are literally right next to each other, and literally worlds apart.

In Charles Dickens' *Hard Times* one of his characters foretells that 'every inch of the existence of mankind, from birth to death, was to be a bargain across a counter'.[7] This prediction, so dreary and bleak, would be a luxury for Miami's poor. For them there is no counter and no bargain, only abandonment by a government and wider society that turns a blind eye to their existence. Blissfully ignored by the over-passes and highways that connect the well-to-do, isolated by fences and ditches, consumed by drugs and despair, they are best neither seen nor heard. Like the inhabitants of 'Vita', they too are human refuse. Zones of social abandonment are not exclusive to the Third/Two-Thirds World only. They can be found in the United States as well. The divide between those included and those excluded from the global economy is not merely a geographic rich-poor polarization, it is also a *social* rich-poor divide that 'cuts across territorial boundaries and geographic regions.'[8] Starting from this claim, this chapter will suggest that a United Statesian liberation theologian works in a material context little different from a liberation theologian from the Third World.[9] While the United States is the wealthiest and most powerful country in the world, it also boasts some of the highest poverty levels of all the industrialized nations. Miami, in reality, is a microcosm for the United States as a whole.

Vita: the United States as a Zone of Social Abandonment

In his Gettysburg Address, Abraham Lincoln memorably proclaimed that 'my dream is of a place and time where America will once again

---

become of the complex stings. "We didn't have to leave," she said. "We could have been there all this time".' *The Miami Herald*, 12 November 2006. See also 'Leadership Void Shown in Fall of Condo Market', *The Miami Herald*, 15 November 2006.

7 From memory.

8 Ankie Hoogvelt, *Globalization and the Postcolonial World: The New Political Economy of Development*, Baltimore: The Johns Hopkins University Press, 1997, p. 64.

9 As I stated in the previous chapter, I prefer 'United Statesian' to 'American' or 'North American'. See p. 12, note 23.

be seen as the last best hope of earth'.[10] For believers in the rosy myth of the American dream, and there are many, that time is now. They take for granted that the United States is the greatest country in the world, destined to shape the globe in its image, they do not question the notion of the United States as a land of opportunity where self-made men (and women) thrive, a promised land for all to emulate.[11] Studies show that compared to Europeans, United Statesians are much more likely to believe that they can improve their standard of living and less than one-fifth see race, gender or class as important for getting ahead.[12] As Bill Clinton once exclaimed that 'the American dream that we were all raised on is a simple but powerful one – if you work hard and play by the rules, you should be given a chance to go as far as your God-given ability will take you.'[13] For believers in this dream, the revelation of poverty and lack across their nation can be shocking.

In what follows, I show that Vita is no stranger to the United States; zones of social abandonment exist, more so, spread, in the most powerful nation on earth. And while Ray Charles once quipped 'affluence separates people. Poverty knits 'em together. You got some sugar and I don't; I borrow some of yours. Next month you might not have any flour; well, I'll give you some of mine', this spread is most definitely not bringing people together.[14] As a prelude, however, a word must be said about the different ways lack can be measured.[15] Poverty can

---

10 Abraham Lincoln, 'Gettysburg Address', can be found online at various sources. For good overviews of his life and political vision see Richard Carwardine, *Lincoln: A Life of Purpose and Power*, New York: Knopf, 2006 and Doris Kearns Goodwin, *Team of Rivals: The Political Genius of Abraham Lincoln*, New York: Simon & Schuster, 2006.

11 For two books that examine the notion of the United States' manifest destiny see Ernest Lee Tuveson, *Redeemer Nation: The Idea of America's Millennial Role*, Chicago: University of Chicago Press, 1968 and William R. Hutchinson and Hartmut Lehmann (eds), *Many Are Chosen: Divine Election and Western Nationalism*, Minneapolis: Fortress Press, 1994.

12 Annette Lareau, *Unequal Childhoods: Class, Race, and Family Life*, Berkeley: University of California Press, 2003, p. 7.

13 From President Clinton's 1993 speech to the Democratic Leadership Council. Cited in Lareau, *Unequal Childhoods*, p. 7. She in turn cites Clinton from Jennifer L. Hochschild, *Facing Up to the American Dream: Race, Class, and the Soul of the Nation*, Princeton, NJ: Princeton University Press, 1995, p. 18.

14 http://www.brainyquote.com/quotes/quotes/r/raycharles134555.html

15 For data from the latest census see http://www.census.gov/Press-Release/www/releases/archives/income_wealth/005647.html. Good books on poverty in the United States include Felicia Kornbluh, *The Battle for Welfare Rights: Politics and Poverty in Modern America*, Philadelphia: University of Pennsylvania Press, 2007; Amy K. Glasmeier, *An Atlas of Poverty in America: One Nation, Pulling Apart, 1960–2003*, New York: Routledge, 2006; Meizhu Lui, Barbara Robles, Betsy Leondar-Wright, Rose Brewer and Rebecca Adamson (eds), *The Color of Wealth: The Story Behind the U.S. Racial Wealth*

be measured by an absolute standard, a relative standard or a combination of both. Absolute measures define a basic-needs bottom line; relative measures define poverty as a condition of comparative disadvantage. In the former extreme differences of income between parts of the population are not taken into account, as long as the absolute basic standard is met, while in the latter such differences would be accounted for. The debate about how to measure poverty, therefore, revolves around whether poverty refers to a basic subsistence standard, the amount of money required to survive, or to economic marginalization; that is, deprivation relative to social norms and standards.[16]

In practice, the United States uses an absolute measure while in most industrialized nations the poverty line is set at a given proportion of the median income rather than being based on a fixed amount of money. I bring this up because the choice for an absolute standard by which poverty is measured carries consequences that are not innocent of political implications. The absolute measure used in the United States has a time and place of birth:

> Within the Kennedy administration, the economist Walter Heller, chairman of the Council of Economic Advisers (CEA), wanted to 'launch a Kennedy offensive against poverty'. The CEA favored doing so within the framework of the broader economic agenda they had been pursuing since 1961, which aimed at faster economic growth and full employment by means of tax cuts. Robert Lampman, a CEA economist at the time, also sought to devise a politically acceptable definition of poverty that would focus less on income inequality and more on the amount needed to achieve a minimum living standard. A narrower income definition would lend itself

Divide, New York: The New Press, 2006; Mark Robert Rank, *One Nation, Underprivileged: Why American Poverty Affects Us All*, Oxford: Oxford University Press, 2004; Keith M. Kilty and Elizabeth A. Segal (eds), *Rediscovering the Other America: The Continuing Crisis of Poverty and Inequality in the United States*, New York: The Hawthorn Press, 2003; John Iceland, *Poverty in America: A Handbook*, Berkeley: University of California Press, 2003; Garth L. Mangum, Stephen L. Mangum, and Andrew M. Sum, *The Persistence of Poverty in the United States*, Baltimore: Johns Hopkins University Press, 2003; and Edward N. Wolff, *Top Heavy: The Increasing Inequality of Wealth in America and What Can Be Done About It*, New York: The New Press, 2002. Also worthwhile are Walter Benn Michaels, *The Trouble with Diversity: How We Learned to Love Identity and Ignore Inequality*, New York: Metropolitan Books, 2006; Barbara Ehrenreich, *Bait and Switch: The (Futile) Pursuit of the American Dream*, New York: Metropolitan Books, 2005 and Barbara Ehrenreich, *Nickel and Dimed: On (Not) Getting By in America*, New York: Owl Books, 2002.

16 Iceland, *Poverty in America*, p. 36.

to the growth-centered economic policy (as opposed to income or wealth redistribution policies) the CEA was advocating.[17]

So, on the one hand, most basically, an absolute measure leads to lower poverty measures, by an absolute standard fewer people enter the radar as poor; more importantly, on the other hand, an absolute measure discourages economic policies geared toward alleviating inequality such as social programmes that might include an income or wealth redistribution component. Instead, the focus falls on growth-centred approaches, such as tax cuts, geared toward facilitating investment and the creation of jobs that would then lift the standard of living of the poor. Anyone familiar with the United States' recent economic history will know how the exclusive reliance on an absolute measure has played itself out.[18] In what follows, I look at data provided by both measures.

The Bottom Rung

By the absolute measure used by the United States government, today there are 34.6 million people, 12.6% of the population, who fall below the poverty line. There are always those, however, who hover dangerously close to the official threshold of poverty. If one were to use 1.25 of the poverty line, thus increasing the poverty level by 25%, over 47.1 million people, 16.5% of the population would be poor, and if one

---

17 Iceland, *Poverty in America*, p. 18. Heller and his colleagues adapted a measure developed by Mollie Orshansky. For a good non-academic overview see John Cassidy, 'Relatively Deprived: How Poor is Poor?', in *The New Yorker*, 3 April 2006, pp. 42–7.

18 To this end the *New York Times* reports: 'Despite the Bush-era expansion, the number of Americans living in poverty in 2005 – 37 million – was the same as in 2004. This is the first time the number has not risen since 2000. But the share of the population now in poverty – 12.6 percent – is still higher than at the trough of the last recession, when it was 11.7 percent. And among the poor, 43 percent were living below half the poverty line in 2005 – $7,800 for a family of three. That's the highest percentage of people in "deep poverty" since the government started keeping track of those numbers in 1975. As for the uninsured, their ranks grew in 2005 by 1.3 million people, to a record 46.6 million, or 15.9 percent. That's also worse than the recession year 2001, reflecting the rising costs of health coverage and a dearth of initiatives to help families and companies cope with the burden. For the first time since 1998, the percentage of uninsured children increased in 2005. The Census findings are yet another indication that growth alone is not the answer to the economic and social ills of poverty, income inequality and lack of insurance. Economic growth was strong in 2005, and productivity growth was impressive. What have been missing are government policies that help to ensure that the benefits of growth are broadly shared – like strong support for public education, a progressive income tax, affordable health care, a higher minimum wage and other labor protections.' 'Downward Mobility', *The New York Times*, 30 August 2006.

were to increase the poverty level by 50% and use 1.50 of the poverty line as measure, 61.1 million people would fall below the poverty line. So by the absolute measure over 34 million people are poor in the United States, while an additional 26 million people live at the edge of the poverty line.[19]

These numbers may be dry, but they quantify a stark reality. What do they mean on a day-to-day basis in terms of, for example, food? In 2002 the poverty level for a family of four was $18,392. The United States government, in turn, assumes that one-third of a family's income goes toward the purchase of food. In this case, therefore, a family at the poverty line would have $6,131 to spend on food per year: 'This comes out to $118 a week, $16.86 a day, or $4.22 a day for each member of that family. Assuming that family members eat three meals per day, this works out to $1.41 per person per meal a day.'[20] That will not buy you much of a meal. Notice, however, that this family suffers what could be called a 'wealthy' poverty; they live at the highest level of what is defined as poverty: 'In 2002, 41% of all poor persons were living in households where the income fell below one-half of their respective poverty threshold. If we take 50% of the poverty threshold for a family of four, this works out to $59 per week for food, and $118 per week for all other expenses.'[21] Do the math. In this case $59 per week translates to $8.42 a day, or $2.1 a day for each family member. If each eats three meals a day it boils down to 70 cents a meal.

The absolute poverty rate of 12.6% of the population, where 34.6 million people are defined as poor, may lull the mind into thinking that poverty is a relatively contained phenomenon. The truth, however, is that the likelihood of experiencing poverty is far greater than that captured by a static measure.[22] At the poverty threshold, by the age of 40, 35.6% of the population has lived at least one year in official poverty. By the age of 60, 48.2% of the population has done so. Finally, by age 75, over half the population, 58.5%, has experienced at least a year in poverty. The percentages rise substantially if you take into account those who hover near the threshold. At the age of 40, 43.6% of the population falls below 1.25 of the poverty line and 51.7% fall below 1.50 of the same line. By the age of 60, the percentages are 56.1 and 64.2%, while, by the age 75, the percentages are 68 and 76. Poverty, therefore, is not a self-contained phenomenon suffered by only a marginal segment of the population. The striking reality is that

---

19 I take this data from Rank, *One Nation*, p. 25.
20 Rank, *One Nation*, p. 23.
21 Rank, *One Nation*, p. 24.
22 What follows draws from Rank, *One Nation*, pp. 92–5.

poverty is an experience that will affect a majority of United States citizens during their lifetime. You should also be aware that the way the absolute measurement is calculated has become harsher over time. In 1959 the poverty threshold for a family of four was drawn at 50% of the median income for a family of four; in 1980, it was drawn at 35% and in 2000 at 28%. In 1964 the federal government calculated that an additional $12 billion dollars given to all families in poverty would lift them up to the poverty line as long as they did not reduce their work income. In the year 2000, however, it would have taken $42.4 billion to meet the same goal.[23] The end result is that being poor today means living much farther from the midpoint than before; poverty, in this sense, is far more severe than it was in the past.[24]

The United States' absolute poverty rate does not compare favourably to those of the rest of the wealthy industrialized world.[25] Only Australia and the United Kingdom, at 17.6% and 15.7%, have higher rates than the United States' 12.6%. France, Canada, Germany, Netherlands, Sweden, and Italy have lower rates, some half as low. The United States also has a high child absolute poverty rate. Approximately 12 million children under the age of 18 live in poverty while 18.2% of children under the age of five live below the poverty line. One in six of all children lives in poverty today, while at least one in four are poor in eight states: Alabama, Arizona, Arkansas, District of Columbia, Louisiana, Mississippi, New Mexico, Tennessee and West Virginia. Remarkably, 31% of all children in Washington DC, the nation's capital, are poor.[26] France, Germany, Netherlands, Canada, Belgium, Austria, Denmark, Finland, Switzerland, Taiwan, and a host

---

23 Mangum, Mangum, and Sum, *Persistence of Poverty*, p. 7.

24 Rank notes that 'if we were to apply in 2001 the economic distance that families in poverty were from the median income found in 1959, the poverty threshold for a family of four would rise from $18,104 to $31,639'. For this data see Rank, *One Nation*, pp. 24–5. He cites Wyoming House of Representatives member Barbara Cubin's analogy between the poor and wolves as an example of the mindset that makes this slide possible: 'The Federal government introduced wolves into the State of Wyoming, and they put them in pens, and they brought elk and venison to feed them every day. This is what I call the wolf welfare program. The Federal Government provided everything that the wolves need for their existence. But guess what? They opened the gates and let the wolves out, and now the wolves won't go. Just like any animal in the species, any mammal, when you take away their freedom and their dignity and their ability, they can't provide for themselves.' Rank, *One Nation*, pp. 36–7.

25 The Luxembourg Income Study (LIS) accumulates information on households from over twenty-five countries and makes such comparisons possible. Both Rank and Iceland use its data. See Iceland, *Poverty in America*, pp. 63–6 and Rank, *One Nation*, pp. 33–6.

26 I take this data from Glasmeier, *Atlas of Poverty*, p. 6.

of other countries do a better job of meeting a child's basic needs than does the United States.[27]

While an absolute measure indicates a clear cut-off threshold, relative measurements remind us that poverty is also contextual. The history of economic thought includes a distinguished list of economists who warn that absolute measures by themselves do an inadequate job of understanding the reality of poverty. In the *Wealth of Nations*, for example, Adam Smith stressed that 'by necessaries I understand not only the commodities which are indispensably necessary for the support of life, but whatever the custom of the country renders it indecent for creditable people, even of the lowest order, to be without'.[28] Similarly, John Kenneth Galbraith once noted that

In part poverty is a physical matter . . . But . . . it is wrong to rest everything in absolutes. People are poverty-stricken when their income, even if adequate for survival, falls markedly behind that of the community. Then they cannot have what the larger community regards as the minimum necessary for decency; and they cannot wholly escape, therefore, the judgment of the larger community that they are indecent.[29]

Social perceptions of poverty are therefore important. So Amartya Sen thinks of poverty as a 'capability failure', the inability to participate fully in society. For him, people with little political voice, little economic and physical security, and little opportunity to improve their lives lack basic capabilities. From this perspective, goods and services are valuable insofar as they help people lead satisfying lives; in highly unequal societies, however, those at the bottom are unable to do so.[30]

Does the United States suffer from capability failure? The reality is that the United States lags even farther behind the rest of the industrialized world when measured by the percentage of people living with

27 See Iceland, *Poverty in America*, p. 65.

28 Smith explains: 'A linen shirt, for example, is, strictly speaking, not a necessary of life. The Greeks and Romans lived, I suppose, very comfortably, though they had no linen. But in the present times, through the greater part of Europe, a creditable day-labourer would be ashamed to appear in public without a linen shirt, the want of which would be supposed to denote that disgraceful degree of poverty which, it is presumed, nobody can well fall into, without extreme bad conduct.' Adam Smith, *An Inquiry Into the Nature and Causes of the Wealth of Nations*, ed. and notes by Edwin Cannan, introd. by Edwin Cannan and Max Lerner, New York: Modern Library, 1937, pp. 351–2.

29 John Kenneth Galbraith, *The Affluent Society*, Boston: Houghton Mifflin, 1984, p. 251.

30 See Amartya Sen, *Development as Freedom*, New York: Knopf, 1999.

less than half of median income. According to this measure the United States has the highest relative poverty rate of 17.8%. Italy is the next closest country at 13.9% followed by the United Kingdom, Canada, Spain, and Israel. Netherlands stands at 7.9%, Australia at 6.7%, and Belgium at 5.5%.[31] Eyed through this measure, one in every four children in the United States lives in poverty, which is the same ratio as in Russia. The high relative poverty rate points to an increasing disparity between the upper and lower class of the population. In the United States, 47% of the country's financial wealth is owned by the top 1% while 70% is held by the top 5%.[32] Household income is also concentrated with the top 5% receiving 49.8% of total household income while the bottom 20% of households in the United States had total incomes of less than 3.4% of that total.[33]

In the last 40 years, the real value of stock prices has increased by a multiple of more than three and the salaries of chief executives of companies have grown by a multiple of eleven. In 1970, the average worker's wage, adjusted for inflation today, was $32,522; that same year the average total pay of the top 100 CEOs was $1,255,000. By 1998, the average wage showed a bare increase to $35,864, while the average total pay of the top 100 CEOs jumped to an incredible $37,509,000; 'in other words, the average income of a top CEO in this country has gone from 39 times the average worker's salary in 1970, to more than 1,000 times what an average workers earns during the year.'[34] Between 1979 and 2000 the average after-tax income of the richest 1% of United Statesians increased by nearly 200%.[35] Yet the level of a production worker's pay and the minimum wage has barely grown.[36] Between 1950 and 1970, for each additional dollar made by those in the bottom 90% of income earners, those in the top 0.01% received an additional $162; from 1990 to 2002, for every added dollar made by those in the bottom 90%, those in the uppermost 0.01% (today around 14,000 households) made an additional $18,000.[37] It's

31 For these numbers see Rank, *One Nation*, pp. 33–4.

32 Rank, *One Nation*, p. 161.

33 Glasmeier, *Atlas of Poverty*, p. x.

34 Rank, *One Nation*, p. 161. Another report states that if worker pay had grown at the same rate as the pay of CEOs, 'in 2004, the average worker would have made $110,136, compared to the actual average of $27,460. Similarly, if the federal minimum wage had grown at the same rate as CEO pay, it would have been $23.03 in 2004, instead of $5.15.' The report can be found at http://www.faireconomy.org and is cited in Michaels, *Trouble with Diversity*, pp. 212–13, endnote 13.

35 Glasmeier, *Atlas of Poverty*, p. 28.

36 Bob Sutcliffe, *100 Ways of Seeing an Unequal World*, New York: Zed Books, 2001, graph 16.

37 John Bellamy Foster, 'Aspects of Class in the United States: An Introduction',

not surprising, therefore, that the United States' GINI coefficient – a simple measure economists use to express inequality – is approaching that of Latin America, the most unequal region of the world.[38] Indeed, income inequality in the United States, the proportion of the richest tenth to the poorest tenth, is greater than income inequality in India.[39] This is a nation literally pulling apart.[40]

African Americans

While whites constitute the majority of the poor at 45%, the probability of being poor follows racial, ethnic and gender lines. The United States does possess a significant African American middle class (based on an income of $40,000 or more) but the number of families below the poverty line and the number of black children living in extreme poverty has risen since the mid-1990s. Today African Americans are almost three times as likely to live in poverty as whites and almost one million black children live in extreme poverty. A child in the United States has an almost one-in-five chance of living in poverty, whereas an African American child has a one-in-three chance of being poor. African American families' income and wealth is half that of white

---

Monthly Review Vol. 58, no. 3, July–August 2006; consulted online at http://www. monthlyreview.org/0706jbf.htm. Foster gets this data from correspondents of *The New York Times*, *Class Matters* (New York: Times Books, 2005), p. 186.

38 Glasmeier, *Atlas of Poverty*, p. x.

39 Sutcliffe, *100 Ways*, graph 41.

40 The pulling apart is also evident through the lens of urban planning and spread of what Steven Flusty calls 'interdictory space, designed to intercept and filter or repel would be users'. He identifies five: stealthy space, space that is hard to find, 'the Poets' Walk garden of Citicorp Plaza, in the heart of downtown L.A.'s central business district's financial core . . . is concealed behind an office tower, a department store entrance kiosk, and a flight of escalators;' slippery space, space that is hard to reach; crusty space, space that can't be accessed because of walls, gates, and check points; prickly space, space that can't be occupied comfortably, 'defended by such bedeviled details as wall-mounted sprinkler heads activated to clear loiterers, or ledges sloped to inhibit sitting', such as 'backless benches with seats at a leg-numbing height of twenty-four inches above ground', designed as 'bum proof benches'; and jitterry space, space that can't be used without being monitored by roving patrols or remote technologies. In each case the result is spaces where the undesirables, the lower classes, are kept out. He goes on to note that public spaces are being 'increasingly supplanted by privately produced (although often publicly subsidized) "privately owned and administered spaces for public aggregation". That is, spaces of consumption, or, most commonly, malls. In these new, "post-public" spaces, access is predicated upon the ability to pay.' The above draws from Steven Flusty, *De-Coca-Colonization: Making the Globe from the Inside Out*, New York: Routledge, 2004, pp. 72–6. For more on the hijacking of public space for private gain see Naomi Klein, *No Logo*, New York, NY: Picador USA, 2000.

families, they are also half as likely to own a home. More than 30% of black families, moreover, have a negative net worth compared with only 13% of white families.[41] In fact, from 1995 to 2001 the net worth of the average African American family fell 7%, while the net worth of the average white family grew 37%.[42] The end result is that while the median net worth, the number at which half the population is above and half below, for whites in 2001 was $120,989, for African Americans it was $19,024.[43]

In any given year, approximately 25% to 30% of the black population lives below the poverty line. Remember that by the age of 40, 35.6% of the general population has experienced at least a year below the poverty threshold. At the same age, however, two-thirds of African Americans will have lived below the official poverty measure. By 60, 48.2% of the general population has lived in poverty, while a clear majority of blacks at 81.9% will have done so. Of African Americans who reach the age of 75, 91% will have suffered below the poverty threshold. In fact, nine out of ten African Americans living a normal lifespan will be poor at some point during their prime working years. By the age of 28, moreover, the African American population will have surpassed the cumulative level of lifetime poverty that whites reach by the age of 75; blacks as a whole experience in 9 years the same risk of poverty that whites face in 56.[44]

In 1950, more than 78% of all black families were two-parent; by 1990 the number had dropped to slightly over 50%. Economic instability, incarceration and mortality are factors in this drop. Today 25% of all jobs pay less than a poverty-level income.[45] Lacking higher education, jobs that will keep someone, or a family, over the poverty threshold are hard to come by. This is bad news; in the year 2000 African American men were more likely to be in jail than in college. In 1980 463,700 black men were enrolled in a college or university while only 143,000 lived behind bars; by 2000 a total of 791,600 were in jail in contrast to only 603,032 enrolled in higher education. Indeed, between 1980 and 2000 three times as many African American men were added to the prison system than were added to the higher education system. Blacks, in fact, are disproportionately represented in the criminal justice system. The data is startling. While they are only 13% of the total population, African Americans are 30% of the people

---

41 The data above is taken from Glasmeier, *Atlas of Poverty*, p. 14.
42 Lui, Robles, Leondar-Wright, Brewer and Adamson, *Color of Wealth*, p. 2.
43 Lui, Robles, Leondar-Wright, Brewer and Adamson, *Color of Wealth*, p. 74.
44 The above is taken from Rank, *One Nation*, pp. 95–7.
45 Glasmeier, *Atlas of Poverty*, p. x.

arrested, 41% of the people jailed, and 49% of all people in prison. One in three African Americans between the ages of 20 and 29 has been in prison while one in ten black men in their twenties and early thirties is currently in jail. An African American male between the ages of 25 and 40 has a one in three chance of spending his most productive working years incarcerated; between the ages of 25 and 29 a black man is nine times more likely to be in prison than a white man of the same age range.[46] These statistics take a physical toll. Amazingly, African American men in Harlem have a lower life expectancy than men in Bangladesh, one of the poorest countries in the world.[47]

Hispanic/Latino(as)

Perhaps because the irruption of Hispanic/Latino(as) into national consciousness is a relatively recent phenomenon, there is far less data available for them as a subgroup than there is for the African American population.[48] What can be said with certainty is the following: since 2005, Hispanic/Latinos have been the largest minority group in the United States. They account for 13% of the total population, more than 35 million people, and during the 1990s they were responsible for almost 40% of the nation's population growth. Estimates have Hispanic/Latino(as) comprising 25% of the total population by the middle of the twenty-first century. Since the Bracero programme, which originated from a treaty between the United States and Mexico, Hispanic/Latino(as) have been recruited to fill labour shortages in low-paying occupations. Bracero itself was designed to allow the recruitment and employment of Mexicans to reduce labour shortages in the context of the second great intracolonial war of the twentieth century.[49] Today, as then, Hispanic/Latino(as) place in the labour market is one of low wages and low prestige. While 31.4% of the total male population in the United States works in professional and managerial occupations, only 14.6% of Hispanic/Latino males do so. Poverty rates for Hispanic/Latino(as) are almost twice the national average at 21.9% and child poverty rates are 10 percentage points above the national average –

---

46 The above data is taken from Glasmeier, *Atlas of Poverty*, p. 16.

47 Paul Farmer, *Pathologies of Power: Health, Human Rights, and the New War on the Poor*, Berkeley: University of California Press, 2003, p. 46 For a good overview of US policy toward African Americans see Lui, Robles, Leondar-Wright, Brewer and Adamson, *Color of Wealth*, pp. 78–121.

48 For a brief but good overview of US policies toward Hispanic/Latino(as) see Lui, Robles, Leondar-Wright, Brewer and Adamson, *Color of Wealth*, pp. 139–76.

49 By which I mean World War Two.

27.8% versus 16.6%. Hispanic/Latino(a) median net worth is lower than that of both whites and African Americans: in 2001 median net worth for the former was $120,989, for the latter it was $19,024, while for Hispanic/Latino(as) it was $11,458.[50] Elderly Hispanics, in turn, are twice as likely to live in poverty as the general elderly population. Of elderly Hispanic/Latino(as) 22% are poor; without social security benefits over 50% would fall below the poverty threshold. The 1990s recession, moreover, was especially harsh toward Hispanic/Latino(as); they lost 25% of their wealth compared to white families.[51]

As was the case with the African American population, the educational scenario for Hispanic/Latino(as) is troubling. In the last three decades real wages for workers without a high-school degree have declined by 19%, while real wages for those with at least some college education have increased by 16%. Failing to graduate from high school is a ticket to a life of economic instability and potential poverty. Despite this fact, graduation rates in schools with predominately minority student populations are almost 18% lower than those in predominately white districts. Drop-out rates, moreover, are highest in the West and the South, areas where Hispanic/Latino(as) are more heavily concentrated. Income, of course, makes a difference. High-school students in the lowest 20% of the family income bracket are six times as likely to drop out of high school as students from families in the top 20% of the income bracket. Children of colour generally are more likely to drop out; but among all groups Hispanic/Latino(as) have by far the highest high-school drop-out rate at 26%, more than three times as high than the white rate and more than double the African American drop-out rate.[52]

Women

In the United States, women compose about 57% of the population living below the poverty threshold.[53] While the majority of poor women are white, a higher percentage of poor women is found among minority populations. Of all poor females, 13.7% are white, 24.4% are Hispanic/Latino, and 26.5% are African American. Women of colour, therefore, are more likely to be poor. Wage discrimination has not been overcome:

---

50 Lui, Robles, Leondar-Wright, Brewer and Adamson, *Color of Wealth*, p. 134.
51 The above data is taken from Glasmeier, *Atlas of Poverty*, pp. 18–19.
52 The data above is taken from Glasmeier, *Atlas of Poverty*, pp. 8–9.
53 Iceland, *Poverty in America*, p. 88.

Not only do some occupations continue to remain highly segregated by gender, but wages in those occupations still show large discrepancies among comparable jobs. For example, janitors, who are primarily men, earned an average wage of $10.00 an hour in 2004, while maids and housekeepers, an occupation that requires similar amounts of training and skill, earned $8.67 an hour. Machinery maintenance workers and nursing aides receive similar amounts of training, but the former earned $16.64 an hour in 2004, while the latter earned $10.53.

Overall, women earn 76 cents on the dollar for every dollar earned by a man; their labour is thus compensated at a lesser rate for the same job performed.[54] Reductions in the wage differential over the past decade, moreover, have had more to do with stagnant male wages rather than rising female compensation. Low pay for women means that they must take two or more jobs to make ends meet; almost 50% of all multiple jobholders are women.[55] On the bright side, women are more likely to go to and graduate from college than men and so are gradually becoming a more important part of the labour force. Still, however, only a minority of women have higher degrees and this trend remains concentrated among white middle- and upper-income women. In 2004 only 23% of all women aged 25 to 64 had a college degree. For black women in this age group, only 14% had a college degree or more, while for Hispanic women the figure is only 9%.[56] Despite greater access to higher education, women with the same level of education still earn

---

54 Stephanie Luce and Mark Brenner, 'Women and Class: What has Happened in Forty Years?', *Monthly Review* Vol. 58, no. 3, July–August 2006. Consulted online at http://www.monthlyreview.org/0706lucebrenner.htm

55 Only an economist could take someone's need to work multiple jobs – and thus rarely see family, barely sleep, wonder whether you'll make ends meet – and spin it into something positive. *The New York Times* once had a piece about how the middle class is being squeezed out of major US Cities: 'The percentage of higher-income neighbourhoods in many places has gone up. In New York, the supply of apartments considered affordable to households with incomes like those earned by starting firefighters or police officers plunged by a whopping 205,000 in just three years, between 2002 and 2005.' So what does an economist have to say about this? 'Firefighters who want to live in high-priced cities can work two jobs,' said W. Michael Cox, chief economist for the Federal Reserve Bank of Dallas. 'I think it's great,' he said. 'It gives you portfolio diversification of your income.' I find it incredible and shameful that Mr Cox can conceive of a parallel between someone wealthy diversifying their stock portfolio and someone working several jobs to get to the end of the month. Janny Scot, 'Cities Shed Middle Class, and are Richer and Poorer for It', 23 July 2006.

56 Stephanie Luce and Mark Brenner, 'Women and Class', http://www.monthlyreview.org/0706lucebrenner.htm

less than men.[57] Overall, however, a woman's chances of being poor are only slightly superior to that of a man.[58] By the age of 40, 36.2% of women and 33.7% of men have lived at or below the poverty threshold; by the age of 60, the percentages are 49.2 and 45; while, by age 75, 59% of women and 55.5% of men have been poor. Gender, by itself, is not a good determinant of your chances of falling below the poverty line for the simple reason that marriage equalizes the risk men and women face thus narrowing down gender differences.[59] Where the difference becomes marked, however, is in the case of single-women households: 35.5% of single mother-led families are poor compared to 19.1% for single-father families.[60] It is troubling, therefore, that female-headed families have grown in the past decades. Approximately 17.6% of all families are headed by a woman. Of these however, only 13.9% are white, 23.4% are Hispanic and 44% are African American.[61] Poverty is most prevalent among African American and Hispanic women because they are more likely to become single-parent householders, live in low-income neighbourhoods and have low levels of education, than for the simple fact of their gender. Examining the high poverty rates for single-parent households is another way to see how the United States lags behind the rest of the industrialized world in caring for its most disadvantaged citizens. Taking a relative poverty rate of 50% of median income, the poverty rate for children in Sweden is approximately 6.7% for single-parent households and 1.5% for dual-parent households. In Finland the percentages are closer at 7.1% and 3.9%. Using the same measure, however, the poverty rate for single-parent families in the United States is a whopping 55.4%.[62]

---

57 The above is taken from Glasmeier, *Atlas of Poverty*, pp. 10–11. She also notes that 'even with a PhD, a woman is likely to earn only $1,000 more than a man with a Bachelor's degree'. On a side note, this is likely due to the fact that women are under-represented in the sciences; they tend to get their PhDs in the humanities where salaries are extremely low in relation to educational attainment. I, in fact, make less money than most of the people I know who only have bachelor degrees.

58 This runs against the grain of the 'feminization of poverty' literature. For one example see Ruth Sidel, *Keeping Women and Children Last: America's War on the Poor*, New York: Penguin, 1996.

59 The above is taken from Rank, *One Nation*, pp. 97–8.

60 www.legalmomentum.org/womeninpoverty.pdf and Rank, *One Nation*, p. 273.

61 Iceland, *Poverty in America*, p. 92.

62 Iceland, *Poverty in America*, p. 94.

Vita, Reviewed

In 1964, in his first State of the Union Address, Lyndon Johnson proclaimed to the nation that his administration 'today, here and now, declares unconditional war on poverty in America . . . Our aim is not only to relieve the symptoms of poverty, but to cure it and, above all, to prevent it.'[63] That war, of course, has not been won. In fact, the United States has either abandoned the battle or, as Bill Moyers suggests, changed the front upon which it is waged:

> Class war was declared a generation ago in a powerful paperback polemic by William Simon, who was soon to be Secretary of the Treasury. He called on the financial and business class, in effect, to take back the power and privileges they had lost in the depression and the new deal. They got the message, and soon they began a stealthy class war against the rest of the society and the principles of our democracy. They set out to trash the social contract, to cut their workforces and wages, to scour the globe in search of cheap labor, and to shred the social safety net that was supposed to protect people from hardships beyond their control. *Business Week* put it bluntly at the time [in its October 12, 1974 issue]: 'Some people will obviously have to do with less . . . it will be a bitter pill for many Americans to swallow the idea of doing with less so that big business can have more.'[64]

In the United States, those born poor will likely stay poor. While if you want to strike it rich beyond your wildest dreams, get into politics. According to the *Financial Times*:

> Once in office elected officials tend to get far richer than they were when they entered politics. They are cut in on various deals. They become unusually successful investors. Empirical investigation reveals that in any given year between 1993 and 1998 senators who played the stock market did remarkably well. It turns out they were prescient in anticipating the market's movements up and down, purchasing a particular stock before it took off like a rocket and dumping stocks just in time. Consider a landmark study in the *Journal of Financial and Quantitative Analysis*, which took eight

---

63 Cited in Mangum, Mangum, and Sum, *Persistence of Poverty*, p. 1.

64 Bill Moyers, 'This is the Fight of Our Lives', keynote speech, Inequality Matters Forum, New York University, 3 June 2004; cited in John Bellamy Foster, 'Aspects of Class in the United States: An Introduction', *Monthly Review* 58.3 (July–Aug. 2006): http://www.monthlyreview.org/0706jbf.htm.

years to complete because there was no data base from which the scholars could work and they had to develop one, gathering and examining data manually. They found that the stock portfolios of a random group composed of tens of thousands of households underperformed the market as a whole by 1.4 per cent annually. Corporate insiders beat the market by 6 per cent. But the senators (including their spouses and children) beat the market by 12 per cent a year. The study reminds one of the findings of U.S. Senate Banking Committee counsel Ferdinand Pecora who in 1933 exposed how J. P. Morgan had reserved shares for certain clients – FDR's secretary of the treasury, the chairmen of both the Republican and Democratic National Committees, and others. It also brings to mind Mark Twain's observation that 'if your congressman comes back to your state to run for re-election and is not a millionaire, he is a fool and should be turned out of office'.[65]

However, if you're not climbing the political ladder recent studies show that intergenerational class mobility is much more limited than previously assumed; the United States is the most class-bound society of all the industrialized nations with the exception of the United Kingdom. *The Wall Street Journal*, no bastion of the underclass, reported in 2005 that

> Although Americans still think of their land as a place of exceptional opportunity – in contrast to class-bound Europe – the evidence suggests otherwise ... the escalators of mobility move much more slowly. A substantial body of research finds that at least 45 per cent of parents' advantage in income is passed along to their children, and perhaps as much as 60 per cent. With the higher estimate, it's not only how much money your parents have that matters – even your great-great grandfather's wealth might give you a noticeable edge today.[66]

Income, however, is only one element in the reproduction of advantage and disadvantage. Other, harder to quantify factors, also play a

---

65 *Financial Times*, 25 February 2004; 'Senators Beat the Stock Market – and Get Rich – With Insider Information', *Washington Spectator*, 1 January 2006.

66 *The Wall Street Journal*, 13 May 2005; cited in Foster, 'Aspects of Class'. Foster goes on to note that according to *The New York Times* 'Bhashkar Mazumber of the Federal Reserve Bank of Chicago ... found that around 65 percent of the earnings advantage of fathers was transmitted to sons.' Tom Hertz, an economist at American University, states that 'while few would deny that it is possible to start poor and end rich, the evidence suggests that this feat is more difficult to accomplish in the United States than in other high-income nations.'

fundamental role: 'the advantages of coming from a more "cultured" home environment, differential access to educational opportunities, the possession of "connections" in the circles of those holding positions of power and prestige, and self-confidence which children absorb from their parents – the list could be expanded and elaborated.'[67]

In the United States, the poor carry the scars of their suffering in the flesh.[68] Physical markers are part and parcel of a health care system that leaves those at the lower rungs of the ladder to decay and die.[69] Approximately forty million United States citizens have no health insurance. Of these, 14.5% are white, 20.8% are African American, and 35.7% are Hispanic/Latino. Not surprisingly, the gap in insurance rates leads to disparities in health outcomes. African Americans and Hispanic/Latinos are more likely than whites to die of cancer, heart disease and diabetes. Maternal mortality rates for black women are almost four times that among white women; infant mortality among black children is twice that for whites. While African American and Hispanic men have higher rates of death due to heart disease they are less likely to receive treatment; similarly, African American women are more frequently diagnosed than white women with late-stage breast

---

67 Paul M. Sweezy, *Post-Revolutionary Society*, New York: Monthly Review Press, 1980, pp. 79–80; cited in Foster, 'Aspects of Class'.

68 The three elements that follow are developed from Susan Starr Sered and Rushika Fernandopulle, *Uninsured in America: Life and Death in the Land of Opportunity*, Berkeley: University of California Press, 2005. For them, these are signs that the United States is developing a social order based on caste. For more on the United States and caste see Michael A. Byrd and Linda A. Clayton, *An American Health Dilemma: Race, Medicine, and Health Care in the United States, 1990–2000*, New York: Routledge, 2002; Ursala Sharma, *Caste*, Philadelphia: Open University Press, 1999; Douglas S. Massey and Nancy A. Denton, *American Apartheid: Segregation and the Making of the Underclass*, Cambridge, MA: Harvard University Press, 1993; Lucile Duberman, *Social Inequality: Class and Caste in America*, Philadelphia: J.B. Lippincott, 1976 and Anthony De Reuck and Julie Knight (eds), *Caste and Race: Comparative Approaches*, Boston: Little, Brown, 1967.

69 There is a large body of research on the reinforcing relationship between poverty and health on both the global and the national (US) level. See, for example, Pedro Roffe, Geoff Tansey, and David Vivas-Egui (eds), *Negotiating Health: Intellectual Property and Access to Medicines*, London: Earthscan, 2006; Sered and Fernandopulle, *Uninsured in America*; Jill Quadagno, *One Nation Uninsured: Why the U.S. Has No National Health Insurance*, Oxford: Oxford University Press, 2005; Meredith Fort, Mary Anne Mercer, and Oscar Gish (eds), *Sickness and Wealth: The Corporate Assault on Global Health*, Cambridge, MA: South End Press, 2004; Farmer, *Pathologies of Power*; Jim Yong Kim, Joyce Millen, Alec Irwin, and John Gershman (eds), *Dying for Growth: Global Inequality and the Health of the Poor*, Boston, MA: Common Courage Press, 2000; World Bank, *The Burden of Disease Among the Global Poor: Current Situation, Future Trends, and Implications for Strategy*, Washington, DC: World Bank, 2000 and Richard Wilkinson, *Unhealthy Societies: The Afflictions of Inequality*, New York: Routledge, 1996.

cancer. In all these cases, health experts agree that access to adequate health services could reduce the disparities. Indeed, 40% of black men and 37% of Hispanic/Latino men die prematurely, in contrast to 21% of white men: 'Illness itself constitutes a physical marker: rotten teeth, chronic coughs, bad skin, a limp, sores that don't heal, obesity, uncorrected hearing or vision deficits, addiction to pain medication – all of these signal caste in basic ways.'[70]

In the United States, the poor do not just suffer unemployment or toil in low-level jobs while lacking health insurance, do not just carry the physical markings of their plight in the flesh, they also carry a moral judgement upon their character. In the United States, 'work has long been construed as a moral virtue; we need only think of the generations of American women who embroidered samplers proclaiming that "idle hands are the devil's playthings".'[71] Sickness is displayed as a personal failure, a failure to 'take care of oneself "properly" by eating the "right" foods or getting "enough" exercise, a failure to get a pap smear . . . a failure of will, or a failure of commitment – rather than society's failure to provide basic services to all its citizens'.[72] The Personal Responsibility Act passed by the United States Congress in 1996, which supplanted Aid to Families with Dependent Children (AFDC) with Temporary Assistance to Needy Families (TANF), serves as an example. This legislation is based on an ideology that makes work and family the centre of a moral vision for the poor. TANF limits aid to a

---

70 Sered and Fernandopulle, *Uninsured in America*, p. 16. The previous health data is taken from pp. 157–9. Relative deprivation – not just absolute poverty – is unhealthy. The *New Yorker* reports: 'In a famous study conducted between 1967 and 1977, a team of epidemiologists led by Sir Michael Maramot, of University College London, monitored the health of more than seventeen thousand members of Britain's Civil Service, a highly stratified bureaucracy. Marmot and his colleagues found that people who had been promoted to the top ranks – those who worked directly for cabinet ministers – lived longer than their colleagues in lower-ranking jobs. Midlevel civil servants were more likely than their bosses to develop a range of potentially deadly conditions, including heart disease, high blood pressure, lung cancer, and gastrointestinal ailments. Initially, some critics suggested that these results could be attributed to differences in behavior: members of the lower ranks were more likely to smoke and drink and less likely to exercise and eat healthily than their better-paid superiors. To test this theory, Marmot and his team have been conducting a follow-up which began in 1985 and continues to this day. This survey has confirmed the results of the first study, and has also suggested that less than a third of the difference in patterns of disease and mortality can be ascribed to behavior associated with coronary risk, such as smoking or lack of exercise. "The higher the social position, the longer people can be expected to live, and the less disease they can expect to suffer," Marmot explained in a recent paper. "This is the social gradient in health."' John Cassidy, 'Relatively Deprived: How Poor Is Poor?', *New Yorker*, 3 April 2006, p. 46.

71 Sered and Fernandopulle, *Uninsured in America*, p. 16.

72 Sered and Fernandopulle, *Uninsured in America*, p. 16.

period of five years, gives a two-year limit to find full-time employment and requires working for 20 to 35 hours per week within two months of first receiving aid. The end result is that millions of people enter the labour market in a position where they are forced to accept low wages, menial tasks, poor hours, and no benefits. Poor women are at a particular disadvantage. Studies have shown that an exceptionally high percentage of women on welfare are victims of domestic violence and/or suffer from a physical or mental disability. TANF makes it harder for women to leave abusive husbands, since 'removing the safety net and forcing welfare mothers to work is actually a way to reinforce all women's proper commitment to marriage and family'.[73] Given the very first sentence of the Personal Responsibility Act, 'marriage is the foundation of a successful society', and a subsequent analysis that pins poverty and crime on poor life choices such as teenage pregnancy, out of wedlock births and single-parent households, this result should surprise no one. TANF also makes it harder for welfare recipients to get proper physical and mental care. Given that they start from a position of illness without health insurance, the probability that a welfare recipient will be able to perform consistently at the workplace is slim. This problem is exacerbated if the person in question is a single mother. Suffering from poor health, they are unable to get health insurance and so 'become entrenched members of the caste of the ill, infirm and marginally employed'.[74] Witness the use of terms such as 'bum' and 'welfare queen' as evidence that poverty and failing health are seen as evidence of a lack of moral virtue.[75] Addressing that lack thus becomes a central element of programmes designed to fight poverty.[76]

---

73 Sharon Hays, *Flat Broke with Children: Women in the Age of Welfare Reform*, New York: Oxford University Press, 2003; cited in Sered and Fernandopulle, *Uninsured in America*, p. 54. They don't give a page of the Hays quotation.

74 Sered and Fernandopulle, *Uninsured in America*, p. 56.

75 Traci West provides another example of the moral stigma attached to poverty and then to race: 'Media images can instill the idea that the term "welfare recipient" refers to an individual with a moral problem, and that "welfare recipient with a moral problem" equals black woman. For instance, a degrading caricature of a black woman shown in the early 1990s on a *Boston Globe* opinion-editorial page depicted the "welfare mother" problem. A drawing of several blackened figures grabbing for cash appeared on this editorial page of the *Globe* beside an article written by columnist Ellen Goodman, entitled "Welfare Mothers with an Attitude". The most prominent silhouette in the center of the illustration was a female with an Afro hairstyle, a wide nose, and a baby on her hip who was also reaching up to get some of the cash . . . The news consumer viewing this page is led to believe that "the welfare problem" is mainly embodied in black, big-nosed females who are greedy for cash like this one, and who sexually reproduce similarly greedy offspring.' Traci C. West, *Disruptive Christian Ethics: When Racism and Women's Lives Matter*, Louisville: Westminster John Knox Press, 2006, p. 86.

76 Traci West suggests taking the same measure by which 'studying, negatively label-

Concluding with the Primacy of Class

In 1978 William Julius Wilson published his now classic *The Declining Significance of Race*, where he argued that 'race relations in America have undergone fundamental changes in recent years, so much so that now the life chances of individual blacks have more to do with their economic class position than with their day-to-day encounters with whites'.[77] For him, after the victories of the civil rights movement, class is now more important than race in determining the life chances of African Americans. This point needs to be stressed. In the United States poverty figures are usually presented according to race and ethnicity; indeed, I myself presented the data in that manner here. Such a mode of presentation, however, overstates racial discrimination as a source of oppression and hides the primary role of class oppression in determining life chances.[78]

---

ing, and disciplining the morality of those struggling with the least resources and under the most destitute of conditions' is the means to evaluate the performance of the poor on welfare and apply it those in power. One, therefore, would support 'policy regulating the lives of all elites with status, power, and wealth, especially policy makers'. She adds: 'This regulation could be based upon, for instance, probing and analyzing the charges of sexual harassment and extramarital liaisons made against Newt Gingrich, the charges of sexual harassment and extramarital sexual liaisons against President Clinton, and Glenn Loury's sexual liaisons that resulted in children by a woman he never married and his alleged physical assault of his extramarital female partner. If public policy is to be created on the basis of "personal responsibility", such sexual behavior (as it has been in welfare policy), wouldn't just public practices mandate scrutiny and regulation of those who actually wield political and economic power in this nation, rather than targeting those with little or none?', West, *Disruptive Christian Ethics*, p. 108. I like this idea. After all, aren't those entrusted with the public good worthy of greater scrutiny?

77 William Julius Wilson, *The Declining Significance of Race: Blacks and Changing American Institutions*, Chicago: University of Chicago Press, 1979, p. 1. For more from Wilson see *The Truly Disadvantaged: The Inner City, the Underclass, and Public Policy*, Chicago: University of Chicago Press, 1987; *When Work Disappears: The World of the New Urban Poor*, New York: Vintage, 1997 and *The Bridge Over the Racial Divide: Rising Inequality and Coalitional Politics*, Berkeley: University of California Press, 1999. For a critical yet constructive response see Melvin Oliver and Thomas Shapiro, *Black Wealth/White Wealth: A New Perspective on Racial Inequality*, New York: Routledge, 1995.

78 Reflecting upon her trip to Russia, Audre Lorde sees bread as the primary concern. She writes: 'Russia does not even appear to be a strictly egalitarian society. But bread does cost a few kopecks a loaf and everyone I saw seemed to have enough of it. Of course, I did not see Siberia, nor a prison camp, nor a mental hospital. But the fact, in a world where most people – certainly most black people – are on a breadconcern level, seems to me to be quite a lot. If you conquer the bread problem, that gives you at least a chance to look around at the others.' Audre Lorde, *Sister Outsider*, New York: Crossing Press, 1984, p. 34.

Of course, this doesn't mean that racial discrimination no longer exists in the United States. In his *Race Matters* Cornel West described parking his 'elegant' car in a midtown Manhattan lot and subsequent inability to hail a cab toward Harlem – they just pass him by – despite wearing an expensive three-piece suit on his way to a photo shoot for his book.[79] Nor do I mean to forget that policies geared toward the working class have historically left out non-whites. During the New Deal, for example, union members were often given preference for public jobs at a time when unions restricted membership to whites. Since the Work Projects Administration was administered locally, projects, especially in the south, benefited only white communities; when the National Industrial Recovery Act of 1932 was passed to halt declining wages in the Depression, plantation owners fired black workers rather than give them a raise; despite the Federal Housing Administration programme, realtors and hostile neighbours shut out African Americans from white neighbourhoods and the Agricultural Adjustment Program distributed its aid almost entirely to white farmers. In essence, the New Deal created a safety net whose benefits went predominately to whites and whose end effect was to widen the gap between them and others groups. The twentieth century's second great intracolonial war further lifted whites. The GI Bill, for example, was meant to provide veterans benefits such as job placement, unemployment compensation, mortgage loans and tuition. Those benefits, however, overwhelmingly went to whites. In fact, the blight of many inner cities can be traced back to the GI Bill. Low interest, long-term mortgages for first-time homeowners, made suburban home ownership cheaper than renting in the inner city. Most of these loans went to white veterans who left the city and its decaying infrastructure to African Americans. The GI Bill helped whites accumulate millions of dollars in equity. Those beneficiaries are 'the parents of baby boomers, and their homes form a substantial part of the record setting $10 trillion in inheritance now being passed down to the baby-boom generation'.[80]

---

79 Walter Been Michaels comments: 'His problem, as the sociologist Annette Lareau brilliantly puts it, is his "inability to signal" his "class position". In situations like this one, Lareau says, "race trumps social class". The obvious irony is that West wants his class to matter on the way to a photo shoot for a book that will be called *Race Matters*.' Michaels, *Trouble with Diversity*, p. 214, endnote 24. He's citing from Lareau, *Unequal Childhoods*, p. 240. See Cornel West, *Race Matters*, New York: Vintage, 1994.

80 This whole paragraph draws from Lui, Robles, Leondar-Wright, Brewer and Adamson, *Color of Wealth*, pp. 252–9. While it lies beyond the scope of this work, we should remember the plight of Japanese Americans during the war: 'The most blatant transfer of assets from people of color to white people during the war was the internment of 110,000 Japanese Americans, two-thirds of them U.S. citizens, from 1942–1945 ...

Race, therefore, does matter, but it matters most importantly because racial discrimination created a racial wealth gap that thus maps onto class inequality. As Dalton Conley has argued:

Many of the behaviors and circumstances that we have come to so closely associate with blackness or whiteness are really more attributable to the class structure of American society. It just happens that this class structure overlays very well onto skin color, which is a lot more visible than someone's investment portfolio.[81]

He stresses that 'it is not race *per se* that matters directly; instead, what matters are the wealth levels and class positions that are associated with race in America'.[82] Indeed, his research shows that the racial divide is more significantly a class divide. When race is taken as the key factor of analysis, African Americans are only 38% as likely as whites to have earned a college degree. But when socioeconomic background is taken into account; that is, when African Americans and whites similar in terms of their age, gender and education levels as well as their parent's educational level, permanent income, net worth and types of assets, are used to determine data, then blacks are just as likely as whites to have completed college. If race is the only variable taken into account, then African Americans are 61% more likely to be expelled or suspended from school. But when socioeconomic status and wealth are equalized the effect of being black emerges as insignificant and class is revealed as the primary determinant. When black and white teenage girls are compared according to race alone, the former are over 12 times more likely to bear a child outside of marriage. However, when socioeconomic status and family background are taken into account African American girls are three times as prone to becoming single mothers. Even when it comes to welfare, common wisdom is off the mark. When welfare is considered on the basis of only race, African Americans are more likely than whites to receive government aid. When class background is taken into account, though, this difference disappears. In all these cases, 'the effects of race are dramatically obscured by the impact of class dynamics and economic resources'.[83]

With Japanese people under deadline to dispose of their homes and business, white neighbors and speculators bought Japanese farms, houses, and businesses at a fraction of their worth, enriching themselves at their interned neighbors' expense.' p. 256.

81 Dalton Conley, *Being Black, Living in the Red: Race, Wealth, and Social Policy in America*, Berkeley: University of California Press, 1999, p. 23.

82 Conley, *Being Black, Living in the Red*, p. 7. His autobiography is also interesting: Dalton Conley, *Honky*, New York: Vintage, 2001.

83 Conley, *Being Black, Living in the Red*, p. 133. In her fascinating study of family

The problem, therefore, is not a lack of formal equal opportunity. The problem is rather the lack of equality of condition that makes a mockery of formal equal opportunity. Take a look at higher education. The politics of higher education, like most of the politics that seeks to be progressive in the United States today, is based on racial/ethnic affirmative action.[84] Universities make a point of highlighting the diversity of their enrollment – the percentage of blacks, Asians, Hispanic/Latino(as) and other minority groups in their student body. Diversity is measured by skin colour or culture, never by class. What if, however, we performed the following experiment?

> We are often reminded of how white our classrooms would look if we did away with affirmative action. But imagine what the Harvard classroom would look like if instead we replaced race-based affirmative action with a genuinely class-based affirmative action. The median family income in the United States today is a little over $54,000 per year; almost 90 per cent of Harvard Students come from families with more than that, so at least half of them would have to

dynamics and child rearing practices Annette Lareau reports that: 'Nevertheless, the role of race was less powerful than I had expected. In terms of the areas this book has focused on – how children spend their time, the ways parents use language and discipline in the home, the nature of the families' social connections and the strategies used for intervening in institutions – white and Black parents engaged in very similar, often identical, practices with their children . . . the biggest differences in the cultural logic of child rearing in the day-to-day behavior of children in this study were between middle-class children on the one hand (including wealthy members of the middle class) and working-class and poor children on the other. As a middle-class Black boy, Alexander Williams had much more in common with *white* middle-class Garrett Tallinger than he did with less-privileged Black boys, such as Tyrec Taylor or Harold McAllister.' Lareau, *Unequal Childhoods*, p. 241. Michaels provides another example of how class maps over race: 'The census report racializes health insurance statistics in the same way it does the poverty rate. The rate for uninsured blacks is 19.7 percent, for whites only 11.3 percent. And a 2005 report called *Closing the Gap: Solutions to Race-Based Health Disparities* (issued by the Applied Research Center in Oakland in collaboration with the Northwest Federation of Community Organizations) tells us that "racial disparities in health constitute a national crisis. Equalizing mortality rates between African Americans and whites alone would have saved five times as many lives as all the advances in medical technology saved between 1991 and 2000." No doubt, the gap between blacks and whites in insurance rates helps account for the gap in mortality rates. But the census report also tells us that the rate of the uninsured among people with annual incomes under $25,000 is 24.2 percent and that among people with annual incomes above $75,000, it's 8.2 percent. This gap is a lot bigger than the racial one (and given the disproportionably large number of poor blacks, it does a lot to explain the racial one). So why is the national crisis the racial disparity in health care? Why isn't it the economic disparity in health care?' Michaels, *Trouble with Diversity*, p. 228, note 1.

84 Here I draw from Michaels. Chapter 3 – 'Richer, not Better' – includes a brilliant analysis of the obsession with racial/ethnic diversity in the US educational system.

go. And almost 75 per cent of Harvard students come from families with incomes over $100,000 per year, although only a little over 20 per cent of American families have incomes that high. So most of them would have to go too. If the income distribution at Harvard were made to look like the income distribution of the United States, over half the people in that room would be gone and a great many of the disappeared would be rich and white. It's no wonder that rich white kids and their parents aren't complaining about diversity. Race-based affirmative action, from this standpoint, is a kind of collective bribe rich people pay themselves for ignoring economic inequality. The fact (and it is a fact) that it doesn't help to be white to get into Harvard replaces the much more fundamental fact that it does help to be rich and that it's virtually essential not to be poor.[85]

Public universities fare little better when it comes to class diversity. *USA Today* recently reported on a study showing that the nation's top public universities 'are becoming disproportionately whiter and richer'. The study goes on to show that 'between 1995 and 2003 flagships and other public research universities decreased grant aid by 13 per cent for students from families with an annual income of $20,000 or less, while increasing by 406% aid to students from families who make more than $100,000'.[86] *The New York Times* reports that students at the University of Florida in Gainesville 'with its historic buildings, lawns and lush vegetation, are so affluent that those who must work to help support themselves are sometimes put off by the fancy cars, the stylish clothes and what they see as a sense of entitlement around them'. In fact, Dr Machen, President of the institution, informed the *Times* that 'he was troubled to discover that the average student's family income was about $100,000'.[87] In fact, as merit-based scholarships continue

---

85 Michaels, *Trouble with Diversity*, pp. 85–6. He's aware that 'the more commonly used figure, median household income per year, is $44,839' (rather than the $54,000 of median family income he chooses to use in the paragraph), p. 215, endnote 1.

86 'Financial Aid Falls Short for Minority, Low-Income College Students', *USA Today*, 21 November 2006.

87 'Public Universities Chase Excellence, at a Price', *The New York Times*, 20 December 2006. The *Boston Globe* reports that in 2007 'US college freshmen are wealthier than at any point in the past 35 years, and the income gap is widening between their families and the rest of the nation . . . This academic year's entering class came from families with income 60 percent greater than the national median, as tuition increases shut out lower-income students, the Higher Education Research Institute at the University of California, Los Angeles, said in a report yesterday. The gap was 46 percent in 1971, according to the study of more than 8 million students compiled over 40 years.' 'College Freshmen Wealthier, Study Says', *Boston Globe*, 10 April 2007.

to replace need-based scholarships the mechanisms set up to help poor children get to college only serve to subsidize the rich:

> Donald Heller and Christopher Rasmussen make this point sharply in their assessment of the effect of the Michigan Award Scholarship Program . . . designed 'to increase access to post-secondary education'. They show that at a school like Grosse Ile High, where 64 per cent of the students qualified for merit scholarships, 94 per cent of the graduating seniors were already heading to college before the program was established. At Hamtramck High School, by contrast, the college participation rate is only 30 per cent and only 14 per cent of the students qualified for the award. So these scholarships don't increase access to college; they mainly provide extra funds for kids who were already going. Furthermore, the kids who are already going are the ones who least need the scholarships in the first place. The median family income in Grosse Ile is $96,226 a year. The median family income in Hamtramck is $30,496 a year. One way you can put it is that where need-based scholarships give money to the poor, merit-based scholarships give money to the deserving. Another way you can put it is that where need-based scholarships give money to the poor, merit-based scholarship give money to the rich.[88]

Harvard itself may have given this some thought: in 2006 it announced that it would no longer ask parents who earn less than $60,000 to

---

[88] Michaels, *Trouble with Diversity*, pp. 87–8. He adds: 'The trend toward merit scholarships has been matched by a move away from race-based scholarships, and while it is no doubt obvious by now that I'm opposed to race-based scholarships it should also be obvious that my opposition to them and to affirmative action more generally has nothing whatever to do with the complaint that it's a form of discrimination against whites. When, for example, the president of the NAACP Legal Defense and Educational Fund responds to recent efforts to open scholarship programs for black students to white students as well, I think he is absolutely right to wonder how anyone can possibly "conclude that the great evil in this country is discrimination against white people", *The New York Times*, 14 March 2006. Where he's wrong, however, is in thinking that the great evil is discrimination against black students instead. Or, more precisely, where he's wrong is in thinking that the problem is one of discrimination. It's poor kids, not black kids, who are being penalized, and they're the victims of bad education, not discrimination. Ideally, all scholarships would be need-based, and the transfer of scholarship money from people who need it to people who don't need it would be ended. In the meantime, however (and on the principle of need), race-based scholarships are preferable to merit scholarships, since if you used race in awarding money, more poor kids would get it. Grosse Ile, for example, is 99 per cent white, whereas Hamtramck is only 61 per cent white.' Michaels, *Trouble with Diversity*, pp. 215–16, note 7. The point, of course, is that the discourse and preoccupation with race impedes a debate about what matters more deeply – class.

help pay for their children's education. This shift will not cost Harvard much. Its dean of admissions was quoted in the student paper the *Crimson* defining middle income Harvard families as those earning between $110,000 and $200,000 and 90 per cent of Harvard students come from families earning more than the median national income of $55,000.[89] Unfortunately, free tuition is no real solution to the problem of differential class access to higher education because what keeps the poor – whether black, Hispanic/Latino(a) or white – out of the best universities is not their inability to pay the bills but rather their inability to qualify for admission. It should come as no surprise that SAT scores correlate with family income, the higher the income the higher your SAT score.[90] Poor children are disadvantaged long before college age. Their parents can't afford to send them to private schools, they can't pay for expensive prep courses, and they can't live in wealthy neighbourhoods where high property taxes ensure the best public schools.[91]

Eugene Lang, multimillionaire and philanthropist, was once asked to give a speech to sixth graders in Harlem. As he drove mesmerized

---

89 Andrew Delbanco, 'Scandals of Higher Education', *The New York Review of Books* LIV, Number 5 (29 March 2007), p. 42.

90 In 2004 students from families earning over $100,000 had an average combined SAT score of 1115, while students from families earning between $30,000 and $40,000 had a combined score of 960. See Michaels, *Trouble with Diversity*, p. 98 and William G. Bowen, Martin A. Kurzweil, Eugene M. Tobin, and Susanne C. Pichler, *Equity and Excellence in American Higher Education*, Charlottesville, VA: University of Virginia Press, 2005, p. 82. For a review of these two books and others dealing with class and the higher education system see Delbanco. Delbanco notes William Chace's (former president of Wesleyan and Emory University) op-ed piece 'A Little Learning is an Expensive Thing', where he imagines himself giving incoming freshmen the 'honest talk' he never had the nerve to give. For example: 'more than half of the freshmen at selective colleges, public and private, come from the highest earning quarter of households. Tell me the ZIP code and I'll tell you what kind of college a high-school graduate most likely attends.' Delbanco, 'Scandals', p. 46.

91 Michaels notes: 'It's sometimes argued that going to elite schools isn't as important as we think because it can be shown that students who were admitted to elite schools but chose (for whatever reason) to go to less elite ones do just as well as the students who actually attend the elite schools. This may be bad news for the elite colleges, but it doesn't affect my point; it just shows that the benefits of inequality have been conferred before college even begins. That's why the real victims are not those who are too poor to pay the tuition at elite schools once they've been admitted (a dying breed, in any event) but those who are too poor to pay for the advantages (the private school, the travel soccer teams, the SAT coaches, etc.) that might get them admitted in the first place (and that will make them successful even if they end up going to less elite colleges). Michaels, *Trouble with Diversity*, pp. 216–17, note 18. For an account of how poor children fall behind in the first three years of their lives see Betty Hart and Todd R. Risley, 'The Early Catastrophe: The 30 Million Word Gap by Age 3', *American Educator*, Spring 2003. Available online at http://www.aft.org/pubs-reports/american_educator/spring2003/catastrophe.html

through the utterly devastated black and Hispanic neighbourhood on his way toward the school he felt that his prepared words rang hollow. He tore up the speech and when standing in front of the children instead announced that if they finished high school he would foot the bill for the college of their choice. In a school district with a drop-out rate of between 50% and 75%, 54 of the 61 sixth graders graduated. Of these, 32 went on to college. What happened? He didn't improve their school or change the neighbourhood, what he did was give them an asset: 'This asset – in the form of a promissory note – served a role that many middle-class adolescents take for granted: it brought college within the realm of possibility.'[92] In addition, Lang set up a foundation that would help realize the promise through extensive tutoring. He thus both changed expectations as well as provided the necessary help that those higher expectations required.[93] What he did, in essence, was set up a programme of class-based affirmative action that happened to map onto race. Class-based affirmative action, however, falls outside the realm of what's possible within US politics. Needless to say, neither is it an option on a global scale. The US economy, like the global economy, forgets the least among us. Our question now, however, is whether liberation theology forgets them as well.

92 Conley, *Being Black, Living in the Red*, p. 65. He tells the Lang story on pp. 64–5.
93 Conley, *Being Black, Living in the Red*, p. 65.

3

The Theological Context of the Liberation Theologian: The Failure of Liberation Theologies

Any kind of Christian theology today, even in the rich and dominant countries, which does not have as its starting point the historic situation of dependence and domination of 2/3 of humankind, with its 30 million dead of hunger and malnutrition will not be able to position and concretize historically its fundamental themes. Its questions will not be the real questions.[1]

In the famous parable of the four signs, Siddhattha Gotama wakes to the true nature of reality. Born into the riches of royalty, prophecy dictates he will become a great religious leader. Determined to thwart destiny, however, his father shields his son from the facts of life that could stir introspection and dissatisfaction with things as they are. In the palace Siddhattha lives surrounded by sensual pleasure – food, women and wine are never lacking – while the city streets are filled with smiling people so that he would never know pain. Siddhattha thus grows up ignorant of old age, disease and death. One day, though, he sets out with his chariot into the city and comes across a grey haired and shrivelled figure trembling over a cane. Amazed, he stares wide eyed at the apparition and turns to his charioteer for an explanation. The figure is an old man, the charioteer explains, the ravages of old age are inescapable. Shaken, Siddhattha returns to the palace. The next day he sets out again and comes across someone whose diseased body oozes from the flesh. He's told that the figure is a sick man and that no one can avoid the affliction of disease. Distraught, Siddhattha heads home. On the third excursion he sees a funeral procession. At first he confuses the procession for a parade but is puzzled by the wailing tears. His charioteer explains that someone has died and that death is the inevitable fate of all things. He returns to the palace stricken with

---

1 Hugo Assmann, *Teología Desde la Praxis de la Liberación*, Salamanca: Ediciones Sígueme, 1973, p. 40.

grief. Finally, on a fourth trip, he comes across a religious wanderer whose peaceful gaze touches the Buddha to be. He resolves to follow the man's example and become a wandering renunciant in search of a solution for life's afflictions. That very night, after taking one last look at his sleeping wife and child, Siddhattha leaves the palace to return no more.[2]

I like Damien Keown's take on the story:

This simple, poignant story is unlikely to be true in the literal sense . . . It might be more useful to read the story as a parable in which palace life represents complacency and self-delusion, and the vision of the four signs the dawning of a realization about the nature of human life. If the Buddha were alive today he would see the four signs all around: every elderly person, every hospital and every funeral would bespeak the brevity and fragility of life, while every church and religious minister would be testimony to the belief that a religious solution to these problems can be found. The parable seems to suggest that although the signs are all around, most people – like the young Buddha – construct mental barriers (the palace walls) to keep unpleasant realities at bay.[3]

Central to the parable, therefore, is the importance of the right perception of reality as a step toward properly encountering the world.[4] Indeed, Marx's famous eleventh thesis on Feuerbach – 'philosophers have only interpreted the world in various ways, the point however is to change it' – is not entirely fair to philosophers past. To change the world you must first interpret it; that is, you must see it correctly. Unless you do so, you are not going to change it at all.

Take the mural of a Mercator map of the world that until last year covered a full wall of the maps department at the University of Miami's library.[5] I would take my students to the mural and use it as an intro-

---

2 For two excellent introductions to Buddhism see Damien Keown, *Buddhism: A Very Short Introduction*, Oxford: Oxford University Press, 1996; and Michael Carrithers, *The Buddha: A Very Short Introduction*, Oxford: Oxford University Press, 2001.

3 Keown, *Buddhism*, pp. 20–1.

4 Right sight, proper perception, is a key theme in classical philosophy as well. Marcus Aurelius writes 'In every contingency *keep before your eyes* those who, when the same thing befell them, were saddened, astonished, resentful. Where are they now? Nowhere.' Marcus Aurelius, *Meditations*, New York: Walter J. Black, 1945, 7:58. Epictetus also states '*Keep before your eyes* every day death and exile, and everything that seems terrible, but most of all death; and then you will never have any abject thought, nor excessive desire.' See his *Encheiridion* or *Manual*, chapter 21.

5 Water damage in the library forced it being painted over.

duction to liberation theology (and as an explanation of why in a theology course they would have to read so much economics and political science). The Mercator projection was devised by Flemish cartographer Gerardus Mercator in 1569 for navigational purposes and is still the most recognized map in the United States. As most of my students confess, when they think of the size of different countries and continents, it's Mercator's picture that comes to mind. In fact, its presence at the entry way of the maps department speaks to its continued power over our consciousness. The map, however, provides a distorted picture of reality. They are often shocked to learn that while in the Mercator projection Greenland looks almost twice as large as Africa, in reality Africa is almost 14 times larger than Greenland. Greenland also looks bigger than China but China is in fact four times larger than Greenland. Western Europe appears as large as South America, but really the latter is almost twice the size of the former. Alaska seems larger than Mexico, yet Mexico is larger than Alaska. If you bunch the Scandinavian countries together – Norway, Sweden, Finland and Denmark – they come out bigger than India yet India is almost three times larger. It dawns on my students that the Mercator makes the wealthy and white parts of the world seem much larger than they really are. They realize that the Mercator gives no sense of how small the islands of wealth and whiteness are in relation to Africa, Latin America, the Middle East and Asia, the poor and non-white majority of the globe. I tell them that liberation theology does for theology what they just did for the mural – unmask its Eurocentric bias. For my students this map is just like Siddhattha's palace walls, an obstacle to seeing the world correctly.[6]

Similarly, this book seeks to see liberation theology correctly. We already know that a Latin American liberation theologian and a United States liberation theologian share the same material context. The material context within which all American liberation theologies work is one of widespread economic deprivation, racial/ethnic humiliation, and gender discrimination. Within this tripartite division of crucial types of oppression, however, economic deprivation is determinative of all others. I thus disagree with Ada Maria Isasi-Diaz when she writes that 'certainly there is no moral primacy among the causes or factors or elements of oppression: there is no one kind of oppression that is

---

6 For a brief excursion on maps in relation to Latino(a) theology see Miguel A. De La Torre and Edwin David Aponte, *Introducing Latino/a Theologies*, Maryknoll, NY: Orbis Books, 2001, pp. 9–11. Another shocking experience can be found at www.globalrichlist.com, a webpage that will calculate your *global* class standing. At $50,000 (before taxes) I stand within the richest 0.98% of humankind.

worse than another, no one face of oppression that is more oppressive than another'.[7] Ellen Wood bluntly and accurately highlights the different status of class oppression among types of oppression:

> The 'difference' that constitutes class as an 'identity' *is*, by definition, a relationship of inequality and power, in a way that sexual or cultural 'difference' need not be. A truly democratic society can celebrate diversities of life styles, culture or sexual preference; but in what sense would it be 'democratic' to celebrate class difference? If a conception of freedom or equality adapted to sexual and cultural differences is intended to extend the reach of human liberation, can the same be said of freedom or equality that accommodates *class* difference?[8]

Class is involved in all social arrangements of oppression; nothing occurs without implicating the material conditions that shape the way individuals and groups locate themselves, and are located, within their societies. Recent work in medical anthropology confirms this key lesson. As Paul Farmer notes, 'diseases themselves make a preferential option for the poor'.[9] Tuberculosis today has an overall cure rate of over 95%. Yet tuberculosis deaths, which currently number in the millions, are found almost exclusively among the poor, whether in the Third/Two-Thirds world or the inner cities of the United States.[10] In the year 2000, preventable and treatable communicable diseases – tuberculosis and other respiratory infections, AIDS, diarrhoeal diseases, perinatal infections – were the cause of 7.7% of deaths among the affluent but the cause of 58.6% of deaths among the world's poor.[11] Crimes such as rape and assault occur among women, but gender alone does not determine who is at risk; it's poor women who are at the greatest risk.[12] Contemporary slavery is not based on ethnic or racial

---

7 Ada Maria Isasi-Diaz, *Mujerista Theology: A Theology for the Twenty-First Century*, Maryknoll, NY: Orbis Books, 2002, p. 109.

8 Ellen M. Wood, *Democracy Against Capitalism: Renewing Historical Materialism*, New York: Cambridge University Press, 1995, p. 258. There is no reason why you couldn't add 'race' to the elements to be celebrated.

9 Paul Farmer, *Pathologies of Power: Health, Human Rights, and the New War on the Poor*, Berkeley: University of California Press, 2003, p. 140.

10 Farmer, *Pathologies of Power*, p. 147.

11 See Farmer, *Pathologies of Power*, p. 320. Here he gets his data from World Bank, *The Burden of Disease Among the Global Poor: Current Situation, Future Trends, and Implications for Strategy*, Washington, DC: World Bank, 2000.

12 See Farmer, *Pathologies of Power*, p. 44. Amy Farmer, Jill Tiefenthaler and Amandine Sambira stress that while domestic violence claims victims in all races and socio-economic classes 'some women are more likely to be victims of abuse than others'.

differences; the key criterion for enslavement today is deprivation: 'the common denominator is poverty, not color.'[13]

This chapter further uncovers the common background of liberation theologies by arguing that a Latin American liberation theologian and a United States liberation theologian also share the same theological context, a common inability to deal successfully with the material context. A liberation theologian today works within a theological context in which there is a proliferation of liberation theologies – black, womanist, Hispanic/Latino(a), Latin American – yet they're all powerless to face the spread of zones of social abandonment. They're powerless because the upsurge of race, ethnicity, gender, and sexuality as organizing axes for liberation theology has blurred the fact that material deprivation, that is, the deprivation that comes from one's class standing in society, remains the most important form of oppression. The economic poor bear the brunt of oppression and yet it's the economic poor that today fall by the wayside of liberation theologies in the Americas. The warning with which this chapter opens is worth repeating:

Any kind of Christian theology today, even in the rich and dominant

---

More specifically, 'women in the lowest income households have 7 times the abuse rates of those in the highest income households'. See 'The Availability and Distribution of Services for Victims of Domestic Violence in the U.S.' at www.waltoncollege.uark.edu/lab/AFarmer/services%20RR%20Feb%202004.doc; cited in Walter Benn Michaels, *The Trouble with Diversity: How We Learned to Love Identity and Ignore Inequality*, New York: Metropolitan Books, 2006, pp. 117–18. Michaels comments: 'For example, one of the main findings of the study I cited above is that facilities to help the victims of domestic violence are disproportionately located in wealthier areas, that in fact there's an almost inverse relationship between the location of such facilities and the location of the population that needs them. But there is, of course, a deeper difficulty as well. By disconnecting the problem of domestic violence from the question of social class, we find ourselves misunderstanding and misrepresenting the problem itself. We fail to see that the problem of domestic violence is importantly a function of the problem of economic inequality; we fail to see that in a society with less poverty there would be less domestic violence.' Michaels, *Trouble with Diversity*, pp. 118–19.

13 On the issue of contemporary slavery see Kevin Bales, *Disposable People: New Slavery in the Global Economy*, Berkeley: University of California Press, 1999, p. 11. See also Ethan Kapstein, 'The New Global Slave Trade', *Foreign Affairs* 85.6 (Nov./Dec. 2006), pp. 103–16. Kapstein describes the mechanism of enslavement: 'What all slaves have in common is that they are forced to work. Slavers typically recruit poor people in poor countries by promising them good jobs in distant places. A recruiter will then offer a victim a generous loan – at an exorbitant interest rate – to help with travel arrangements, papers, and locating a job in the new community. On arrival, the promised job never materializes, and thus the large debt – up to several thousand dollars – can never be repaid. The victim is then stripped of all travel documents, given a false identity, and forced into a job. He or she – and his or her family – are threatened with disfigurement or death should the slave try to alert the authorities or escape. If they are paid at all, slaves get the bare minimum required for survival.' p. 106.

countries, which does not have as its starting point the historic situation of dependence and domination of 2/3 of humankind, with its 30 million dead of hunger and malnutrition will not be able to position and concretize historically its fundamental themes. Its questions will not be the real questions.[14]

Let us, therefore, clear the ground, so the real questions can again be asked.

The Poverty of Liberation Theologies

In *The Poverty of Philosophy* Marx develops an incisive, and tongue-in-cheek, critique of his fellow economists. He writes:

> Economists have a single method of procedure. There are only two kinds of institutions for them, artificial and natural. The institutions of feudalism are artificial institutions, those of the bourgeoisie are natural institutions . . . They are eternal laws which must always govern society. Thus there has been history, but there is no longer any.[15]

Here economists make up in hubris what they lack in historical sensibility. Their epoch is the final stage in social development; humanity finally has it right.[16] But what if the facts on the ground suggest otherwise? How did economists deal with increasing class struggle in the context of 'natural' institutions? Some, Marx writes, created the *fatalist* school of economics. Fatalist economists take the historical categories of capitalist relations, turn them into eternal laws, and proceed to show why these laws are the end-all of progress. For them the future is bright, 'poverty is in their eyes merely the pang which accompanies very childbirth, in nature as in history'.[17] Those who take to heart society's problems joined the *humanitarian* school. This school 'counsels the workers to be sober, to work hard and to have few

---

14 Assmann, *Teología Desde la Praxis*, p. 40.

15 Karl Marx, *The Poverty of Philosophy*, New York: International Publishers, 1974, p. 102. He can't resist poking fun at theologians: 'In this they [economists] resemble the theologians, who likewise establish two kinds of religion. Every religion which is not theirs is an invention of men, while their own religion is an emanation from God.'

16 For a contemporary expression of this idea see Francis Fukuyama, *The End of History and the Last Man*, New York: Free Press, 1992 and 'The End of History', *The National Interest* Summer (1989), pp. 3–18.

17 Marx, *Poverty of Philosophy*, p. 105.

children; it advises the bourgeois to put a reasoned ardour into production'.[18] It seeks individual and personal solutions to collective social problems. Finally, members of the *philanthropic* school deny at the level of theory the existence of class struggle and social misery at the level of practice. For fatalists poverty is a passing malady; for humanitarians it's an individual failing, and for philanthropists it's ultimately non-existent. For all, poverty is never truly taken seriously.

Unfortunately, contemporary liberation theologians do not take poverty seriously either. They too have a characteristic method of procedure. Liberation theologians claim that they are focused on the material poor and they insist that a liberation with a central socio-economic component is their goal. Yet they then proceed to set up their theologies in such a way that the focus is lost and the goal cannot be realized – they make promises they can't keep. While Marx essentializes his economists into schools of thought (suggesting that they are irredeemable) we need not go so far. Liberation theologians merely suffer from debilitating conditions which cause them to ignore the primary oppression that comes from a person's class standing. There are four such conditions that need to be overcome to restore liberation theology to health – I call them monochromatism, amnesia, gigantism and naiveté. Often found together, it's useful for analytical purposes to examine them separately. In what follows, I uncover examples of these conditions in the work of prominent liberationists. My intention, however, is not to critique this or that particular theologian. Neither is it to provide an exhaustive catalogue of these conditions. I merely seek to provide representative examples so that the reader can identify them on his/her own in the future.

Monochromatism

Monochromatism is the most important debilitating condition found in US liberation theologies as it afflicts black, womanist and Hispanic/ Latino(a) production indiscriminately. Theologians with monochromatism suffer from a limited range of vision. Depending on the strain they see only black and white, or brown and white, or theological and non-theological. Monochromatism is thus evident when theologians of a particular ethnic or racial group refuse to look beyond the parameters of that group, as well as the parameters of their discipline, for tools and resources useful to the cause of liberation. Theologians with monochromatism, therefore, stress the goal of liberation, but dramati-

---

18 Marx, *Poverty of Philosophy*, p. 105.

cally limit the pool of resources they can draw upon to actually engage the task. In the end, colour of membership and membership in a professional guild takes priority over liberation from material blight.

While today all US liberation theologies suffer from monochromatism, its origins lie within black theology and can be traced back to the critical response to James Cone's *Black Theology and Black Power* and *A Black Theology of Liberation*. Both ground-breaking texts were written in the shadow of Martin Luther King Jr's assassination and the riots that subsequently engulfed the United States. In both, Cone makes the Black Power struggle for political liberation central to his theology. As he once thundered: 'Christianity is not alien to Black Power; it is Black Power.'[19] At the same time, however, Cone remained indebted to white European theologians such as Karl Barth and Paul Tillich and continued to pay homage to the traditional categories of Christian theology. To this end Albert Cleage noted that Cone takes 'white Christians as far as they are able to go (and then some) in interpreting Black theology within the established framework which they can accept and understand'.[20] And his brother Cecil Cone spoke of an 'identity crisis' of black theology in stark terms. For him, those

> who are infatuated with the themes of liberation, freedom, and equality in the social structures . . . must begin to realize that they are being influenced more by Euro-American conceptions of freedom than the religious freedom of the black religious experience. Black Power, despite its positive affirmations of blackness and freedom, owes more in its origin to Europe than to Africa.[21]

Many of his black colleagues, therefore, thought his approach did not go far enough in its assault of theology as a white European stronghold. Cone himself recognized that the most powerful critique he received was that his theology was 'black in name only and not in reality. To be

19 James Cone, *Black Theology and Black Power*, Maryknoll, NY: Orbis Books, 1997, p. 35.

20 Albert Cleage, *Black Christian Nationalism: New Directions for the Black Church*, New York: William Morrow, 1972, p. xvii.

21 Cecil Cone, *The Identity Crisis in Black Theology*, Nashville: AMEC, 1975, p. 142. James Cone comments: 'When black scholars said that what I call black theology was nothing but white theology painted black, I was deeply wounded. Even my brother, Cecil, attacked me in his book, *The Identity Crisis in Black Theology*. He claimed that I was more accountable to the academic standards of white theology than to the spiritual life of the black church. That was absurd – almost too silly to warrant a serious response.' James Cone, 'The Vocation of a Theologian', in Linda E. Thomas (ed.), *Living Stones in the Household of God: The Legacy and Future of Black Theology*, Minneapolis: Fortress Press, 2004, p. 208.

black in the latter sense, you must derive the sources and norm from the community in whose name you speak.'[22]

This argument is made most extensively by Gayraud Wilmore, the intellectual father of monochromatism. He and the early Cone possess contrasting understandings of blackness. For Cone, 'being black in America has very little to do with skin color. To be black means that your heart, your soul, your mind, and your body are where the dispossessed are . . . being reconciled to God does not mean that one's skin is physically black. It essentially depends on the color of your heart, soul and mind.'[23] Wilmore, however, disagrees with Cone's attempt to make blackness symbolic of all those who are oppressed or side with the oppressed. He asks 'whether black theology is simply the blackenization of the whole spectrum of traditional or classic Christian theology, with particular emphasis upon the liberation of the oppressed, or is it singular, is it something else? In other words, does it find in the experience of the oppression of blacks in the Western world, *as black*, a singular religious meaning?'[24] His answer leaves little doubt as to his differences with Cone: 'Simply being oppressed, or psychologically and politically in empathy with the dispossessed, does not deliver one into the experience of blackness any more than putting on a blindfold delivers one into the experience of being blind.'[25]

For Wilmore, black theology in its quest for black freedom must use black theological resources. The task ahead is to draw from Scripture, the early black church, the traditions of the black community, the writings of black preachers and black men and women now and past, and the traditional religions of Africa, to develop a black hermeneutic. This black hermeneutic would unpack

> the mythology, folklore, and ethical norms of the black community as reflected in its oral tradition and literature, in order to uncover the ways in which blacks have linguistically and otherwise commu-

---

22 James Cone, *Black Theology and Black Power*, pp. xi–xii.

23 James Cone, *Black Theology and Black Power*, p. 151. Gayraud S. Wilmore cites this passage *Black Religion and Black Radicalism: An Interpretation of the Religious History of Afro-American People*, Maryknoll, NY: Orbis Books, 1983, p. 217. He also cites Cone from *A Black Theology of Liberation*: 'The focus on blackness does not mean that *only* black suffer as victims in a racist society, but that blackness is an ontological symbol and a visible reality which best describes what oppression means in America . . . Blackness, then, stands for all victims of oppression who realize that their humanity is inseparable from man's liberation from whiteness.' James H. Cone, *A Black Theology of Liberation*, C. Eric Lincoln Series in Black Religion, Philadelphia: J. B. Lippincott Company, 1970, pp. 27–8.

24 Wilmore, *Black Religion and Black Radicalism*, pp. 217–18.

25 Wilmore, *Black Religion and Black Radicalism*, p. 218.

nicated their provisional and ultimate concerns and solutions in an exploitative and racist society . . . Only so shall we be able to unlock the secrets of the people's experience and develop a theology of humanization and liberation that will make contact with and be validated by that experience.[26]

Only then can the uniqueness of the black experience be given its just due. James Cone is the most famous of black liberation theologians but Gayraud Wilmore is the most influential. It is his project that has come to dominate black theology. As he more recently noted:

The theology of blackness . . . is a thinking and praxis that must draw its essential sustenance and energy from a specific culture that was fused long ago out of the bits and pieces found in that special corner of the basement where black people languished. That is what the second generation of black, Afrocentric, and womanist theologians, like Delores S. Williams, Cain Hope Felder, Dwight N. Hopkins, Forest Harris, Jacquelyn Grant, and Diana L. Hayes, are trying to draw from when they research African traditional religions, the slave narratives, the spirituals and the blues, or explore the impertinence and toughness of black mamas who not only have stopped working in Miss Daisy's kitchen, but wouldn't be caught driving her through Atlanta's Piedmont Park.[27]

---

26 Wilmore, *Black Religion and Black Radicalism*, p. 237. As he puts it in another essay: 'And because such a theology sees the variegated expressions of the people's revolutionary situation – its music, art, folklore, social, economic and political life – as its true cultural matrix, it seeks concrete indigenization in black culture as a whole, and its basic authority in the black experience.' Gayraud Wilmore, 'Black Theology: Its Significance for Christian Mission Today', *International Review of Mission* 63 (April 1974), p. 219. See also Gayraud Wilmore, 'Reinterpretation in Black Church History', *The Chicago Theological Seminary Register* LXXIII.1 (Winter 1983), pp. 25–37.

27 Gayraud S. Wilmore, 'Black Consciousness: Stumbling Block or Battering Ram?' in Joerg Rieger (ed.), *Liberating the Future: God, Mammon and Theology*, Minneapolis: Fortress Press, 1998, p. 94. Cone takes note for works after *Black Theology and Black Power* and *A Black Theology of Liberation*. His *The Spiritual and the Blues* and *The God of the Oppressed* make a point to speak from his experience growing up in a black church in Bearden, Arkansas. His brother Cecil points out that in *The God of the Oppressed* Cone 'himself indicates that "something important is missing" in his former works: "They did not show clearly enough the significance of Macedonia A.M.E. Church and the imprint of that community upon my theological consciousness." Cone not only begins this book with his Bearden experience but struggles to make that experience the guiding norm throughout his work. This is especially evident in the selection and interpretation of his primary sources: songs, sermons, testimonies, and slave narratives of the black religious tradition.' Cecil Cone, *The Identity Crisis in Black Theology*, p. 121. I should note that Wilmore doesn't intend his approach to be apolitical. In his words: 'It is important to note that while the critique and reformation of the political order (social

The problems with monochromatism come to the fore in black theology's pre-eminent second-generation representative, Dwight Hopkins.[28] Indeed, monochromatism colours the whole of Hopkins' oeuvre, leading to a tension in his work. On the one hand, Hopkins repeatedly states that his focus is on the black poor. Who, we might ask, are the poor he focuses on? In his *Heart and Head* Hopkins is clear:

> The *poor* indicates first the material poor; those who own or control no wealth. For instance, if two people work at a job and they both earn $20,000 a year, it would seem that they are equal. But what if one of those persons owns an oil field in Colorado or Texas? Let's say that both people are fired from their job and lose their income of $20,000. Both people will not suffer equally. Why? Because the one who owns and controls the oil field still has wealth.[29]

Given this focus on the material poor, Hopkins stresses class as the normative thread that runs throughout black theology.[30] He tells us

transformation) is basic to what black theologians have set forth . . . the basic strategy is *cultural*. This is to say that the controlling concept has to do with the whole gamut of human activity and involves a structural and dynamic renewal that goes beyond the pragmatic ends and shallow motivations of electoral politics . . . To speak of the mission and strategy of the black church as cultural rather than political is not to deny the political, but to subsume it in a larger context; and it is in precisely such a context that we can see how the spiritual dimension of life impinges upon the problems and possibilities of social transformation.' Gayraud Wilmore, 'The Vocation of the Black Church', in William K. Tabb (ed.), *Churches in Struggle: Liberation Theologies and Social Change in North America*, New York: Monthly Review Press, 1986, p. 248.

28 For Hopkins see Dwight Hopkins, *Being Human: Race, Culture, and Religion*, Minneapolis: Fortress Press, 2005; *Heart and Head: Black Theology – Past, Present and Future*, New York: Palgrave, 2002; *Down, Up, and Over: Slave Religion and Black Theology*, Minneapolis: Fortress Press, 2000; *Introducing Black Theology of Liberation*, Maryknoll, NY: Orbis Books, 1999; *Shoes That Fit Our Feet: Sources for a Constructive Black Theology*, Maryknoll, NY: Orbis Books, 1993 and *Black Theology in the U.S.A. and South Africa: Politics, Culture, and Liberation*, Maryknoll, NY: Orbis Books, 1989. He has also edited a number of works including *Black Faith and Public Talk: Critical Essays on Jame's Cone's Black Theology and Black Power*, Maryknoll, NY: Orbis Books, 1999; Dwight Hopkins and George Cummings (eds), *Cut Loose Your Stammering Tongue: Black Theology in the Slave Narratives*, Maryknoll, NY: Orbis Books, 1991 and Simon Maimela and Dwight Hopkins (eds), *We Are One Voice*, Cape Town: Skotaville Publishers, 1989. His influence can be seen in the fact that a review essay on 'Contemporary Black Theology' is in reality a review of his work alone. See Kameron J. Carter, 'Contemporary Black Theology: A Review Essay', *Modern Theology* 19.1 (Jan. 2003), pp. 117–38.

29 Hopkins, *Heart and Head*, p. 24.

30 Dwight Hopkins and Linda Thomas, 'Womanist Theology and Black Theology: Conversational Envisioning of an Unfinished Dream', in Eleazar Fernandez and Fernando Segovia (eds), *A Dream Unfinished: Theological Reflections on America from the Margins*, Maryknoll, NY: Orbis Books, 2001, p. 86.

that 'we must avoid an amorphous type of black theology that omits the crucial phrase of *liberation of the poor*. In ambiguity lies the danger.'[31]

On the other hand, Hopkins wants to make sure that his liberation theology is properly black. In *Being Human* he also asks: 'A black theology of liberation is a specific God-talk and God-walk. But what makes it black?'[32] The answer to this question are black theology's sources – black sources make black theology black. Hopkins, in particular, makes slave narratives the basis for ensuring the blackness of his theology. As he writes in *Cut Loose Your Stammering Tongue*: 'As a living source and a medium of God's word in action, they [the narratives] compel black theology to deepen further its reliance on indigenous resources in the African American community, thereby commanding black theology to cut loose its stammering tongue.'[33] Slave narratives are the remedy for the corrupting effects of the white academy:

> black slaves remove obstacles from our 'God-talk' by imbuing us with their unique liberation practice, world-view, language, thought patterns, and theological common sense. In contrast, years of white education, particularly white theological training, have infused an alien and unnatural method of thinking into the subconscious of African American religious thought.[34]

They are also the way to reconnect theology with blackness: 'Consequently, we who attempt to talk about the liberating faith of oppressed

---

31 Hopkins, *Heart and Head*, p. 162.
32 Hopkins, *Being Human*, p. 8.
33 Dwight Hopkins, 'Introduction', *Cut Loose Your Stammering Tongue*, pp. xv–xvi. Or as George Cummings puts it in the same volume: 'Concomitantly, the slave narratives provide a means to return to the religious genius of the ancestors, who were forcibly taken from Africa and made to serve in the brutal crucible of chattel slavery. The narratives provide us with insight concerning the religious and cultural world-views that informed black slaves' theological interpretation of their experience and can be the basis upon which contemporary black theologians can incorporate the 'thematic universe' of the black oppressed into their discourse.' George Cummings, 'Slave Narratives, Black Theology of Liberation (USA), and the Future', in Hopkins and Cummings (eds), *Cut Loose Your Stammering Tongue*, p. 138. In the introduction to the second edition Will Coleman states that 'the emergent "dialogue" between the slave narratives and contemporary black theology could be characterized as reassessing the true foundation for a constructive black theology of liberation. In lieu of relying on the sources, norms, and methodologies of Eurocentric theologies, this archeological strategy is a return to the images, vernacular, and style of speech that originates from within the African American soul and the collective experience of enslavement.' Will Coleman, 'Introduction', in Hopkins and Cummings (eds), *Cut Loose Your Stammering Tongue*, p. xi.
34 Hopkins, 'Introduction', p. xvi.

black folk and allow that same empowering belief and spirituality to talk through us must return to our theological beginnings. In a sense, the slave's religious stories are a calling for us to write our way back home.'[35] By retrieving voices marginalized from the historical and theological record, the turn toward the slave narratives ensures the blackness of theology.

The problem, however, is that Hopkins' focus on blackness seeps into all of his other sources. Remember that Hopkins does in fact want to focus on the material poor; he embraces the preferential option for the poor as a central element of black theology, an option which he tells us involves a 'faith engaged in a radical redistribution of power and wealth on behalf of those whose voices aren't taken seriously in the United States'.[36] For this reason,

> one of the key challenges for black theology is to understand adequately the negative effects of U.S. monopoly capitalism on African American poor and working communities. Faith and practice based on liberation theology must include the need for freedom from the oppressive control of global capital.[37]

He obviously desires a theology that can address these concrete political and economic issues. Yet the six sources that he makes central to black theology in *Introducing Black Theology* – the Bible, the African American Church, a faith tradition of struggle for liberation, culture (art, literature, music, folktales, black English, and rhythm) and radical politics – make the development of such a theology a close to impossible task.[38]

Ultimately, the focus of Hopkins' sources is the fostering of identity and the safeguarding of orthodoxy. Thus black identity is fostered through the black church and black culture; religious orthodoxy is safeguarded by the primary status of the Bible and the black church. Radical politics is included as a source but it's a radical politics without a compass. Hopkins states that 'here politics is the ability to determine the direction that the African American community can pursue'.[39] Yet how is that direction to be determined without the incorporation of a more concrete social analysis and the development of a more concrete social vision? So, for example, in *Shoes that Fit Our Feet*, Hopkins

---

35 Hopkins, 'Introduction', p. xvi.
36 Hopkins, *Heart and Head*, p. 61.
37 Hopkins, *Heart and Head*, p. 49.
38 Hopkins, *Introducing Black Theology of Liberation*, pp. 42–6.
39 Hopkins, *Introducing Black Theology of Liberation*, p. 45.

correctly writes that 'a constructive and contemporary black theology of liberation needs a prophetic social analysis and social vision'.[40] To address these needs Hopkins has, at times and in his earlier work, explicitly incorporated political economy into black theology's sources:

> While interacting with other disciplines, theology seeks to discover how best to get at divine vocation for concrete liberation. For instance, political economy surfaces the issue of power control of politics, culture, and economics . . . Furthermore, political economy paints the constructive contours of the new democratic society.[41]

But even when making political economy constitutive of black theology Hopkins refuses to turn to the best current social, political, legal and economic theory, preferring instead to place his focus on safeguarding the blackness of his sources. So when delving into political economy in *Shoes that Fit Our Feet* all he does is review ideas from Martin Luther King Jr and Malcolm X. Another essay focuses on Foucault and Cone as sources for a political vision – Foucault for his micro-analysis of power relations and Cone for his macro-analysis.[42]

The same problem ensues. Why this insistence on staying within the parameters of blackness when it comes to social analysis and political construction? Why not turn to contemporary social theory of different colours? While Martin Luther King Jr, Malcolm X and James Cone are obvious potential sources for black theology, they are not the most current nor the most useful resource if one is interested in developing a political and economic vision of content applicable to the twenty-first century. Furthermore, in a section titled 'Communal Political Economy' in *Being Human*, he glides through the views of theologians such as Kim Yong-Bock of Korea, Mary Getui of Kenya, Laurenti Magesa of Tanzania, Mario Castillo of Cuba, Ambrose Mayo of Zimbabwe and Kwame Gyekye (he doesn't say where Gyekye is from) when it comes to work and the economy. So when dealing with 'political economy' he now restricts his sources to blackness *and* theology. Are there no black African or Third World social scientists and social theorists to which

---

40 Hopkins, *Shoes That Fit Our Feet*, p. 170.

41 Dwight Hopkins, 'Black Theology and a Second Generation: New Scholarship and New Challenges', in James Cone and Gayraud Wilmore (eds), *Black Theology, A Documentary History: Volume II 1980–1992*, Maryknoll, NY: Orbis Books, 1993, p. 64. See also Dwight Hopkins, *Shoes That Fit Our Feet*, pp. 215–17 as well as chapters 4–5.

42 See Dwight Hopkins, 'Postmodernity, Black Theology of Liberation and the USA: Michel Foucault and James H. Cone', in David Batstone, Eduardo Mendieta, Lois Ann Lorentzen, and Dwight Hopkins (eds), *Liberation Theologies, Postmodernity, and the Americas*, New York: Routledge, 1997, pp. 205–21.

one can turn? It would seem that turning to the work of social scientists when dealing with political economy is an obvious move. Monochromatism, therefore, keeps Hopkins from looking beyond blackness and theology for tools that might aid the cause of liberation.[43] Seeing only black or not black, seeing theological or not theological, the range of resources available to his theology is severely limited – limiting too his theology's relevance for the liberation of the material poor.[44]

---

43 Hopkins, *Being Human*, pp. 91–8.

44 For a trenchant outsider critique (with whose general parameters I am in agreement) see Alistair Kee, *The Rise and Demise of Black Theology* (Aldershot, England: Ashgate, 2006), paperback version available from SCM Press, 2007. Victor Anderson's work remains the most powerful insider critique of Black theology. In particular, see 'Critical Reflection on the Problems of History and Narrative in a Recent African-American Research Program', in Eleazar Fernandez and Fernando Segovia (eds), *A Dream Unfinished: Theological Reflections on American from the Margins*, Maryknoll, NY: Orbis Books, 2001, pp. 37–51; '"We See Through a Glass Darkly": Black Narrative Theology and the Opacity of African American Religious Thought', in Anthony B. Pinn and Benjamín Valentín (eds), *The Ties That Bind: African American and Hispanic American/Latino/a Theologies in Dialogue*, New York: Continuum, 2001, pp. 78–93 and *Beyond Ontological Blackness: An Essay on African American Religious and Cultural Criticism*, New York: Continuum, 1995. In *Beyond Ontological Blackness* Anderson critiques a definition of blackness where it is intrinsically tied to oppression. To do so allows whiteness to define blackness. Black identity so constituted is not self-constituted, but remains a legacy of white supremacy. In addition, such a definition blurs the class distinctions found within the black community: 'To make suffering, rebellion, and survival essential marks of black existence, it seems to me, trivializes the nature of oppression many blacks genuinely experience by the absurdity that anyone who is black is also oppressed' p. 103. In 'Critical Reflection', Anderson focuses on Hopkins and others who have attempted to ground Black theology in slave narratives. He remains opposed to the project because it too easily draws an equivalence between the slave's sayings and struggles with the rhetoric of contemporary black liberation theology. In the process he furthers his reflections on the class stratification of the black community: 'What is clear is that the fragility of black liberation theology in the United States is being tested by a class differentiation that is nonreducible to the racial categories of white over black. Rather, class differentiation cuts across various levels of the black community itself, raising the question whether the black community may not be facing an incommensurability of values and interests among the various classes that now define the black community . . . The contemporary challenge to alienated black theologians is whether they can speak univocally for the poor and underclass and express the real interests of the black community today out of their internal resources' p. 40. Furthermore: 'The historical question, today, is: What have African-American theologians to say to and do with the public lives of a growing poor, urban underclass whose lives are characterized by homelessness and pervasive poverty and who are themselves undereducated, underemployed, and over incarcerated? The need is for livable and affordable homes, protection from black-on-black violence, effective education that yields employment, and justice in criminal prosecution' p. 51. It is clear that Anderson does not believe that black theology as currently constituted can deal with this reality. His critique, moreover, has not received the attention it deserves within black theology. I agree with his critique of ontological blackness and its powerlessness to deal with class realities, but we part ways on the solution. Anderson does not move black theology toward sources outside of blackness. Instead, he seeks to expands the sources of

Amnesia

Amnesia is the most general of the debilitating conditions afflicting liberation theology. Unlike monochromatism, amnesia has no founder or genealogy. Theologians with amnesia forget the problems they seek to tackle and the goals they want to pursue. Amnesia can occur within one work or between works; in either case, there are three steps: first, the theologian stresses that poverty is a key problem to be addressed and that social liberation is a key goal to be realized. Second, the theologian forgets the first step and chooses sources for theological construction that keep the problem from truly being tackled and the goal from really being achieved. Finally, the cultural advancement of a particular ethnic group replaces social liberation as the goal of theology.

Maria Pilar Aquino, the pre-eminent Latina feminist theologian, provides my first example.[45] Throughout her career, Aquino has writ-

---

blackness: 'the adequacy of African-American theology, today, depends on its ability to take into itself the widest ranges of sources from black history and culture. Such sources include storytelling, myth-making, memory, recovering, theologizing black culture, dancing, shouting in churches and fields, leaping on stage, engaging music that uplifts the spirit and music that evokes not only black tragedies but human ones in general, and making and watching films depicting both the struggles of blacks toward freedom and the often ironic and comedic realities of black life' p. 49. In the end, therefore, Anderson does not overcome monochromatism but rather calls black theologians to explore other sources of blackness. For an argument that black theology's understanding of blackness excludes black Hispanic/Latino(as), while Hispanic/Latino(a) theology's understanding of its own identity excludes black Hispanic/Latino(as) see Michelle A. Gonzalez, *Afro-Cuban Theology: Religion, Race, Culture, and Identity*, Gainesville: University Press of Florida, 2006.

45 Aquino's foundational body of works includes edited volumes such as Luiz Carlos Susin and Maria Pilar Aquino (eds), *Reconciliation in a World of Conflicts*, London: SCM Press, 2003; Maria Pilar Aquino, Daisy Machado, and Jeanette Rodriquez, *A Reader in Latina Feminist Theology: Religion and Justice*, Austin, TX: University of Texas Press, 2002; Maria Pilar Aquino and Mieth Dietmar (eds), *The Return of the Just War*, London: SCM Press, 2001; Maria Pilar Aquino and Roberto Goizueta (eds), *Theology: Expanding the Borders*, Mystic, CT: Twenty-Third Century Publications, 1998. Her own books include, *La Teología, la Iglesia y la Mujer en América Latina*, Chapinero, Santa fe de Bogota, Colombia: Indo-American Press Service, 1994; *Our Cry for Life: Feminist Theology from Latin America*, Maryknoll, NY: Orbis Books, 1993, originally published in Spanish as *Nuestro Clamor por la Vida: Teología Latinoamericana Desde la Mujer*, San José, Costa Rica: Departamento Ecuménico de Investigaciones (DEI), 1992; and programmatic essays such as 'Latina Feminist Theology: Central Features', in Maria Pilar Aquino, Daisy Machado, and Jeanette Rodriguez (eds), *A Reader in Latina Feminist Theology: Religion and Justice*, Austin: University of Texas Press, 2002, pp. 133–60; 'Theological Method in U.S. Latino/a Theology: Toward an Intercultural Theology for the Third Millennium', in Orlando O. Espin and Miguel H. Diaz (eds), *From the Heart of Our People*, Maryknoll, NY: Orbis Books, 1999, pp. 6–48; 'Latin American Feminist Theology', *Journal of Feminist Studies in Religion* 14.1 (Spring 1998), pp. 87–107; 'The Collective "Dis-Covery" of Our Own Power: Latin American Feminist Theology', in

ten several programmatic statements outlining the basic contours of Latino/a theology.[46] It's in her most recent statement, 'Latina Feminist Theology: Central Features' that amnesia is most evident. Aquino writes that 'Latina/Chicana feminism is a critical framework to analyze systematic injustice, both locally and globally, to determine effective strategies for its elimination and the actualization of authentic justice.'[47] Given this liberationist thrust, Aquino provides an analysis of the 'material geopolitical' context which determines the method, the principles for theologizing and the tasks for Latina theology.[48] The first level is characterized by global poverty, inequality, social exclusion, and social insecurity brought about by 'the current capitalist, neoliberal global economic paradigm.'[49] The second level is characterized by poverty in the United States and the fact that the poverty rates for children, minorities and families headed by women are well above average of the United States as a whole. The third level is characterized by the exclusion of Latina women from theological activity. Aquino begins, therefore, with an examination of the economic and social context which Latina theology must deal with.[50]

Following her analysis of Latina theology's context, Aquino moves to highlight its central features. These features include preconditions such as 'entering *Nepantla*; fostering *la facultad*; *honesty* with the real; *empapamiento* of hope; and an *evolving* truth'.[51] Entering *Nepantla* means that the theologian must be willing to explore God and ourselves from the borders; *la facultad* stresses that the theologian must have the capacity to transform and relocate him or herself to best make signs to the dispossessed and keep theology vital and dynamic; *honesty* with the real requires recognizing that the world is marred by injustice; *empapamiento* refers to the need to saturate oneself with hope to better engage the transformative imagination; finally, *evolving* truth means that truth is not given once and for all but is the evolving product of culturally plural truths. Latina theology's central features also include, among the major methodological characteristics and principles, a focus on the varied daily life experiences (*la vida cotidiana*) of

---

Ada Maria Isasi-Diaz and Fernando F. Segovia (eds), *Hispanic/Latino Theology: Challenge and Promise*, Minneapolis: Fortress Press, 1996, pp. 240–60 and 'Directions and Foundations of Hispanic/Latino Theology: Toward a Mestiza Theology of Liberation', *Journal of Hispanic/Latino Theology* 1.1 (1993), pp. 5–21.

46 See the essays cited in the previous note.
47 Aquino, 'Latina Feminist Theology', p. 136.
48 Aquino, 'Latina Feminist Theology', p. 140.
49 Aquino, 'Latina Feminist Theology', p. 140.
50 Aquino, 'Latina Feminist Theology', pp. 140–5.
51 Aquino, 'Latina Feminist Theology', p. 149, italics original.

excluded women as the starting point for critical reflection; a focus on popular religion as both oppressive and liberative; the feminist option for the poor and the oppressed; as well as the claim that salvation should be understood as 'liberation from every oppression'.[52]

Given the focus on Latina theology's material geopolitical context and the elements outlined above, her description of Latina theology's four main tasks comes as a surprise. The first task lies in developing further Latina theology's theological foundations by bringing a feminist critical approach to its sources – *mestizaje*, popular religion, Scripture, the Magisterium, interdisciplinary studies, intercultural theories and philosophical hermeneutics. The second task lies in Latina women continuing to claim their right to intellectual construction and the development of means and resources for the theological education of Latinas. The third task is drawing a closer connection between theology and spirituality in feminist terms. Finally, the fourth task lies in continuing the theological analysis of capitalist neoliberal globalization on the life of grassroots Latinas.[53]

Amnesia is now evident. While Aquino began her essay by highlighting the 'material geopolitical' context which is supposed to determine the method, the principles for theologizing and the tasks for Latina theology, as the essay develops, the background of global economic marginalization as well as the marginalization of the United States' poor recedes from view while the theological exclusion of Latinas comes to the forefront. This happens in two main ways: first, Aquino explicitly relegates the critique of economic conditions to the fourth task Latina theology must tackle. Access to theological education and intellectual construction comes first. So does developing further the foundation of Latina theology. Helping people become theologians is given priority over helping people lift themselves from social misery. Obviously, a class choice has been made. It seems, therefore, that the focus of Latina theology is middle-class Latinas, rather than the poor. Second, among the sources she names for Latina theology – *mestizaje*, popular religion, Scripture and Magisterium, interdisciplinary studies, and philosophical hermeneutics – disciplines that might help tackle global and local economic marginalization are conspicuously absent. Political economy and legal theory seem like obvious tools for a theology seeking to respond to her 'material geopolitical' context, yet Aquino stresses elements that ensure her a place within the dominant religious and academic orthodoxy.[54] The end result of these moves is a

---

52 Aquino, 'Latina Feminist Theology', p. 151.
53 Aquino, see, 'Latina Feminist Theology', pp. 153–4.
54 Let's not forgot the furious criticism early Latin American liberation theology faced

theological focus that deals almost exclusively with seeking to address cultural marginalization through integration at the level of the academy, exemplified in one instance by Aquino's penchant for incorporating words from Nahuatl and Spanish into a North Atlantic theological discourse dominated by English, French and German.

Let me stress that I wholeheartedly support feminist theological projects and agree with Aquino that the cultural exclusion of Latinas in the United States as well as their under-representation in the academy are problems that must be addressed. I also agree that English, French and German have dominated theology for too long. Aquino is right to try to give Latinas a voice. But this focus is too narrow and makes scarcely visible either global poverty or the poverty of the vast majority of Latinas in the United States. By the end of the essay the 'material geopolitical context', rather than addressed, has been forgotten. Aquino writes that 'salvation is understood by Latina Feminist theology as liberation from every oppression' and that 'the historical process of liberation from poverty, social injustice, and exclusion becomes the most effective and credible manifestation of God's salvation'.[55] Yet the tasks she outlines for Latina theology as well as the elements that make it up relegate liberation from poverty and social injustice to an afterthought. What really has priority is the inclusion of Latinas into the United States' mainstream. This is not a theology of liberation, it is a theology of inclusion for the middle class.[56]

---

for using dependency theory. For the Vatican, the use of dependency theory placed liberation theology outside the realm of religious orthodoxy; for the North Atlantic academy, the use of dependency theory placed liberation theology outside the realm of what could be called theological orthodoxy. For the former, liberation theology was heretical for a supposed espousal of an atheist Marxism; for the latter, liberation theology was more sociology or politics than theology. Marcella Althaus-Reid is correct when she suggests that liberation theology was an 'indecent' theology – one that questioned the limits of theological, political and economic reason. Aquino's Latina theology, as stated in this programmatic essay, is decent. On indecent theology see, most recently, Marcella Althaus-Reid, *The Queer God*, New York: Routledge, 2003, as well as Marcella Althaus-Reid, *Indecent Theology: Theological Perversions in Sex, Gender and Politics*, New York: Routledge, 2000. For an essay that deals with the relationship between indecent theology and liberation theology see her 'From Liberation Theology to Indecent Theology: The Trouble with Normality in Theology', in Ivan Petrella (ed.), *Latin American Liberation Theology: The Next Generation*, Maryknoll, NY: Orbis Books, 2005, pp. 20–38.

55 Aquino, 'Latina Feminist Theology', p. 151.

56 The same issue with the disciplines chosen emerges in another statement on method. In 'Theological Method in U.S. Latino/a Theology: Toward an Intercultural Theology for the Third Millennium' Aquino again stresses 'the option for the poor and oppressed' and engages in a critique of neoliberal globalization but when it comes to the disciplines that could aid in the struggle for liberation – 'relational theological anthropology', 'intercultural liberation philosophy', 'critical theories of systemic analysis', such as 'critical feminist and ecologic theories' – are the only ones mentioned. I'm not saying that these

Benjamín Valentín provides my second example.[57] Valentín's *Mapping Public Theology* is the only book-length critique of Hispanic/Latino(a) theology undertaken by an insider; a critique, moreover, with which I am in full agreement.[58] Indeed, his criticism of Hispanic/Latino(a) theology can be applied to Aquino above and is echoed in my criticism of liberation theologies generally. We share, for example, an evaluation of current liberationist production:

> the irony of the contemporary intellectual scene is that in a time when the need for comprehensive and integrative thought has increased, liberationists and progressives have generally taken to circumscribing their ambitions and visions, choosing to dedicate themselves principally to the promotion of particular cultural and identity commitments.[59]

We also share the belief that 'the emphasis on specific localization that undergirds much of our liberationist discourse, which lends itself to an insular attachment with matters of culture, identity and difference, is too narrow to foster the kinds of overarching and harmonizing emancipatory visions that the goal of social justice requires in

---

disciplines should not be considered, but why not also consider economics, legal theory, sociology and political science? Aquino, 'Theological Method in U.S. Latino/a Theology', p. 40.

57 For Valentín see Benjamín Valentín (ed.), *New Horizons in Hispanic/Latino(a) Theology*, Cleveland, OH: The Pilgrim Press, 2003; *Mapping Public Theology: Beyond Culture, Identity, and Difference*, Harrisburg, PA: Trinity Press International, 2002; Anthony Pinn and Benjamín Valentín (eds), *The Ties That Bind: African American and Hispanic American/Latino/a Theologies in Dialogue*, New York: Continuum, 2001 and Benjamín Valentín, 'Nuevos Odres para el Vino: A Critical Contribution to Latino/a Theological Construction', *Journal of Hispanic/Latino Theology* 5.4 (1998), pp. 30–47.

58 For book-length overviews of Hispanic/Latino(a) theology see Luis G. Pedraja, *Teología: An Introduction to Hispanic Theology*, Nashville, TN: Abingdon Press, 2003; for article length overviews see Justo L. Gonzalez, 'Latino/a Theology', in Miguel A. De La Torre (ed.), *Handbook of U.S. Theologies of Liberation*, St Louis: Chalice Press, 2004, pp. 204–17; John Ford, 'Hispanic/Latino Theology – En Marcha!', *Religious Studies Review* 29.1 (2003), pp. 35–42 and Michelle Gonzalez, 'Latino/a Theology: Doing Theology Latinamente', *Dialog: A Journal of Theology* 41.1 (Spring 2002), pp. 63–72. Hispanic/Latino(a) theologians have also produced a host of edited volumes. See, for example, Edwin David Aponte and Miguel A. De La Torre (eds), *Handbook of Latina/o Theologies*, St Louis: Chalice Press, 2006; Alvin Padilla, Roberto Goizueta, and Eldin Villafane (eds), *Hispanic Christian Thought at the Dawn of the 21st Century: Apuntes in Honor of Justo L. Gonzalez*, Nashville: Abingdon Press, 2005; Orlando O. Espin and Miguel H. Diaz (eds), *From the Heart of Our People*, Maryknoll, NY: Orbis Books, 1999 and Isasi-Diaz and Segovia (eds), *Hispanic/Latino Theology*.

59 Valentín, *Mapping Public Theology*, p. xi.

our time'.[60] Indeed, for Valentín as for myself, 'our theologies need to be guided by broad sociopolitical imagery and analysis'.[61] To do so, however, 'Hispanic theologians must bear in mind that U.S. Latino/as suffer injustices that are traceable not only to the denigration of their culture, but also to socioeconomic exploitation and inequity. It is vital, therefore, that we extend sustained and mature attention to matters of economic justice in our theologies.'[62] The core of his critique, moreover, lies in the claim that Hispanic/Latino(a) theology, as currently configured, is incapable of producing a true liberation theology. His blunt confession toward the end of this book is worth quoting more fully:

> We can pretend that our current particularist, identity- and culture-based theologies of liberation will somehow produce a liberationist movement that will raise the living standards for Latino/as and members of other social groups, and will somehow bring to bear meaningful broad-based pressure on the unjust institutional structures of society, but the evidence thus far has been overwhelmingly to the contrary. After three decades of our discursive and activistic affiliation with the paradigm of identity and a cultural politics of difference, the poor have become poorer while the truly wealthy have become wealthier, racism continues to permeate institutional life, and cultural oppression and sexism continue to exist.[63]

Given the direction of his critique in *Mapping Public Theology*, one would expect Valentín's subsequent work to move in the direction of developing a Hispanic/Latino(a) theology that focuses less on culture and more on class in order to deal with the issue of material poverty and build bridges between different ethnic/racial groups. Yet in an essay tantalizingly titled '¿Oye, ¿Y Ahora Qué?/ Say, Now What? Prospective Lines of Development for U.S. Hispanic/Latino(a) Theology', he falls into the same traps he highlighted in others. While one part of the essay reiterates his critique that 'Hispanic/Latino(a) theology has lagged behind in its scrutiny of issues related to socioeconomic injustice and political disparities that exist in our society' and therefore 'it is vital . . . that we extend sustained and mature attention to socioeconomic injustice, which is rooted in the political-economic structure

---

60 Valentín, *Mapping Public Theology*, p. xiv.
61 Valentín, *Mapping Public Theology*, p. 83.
62 Valentín, *Mapping Public Theology*, p. 78.
63 Valentín, *Mapping Public Theology*, p. 139.

of society,' no move is made in that direction.[64] Instead, the bulk of
the essay is taken up with developing further the Hispanic/Latino(a)
identity of such theology. For example, Valentín argues that Hispanic/
Latino(a) theologians should move from mere cultural approbation to
cultural incorporation so that they 'push forward our cultural emphasis by moving from a mere honoring of the concept of culture to the
utilizing of Latino(a) cultural production in our theologies'.[65] He suggests that 'sustained engagement with U.S. Latino(a) literature, music,
art, film, drama, comedy and other such cultural expressions and
practices could serve to proffer an existential historicity, a contextuality, a corporeality, and a palpable "Latinidad" to our theologies'.[66] In
an essay that promises to outline prospective paths of development,
ensuring the Hispanic/Latino(a) identity of theology emerges as the
paramount issue: 'I dare say that without such an artifactual, cultural encounter and incorporation our theologies run the risk of being
"Latino(a)" just in name . . .'[67]

Despite the powerful critique he develops in *Mapping Public Theology*, Valentín's focus here is no broader than that of the bulk of Hispanic/
Latino(a) theology he criticizes. And despite his call for 'more serious
efforts of social theorizing' and his assertion that 'Latino(a) theology
should also be willing to traverse the boundaries of group knowledge
and interest in order to envision and articulate a social ontology that
can more tangibly enable relationships across local personal and group
difference', his only suggestion to this end is to 'be more willing to
entertain the potentiality both of relational theologies and of dialogi-
cal exchange with theologians and religious scholars of other culturally
and ethnically defined groups'.[68] Why limit oneself to meetings with
other theologians and scholars of religious studies? If one is interested
in more serious efforts toward social theorizing, meeting with critical
social scientists – economists, sociologists, legal theorists – is in order.
One might want to incorporate economics, political science and a host
of the other social sciences in addition to Latino(a) film and comedy.
Here Valentín, like Aquino, refuses to look beyond ethnicity and traditional definitions of theology. He seems to have forgotten his own best
work. In this case, moreover, amnesia shades into monochromatism

---

64 Benjamín Valentín, '¿Oye, Y Ahora Qué?/Say, Now What? Prospective Lines of
Development for U.S. Hispanic/Latino(a) Theology', in Valentín (ed.), *New Horizons
in Hispanic/Latino(a) Theology*, Cleveland, OH: The Pilgrim Press, 2003, pp. 112 and
113 respectively.
65 Valentín, '¿Oye, Y Ahora Qué?', p. 107.
66 Valentín, '¿Oye, Y Ahora Qué?', p. 107.
67 Valentín, '¿Oye, Y Ahora Qué?', p. 107.
68 Valentín, '¿Oye, Y Ahora Qué?', p. 117.

of ethnicity and guild, whose pernicious effects are by now evident in Hispanic/Latino(a) theologies as well.[69]

Gigantism

Latin American liberation theologians are particularly prone to gigantism.[70] Theologians suffering from gigantism see giant and monstrous forces oppressing the material poor. Unlike the amnesiac, therefore, the theologian suffering from gigantism does not forget to focus on class. Quite the contrary, economic conditions and social liberation are always the main focus. As Leonardo and Clodovis Boff stress:

> the socioeconomically oppressed (the poor) do not simply exist alongside other oppressed groups, such as blacks, indigenous peoples,

---

69 While he doesn't use the term 'amnesia', Manuel Mejido provides a powerful critique of Roberto Goizueta's aesthetic project which is similar in spirit to what I have outlined in relation to Aquino and Valentín. See Manuel Mejido, 'A Critique of the "Aesthetic Turn" in U.S. Hispanic Theology: A Dialogue with Roberto Goizueta and the Positing of a New Paradigm', *Journal of Hispanic/Latino Theology* 8.3 (2001), pp. 18–48. I am in general agreement with Mejido's take on Hispanic/Latino(a) theology. For more from him see Manuel Mejido, 'Beyond the Postmodern Condition, or the Turn Toward Psychoanalysis', in Ivan Petrella (ed.), *Latin American Liberation Theology: The Next Generation*, Maryknoll, NY: Orbis Books, 2005, pp. 119–46; 'The Fundamental Problematic of U.S. Hispanic Theology', in Valentín (ed.), *New Horizons in Hispanic/Latino(a) Theology*, Cleveland, OH: The Pilgrim Press, 2003, pp. 163–80 and 'Propaedeutic to the Critique of the Study of U.S. Hispanic Religion: A Polemic Against Intellectual Assimilation', *Journal of Hispanic/Latino Theology* 10.2 (2002), pp. 31–63. Roberto Goizueta's main work is *Caminemos con Jesus: Toward a Hispanic/Latino Theology of Accompaniment*, Maryknoll, NY: Orbis Books, 1995. For another critique of Goizueta with which I sympathize, and which extends to Hispanic/Latino(a) theology more generally, see Christopher D. Tirres, '"Liberation" in the Latino(a) Context: Retrospect and Prospect', in Valentín (ed.), *New Horizons in Hispanic/Latino(a) Theology*, Cleveland, OH: The Pilgrim Press, 2003, pp. 138–62.

70 For a sampling of classic texts in English translation see Gustavo Gutiérrez, *A Theology of Liberation: History, Politics and Salvation*, trans. Caridad Inda and John Eagleson, New York: Maryknoll, 1985; José Míguez Bonino, *Doing Theology in a Revolutionary Situation*, ed. William H. Lazareth, Confrontation Books, Philadelphia: Fortress Press, 1975; Juan Luis Segundo, *The Liberation of Theology*, Maryknoll: Orbis Books, 1985; Hugo Assmann, *Theology for a Nomad Church*, trans. Paul Burns, Maryknoll, NY: Orbis Books, 1975 and Franz Hinkelammert, *The Ideological Weapons of Death: A Theological Critique of Capitalism*, Maryknoll, NY: Orbis Books, 1986. For recent work see Mario Aguilar, *The History and Politics of Latin American Theology, Volume I*, London: SCM Press, 2007 and Mario Aguilar, *The History and Politics of Latin American Theology, Volume II*, London: SCM Press, 2008; Ivan Petrella, *The Future of Liberation Theology: An Argument and Manifesto*, London: SCM Press, 2006 and Ivan Petrella (ed.), *Latin American Liberation Theology: The Next Generation*, Maryknoll, NY: Orbis Books, 2005.

women . . . It is one thing to be a black taxi-driver, quite another to be a black football idol; it is one thing to be a woman working as a domestic servant, quite another to be the first lady of the land; it is one thing to be an Amerindian thrown off your land, quite another to be an Amerindian owning your own farm.[71]

Unlike the theologian blinded by monochromatism, theologians stricken by gigantism do not limit the range of tools used for liberation. They eagerly embrace recent work from political economy and other social sciences. Their obsession with the gigantic forces oppressing the poor, however, is paralysing. It operates in three steps: first, the theologian asserts the focus on economic oppression and social liberation. Second, the theologian presents a picture of the causes of oppression in which they are of such magnitude that they seem practically insurmountable. Third, given the intractable conditions of oppression, paralysis ensues.[72]

Gigantism has its roots in early Latin American Liberation Theology's espousal of Andre Gunder Frank's brand of dependency theory. In Frank's words,

underdevelopment [in Chile] is the *necessary product* of four centuries of capitalist development and of the internal contradictions of capitalism itself. These contradictions are the expropriation of economic surplus from the many and its appropriation by the few, the polarization of the capitalist system into metropolitan center and peripheral satellites, and the continuity of the fundamental structure of the capitalist system throughout the history of its expansion and transformation, due to the *persistence or re-creation* of these contradictions *everywhere and at all times*.[73]

Following Frank in his classic *A Theology of Liberation* Gustavo Gutiérrez argued that 'the poor countries are becoming ever more clearly aware that their underdevelopment is only the by-product of

---

71 Clodovis Boff and Leonardo Boff, *Introducing Liberation Theology*, Maryknoll, NY: Orbis Books, 1987, p. 29.

72 I trace the origins of gigantism within Latin American liberation theology more fully in chapter 3 of my *The Future of Liberation Theology*. The best book-length treatment of Latin American liberation theology and capitalism remains Jung Mo Sung, *Economía: Tema Ausente en la Teología de la Liberación*, San José, Costa Rica: DEI, 1994.

73 Andre Gunder Frank, *Capitalism and Underdevelopment in Latin America: Historical Studies of Chile and Brazil*, New York: Monthly Review Press, 1967, p. 72; emphasis added.

the development of other countries, because of the kind of relationship which exists between the rich and poor countries'.[74] Capitalism is defined as intrinsically exploitative:

> It has become ever clearer that underdevelopment is the end result of a process ... The underdevelopment of the poor countries, as an overall social fact, appears in its true light: as the historical by-product of the development of other countries. The dynamics of the capitalist economy lead to the establishment of a center and a periphery, simultaneously generating progress and growing wealth for the few and social imbalances, political tensions, and poverty for the many.[75]

Given this reality, Gutiérrez follows dependency theory to claim that 'autonomous Latin American development is not viable within the framework of the international capitalist system'.[76] He remains decisively opposed to reformist measures: 'Hence we speak of social revolution, not reform, of liberation, not development, of socialism; not the modernization of the existing system.'[77] And thus concludes: 'It is a matter of opting for revolution and for socialism ... Only the overcoming of a society divided in classes, only a political power at the service of the great majorities, only the elimination of private appropriation of wealth generated by human labor can give us the bases for a more just society.'[78] Notice gigantism at work: for Gutiérrez, capitalism is a global system that fosters development for the few and underdevelopment for the many. It is a giant that encompasses the whole globe, both developed and underdeveloped countries fall under its grasp. Capitalism necessarily produces underdevelopment, this necessity is part of capitalism's very definition. Capitalism, moreover, cannot be reformed, only superseded; a revolution is required to liberate Latin America from dependency. This is truly an awesome enemy.

Today gigantism can be divided into two related types, gigantism deriving from abstraction and gigantism deriving from demonization. In the former, the theologian identifies the causes of material poverty with such abstraction that they are impossible to tackle. Thus the poor suffer from evils produced by 'capitalism', 'neoliberalism', or 'globali-

---

74 Gutiérrez, *Theology of Liberation*, p. 26.
75 Gutiérrez, *Theology of Liberation*, p. 84.
76 Gutiérrez, *Theology of Liberation*, p. 88.
77 Gustavo Gutiérrez, *Praxis de Liberación y Fe Cristiana*, Madrid: Zero, 1974, p. 32.
78 Gutiérrez, *Praxis de Liberación*, pp. 20, 33; translation is my own.

zation', terms that are used as place markers for the cause of oppression but which are rarely carefully examined and concretely defined.[79] The very vagueness of abstraction as a technique, moreover, ensures that the place markers will be seen as capturing society as a whole. Witness Pablo Richard's statement that 'it is not possible to live *outside* the system, since globalization integrates everything, but it is possible to live *against* the spirit of the system'.[80] In this case, the main trait of this opponent is that it remains vaguely defined as a 'system' which it is impossible to escape. Capitalism, moreover, has completely taken over the political sphere as well:

> For *el pueblo* [the people] (the popular sectors, social movements at the base) political power has become impossible (the system does not allow for the orientation of political power in benefit of popular interest), political power has become *irrelevant* (since everything is determined by market logic and it is impossible to govern against that logic).[81]

Now, instead of capitalism, the preferred term is globalization. But Richard's understanding of the opponent is really no different than Gutiérrez's. Globalization is still all-encompassing and inherently exploitative. In fact, Richard is at a disadvantage; he lacks the socialist alternative Gutiérrez thought viable. Given this lack and the enemy's awesome scope and power, small wonder that the only possible resistance he can envision is a vague shift in attitude that leaves the actual structures of oppression untouched.

With demonization – the name says it all – gigantism is taken to the extreme. Following this line, Leonardo Boff, in a commentary on the Lord's Prayer, declares that the petition to deliver us from evil should be translated as 'deliver us from the evil one . . . He has a name; he is the capitalism of private property and the capitalism of the state.'[82] Another example is Hinkelammert's claim that 'the world which now appears and announces itself is a world where there is only "one lord" and "master", where there is only one system . . . There is no place of

---

79 For the study that most influenced my line of thinking in relation to this issue see J. K. Gibson-Graham, *The End of Capitalism (as we Knew It): A Feminist Critique of Political Economy*, Cambridge: Blackwell Publishers, 1996.

80 Pablo Richard, 'Teología de la Solidaridad en el Contexto Actual de Economía Neoliberal de Mercado', in Franz Hinkelammert (ed.), *El Huracán de la Globalización*, San José, Costa Rica: DEI, 1999, p. 228, italics in original.

81 Richard, 'Teología de la Solidaridad', p. 233, italics in original.

82 Cited in Iain Maclean, *Opting for Democracy: Liberation Theology and the Struggle for Democracy in Brazil*, New York: Peter Lang, 1999, p. 142.

asylum . . . The empire is everywhere. It has total power and knows it.'[83] Capitalism appears metaphorically as an all-encompassing and absolute empire that cannot be escaped. Look also at Hinkelammert's claim that 'today we are before a system of domination which includes even our souls, and which tries to suffocate even the very capacity for critical thinking'.[84] Here capitalism becomes the devil itself; nothing, not even our souls, lies beyond its scope. Capitalism's ability to possess our very being is taken to the limit in the following statement from Boff:

> the dominant system today, which is the capitalist system . . . has developed its own ways of collectively designing and constructing human subjectivity . . . The capitalist and mercantile systems have succeeded in penetrating into every part of the personal and collective human mind. They have managed to decide the individual's way of life, the development of the emotions, the way in which an individual relates to his or her neighbors or strangers, a particular mode of love or friendship, and, indeed, the whole gamut of life and death.[85]

Theologians suffering from gigantism see capitalism everywhere and as responsible for everything. Within this conception even envisioning a means of negative resistance is a close to impossible task. Where can one anchor change if the enemy is so powerful and all encompassing? Paralysis ensues.

Naiveté

Naiveté is the last of the debilitating conditions to which liberation theologians are prone. Intimately related to amnesia, monochromatism and gigantism, naiveté is often a consequence of these. If you choose your sources according to colour or guild you are prone to naiveté;

---

83 Franz Hinkelammert, 'Changes in the Relationships Between Third World and First World Countries', in K. C. Abraham and Bernadette Mbuy-Beya (eds), *Spirituality of the Third World*, Maryknoll, NY: Orbis, 1994, pp. 10–11; cited in Daniel M. Bell Jr, *Liberation Theology After the End of History: The Refusal to Cease Suffering*, London: Routledge, 2001, p. 67.

84 Franz Hinkelammert, 'Determinación y Auto constitución del Sujeto: Las Leyes Qué Se Imponen a Espaldas de los Actores y el Orden por el Desorden', *Pasos* 64 (March–April 1993), p. 18.

85 Leonardo Boff, *Ecology and Liberation: A New Paradigm*, New York: Orbis Books, 1995, pp. 33–4.

if you forget to include sources within your theology that allow for concrete socio-economic and political analyses you should be wary of naiveté; finally, if you see an all-encompassing monster as the cause of oppression you will likely fall prey to naiveté. While the ailments examined thus far often taint an entire work or body of works, naiveté is more elusive and will lie dormant until circumstances are ripe for its emergence. Look for it when liberation theologians suffering from previous conditions try to outline paths of societal reform or means of resistance to an unjust status quo. At this point worldly and sophisticated theologians, stricken by naiveté, suddenly become ingenuous, credulous and succumb to wishful thinking and/or poetic rapture in which rhetoric is pumped up to mask an absence of ideas.

Womanist theology, like its black male counterpart, makes retrieving the black voice a central element of theology and blackness the ultimate judge of its sources.[86] As Linda Thomas stresses:

> womanist theology draws on sources that range from traditional church doctrines, African American literature, nineteenth-century black women leaders, poor and working-class black women in holiness churches, and African American women under slavery. In addition, other vital sources include the personal narratives of black women suffering domestic violence and psychological trauma, the empowering dimensions of conjuring and syncretic black religiosity, and womanist ethnographic approaches to excavate the life stories of poor women of African descent in the church.[87]

---

86 For the foundational edited collection of womanist essays see Emilie M. Townes (ed.), *A Troubling in My Soul: Womanist Perspectives on Evil and Suffering*, Maryknoll, NY: Orbis Books, 2002. For book-length works, Traci C. West, *Disruptive Christian Ethics: When Racism and Women's Lives Matter*, Louisville, KY: Westminster John Knox Press, 2006; the essays collected in: Emilie M. Townes, *In a Blaze of Glory: Womanist Spirituality as Social Witness*, Nashville: Abingdon Press, 1995; Katie Geneva Cannon, *Katie's Canon: Womanism and the Soul of the Black Community*, New York: Continuum, 1995; Marcia Y. Riggs, *Awake, Arise and Act: A Womanist Call for Black Liberation*, Cleveland, OH: The Pilgrim Press, 1994; Delores Williams, *Sisters in the Wilderness: The Challenge of Womanist God-Talk*, Maryknoll, NY: Orbis Books, 1993 and Jacquelyn Grant, *White Women's Christ and Black Women's Jesus: Feminist Christology and Womanist Response*, Atlanta, GA: Scholars Press, 1989. For book-length overview see Stephanie Y. Mitchem, *Introducing Womanist Theology*, Maryknoll, NY: Orbis Books, 2002. For an article-length overview consult Emilie M. Townes, 'Womanist Theology', *Union Seminary Quarterly Review* 57.3–4 (2003), pp. 159–75.

87 Linda E. Thomas, 'Womanist Theology, Epistemology, and a New Anthropological Paradigm', in Linda E. Thomas (ed.), *Living Stones in the Household of God: The Legacy and Future of Black Theology*, Minneapolis: Fortress Press, 2004, p. 39.

It seems that nothing but the black experience is allowed.[88] Given this limitation, even Emilie Townes, one of the best of womanist theologians, is hard pressed to develop concrete avenues of resistance and reform to the status quo against which she rails. Her 'Living in the New Jerusalem: The Rhetoric and Movement of Liberation in the House of Evil', published in *A Troubling in My Soul*, the foundational collection of womanist essays she herself edited, is one example. That she understands womanist theology as liberation theology is clear from her statement that 'the socioethical claim guiding and informing my argument is that womanist ethical reflection rejects suffering as God's will and understands suffering as outrage'.[89] As such, the bulk of the

---

88 Katie Cannon's description of a debate with Cheryl J. Sanders over the womanist use of feminist resources, where the former, with other scholars, is a respondent to a lead paper by the latter, illuminates what is at stake. Cannon quotes Sanders referring to the replies to her paper as follows: 'The fact that almost all of their footnotes are derived from the writings of black women sends the important signal that we are appreciating, analyzing and appropriating our own sources, and also those of black men, without appealing for the most part to white sources for sanction and approval of what we ourselves have said. This observation is especially significant in view of the fact that in a racist society, self-hatred manifests itself as unmistakably in the academy as in the ghetto when we are pressured to employ our oppressors' criteria to evaluate our own work and worth. To see black women embracing and engaging our material is a celebration in itself.' Then she comments: 'After reading and analyzing the above statement by Sanders I realized that of the four other respondents in the roundtable discussion I made more references to and cited more sources by White woman scholars than any of the other womanist respondents . . . By using the scholarship of White feminist liberationists to frame and substantiate the theoretical requisites for rejecting patriarchal intrusions in the predicament of African American women, am I running the risk of lobotomizing womanist ethics and diminishing Black women agents and agency? Within the terms of the controversy, we need to ask: Is it appropriate for Black women to use analytical modes of exposing and criticizing domination and exploitation created by women with different social identities? . . . The implied accusation in Sander's rejoinder was a shocking and terrifying disorientation for me. I knew I had fashioned an original, concise, and powerful critique of Sanders's essay, and yet her closing statement suggests that my response was somehow bogus relative to her criterion of womanist accountability. Did using quotations from the writings of Beverly W. Harrison and Elisabeth Schüssler Fiorenza to shape and substantiate my theoretical argument manifest self-hatred, or did it make me a fraud?' Her conclusion: 'Every reflective and well-intentioned African American scholar who is consciously concerned with "the liberation of a whole people" must work to eradicate the criterion of legitimacy that implicitly presumes an absolute incompatibility between womanist critical scholarship and White feminist liberationist sources. As one of the senior womanist scholars, I am issuing advance warning to new womanist scholars, both actual and potential, that Sanders's devaluation of credibility consequent on such a conservative framework of Black-sources-only encourages guesswork, blank spots, and time consuming busy work, the reinvention of the proverbial wheel over and over again.' Needless to say, I agree with Cannon. Cannon, *Katie's Canon*, pp. 130–1. For another take on this issue see Delores Williams, 'Womanist/Feminist Dialogue', *Journal of Feminist Studies in Religion* 9.2 (Spring–Fall 1993), pp. 67–73.

89 Emilie M. Townes, 'Living in the New Jerusalem: The Rhetoric and Movement

essay is a compelling and wide-ranging examination of the roots of black women's suffering within a male dominated African American society. Townes, however, also categorically states that uncovering the sources of suffering is not enough: 'a womanist ethic is never content to merely react to the situation: it seeks to change the situation.'[90] She asks: 'What is the society we are trying to create? What does it look like? . . . These are questions a womanist ethic to combat evil takes on individually and collectively. Any discussion of evil and injustice that does not keep these questions in mind easily degenerates to theory and prospect rather than as a blueprint for justice.'[91] She answers her own questions as follows:

> The horizon a womanist ethic works toward is a society that respects the rights and humanity of all peoples and nature. It is a society that provides adequate education, health care, and income opportunities. The society that is part of the New Jerusalem respects and cares for the young and the elderly. It is a society that is rich in diversity through its cultural, racial, and ethnic groups. It is a society in which women and men learn to build healthy relationships with one another. It is a society that does not dwell on sexual orientation or life-style. It is a society that addresses the roots of its problems instead of building prison after prison as a vain panacea. It is a society that is uncompromisingly rooted in justice and fueled by people who use their hope to construct and enact meaningful and significant social change.[92]

Note the vagueness of Townes' analyses at this point. Stricken by naiveté, her essay has moved from an incisive analysis of suffering to mere rhetoric. She provides neither the blueprint for justice she seeks nor the theory and prospect she derides.[93]

---

of Liberation in the House of Evil', in Emilie M. Townes (ed.), *A Troubling in My Soul*, p. 78.

90 Townes, 'Living in the New Jerusalem', p. 84.

91 Townes, 'Living in the New Jerusalem', p. 89.

92 Townes, 'Living in the New Jerusalem', p. 89.

93 Naiveté is also found in Townes' influential *In a Blaze of Glory*. Once again, the bulk of the book is a powerful retrieval of the African American women's club movement and examination of black women's literature made to serve an incisive presentation of contemporary black suffering. It ends, however, with another display of naiveté. She opens the final chapter by writing: 'Apocalyptic vision. Eschatological Hope. These twin concepts move within womanist spirituality. The apocalyptic vision evolves from crisis and martyrdom. It is a theo-ethical, sociopolitical manifesto that refuses to accept or tolerate injustice. It seeks to overcome the discrepancy (and attendant craziness) between what is and what should be – the discrepancy between empirical reality and legitimate

Witness also Marcia Riggs' *Awake, Arise and Act*. The book opens with a decisively liberationist thrust:

> Black liberation may be described as the desire of black citizens to achieve more than integration into U.S. society. That is, whereas integration seeks inclusion of Blacks in terms of reform within U.S. society, black liberation seeks the inclusion of blacks in terms of radical change in society itself. To reiterate: the aim of black liberation is to transform the structure of U.S. society, recognizing structural barriers grounded in institutional racism and capitalist exploitation.[94]

She seeks to provide a radical focus; integration is not enough. The political and economic liberation sought, moreover, requires that blacks understand themselves as a unified community. For her, black liberation

> refers to collective advancement for Blacks with the goal of transforming the economic and political structure of American society. The goal is ideologically nationalistic in that it emphasizes the need for black people to engender and sustain a communal identity. Black communal consciousness is critical to an ethic for black liberation.[95]

Given that Riggs believes that black community is necessary to achieve liberation, her focus falls on an urgent issue – the *lack* of black communal identity. Blacks, she notes, are divided by class: 'the social stratification of Blacks is a factor that undermines black communal consciousness and, consequently, black liberation.'[96] In the process of tracing the origin and development of social stratification Riggs finds that it dates all the way back to slavery: 'free blacks often developed social distinctions within their own ranks ... premised upon their varied origins, ownership of property, income, occupation, skin color, and education.'[97] In fact, it seems that blacks have never possessed the communal consciousness she seeks. In the late nineteenth and early twentieth century 'the mixed black response which began in slavery

---

expectations.' But then her attempt to 'overcome the discrepancy' remains a call to spirituality that is best described as a sermon. Townes, *In a Blaze of Glory*, p. 121.

94 Riggs, *Awake*, p. 11.
95 Riggs, *Awake*, p. 12.
96 Riggs, *Awake*, p. 12.
97 Riggs, *Awake*, p. 24.

was exacerbated by hardening caste-class oppression,' and later 'even the sons and daughters of the black middle class protagonists of the civil rights movement . . . a "Liberated Black Elite" . . . join the rest of society in writing off the black masses.'[98] To deal with this issue Riggs retrieves the nineteenth-century black women's club social movement as a model for an ethic that could overcome social stratification and serve as a foundation for the creation of a black communal consciousness. The club, she tells us, provides a useful model because its leaders were elite blacks who exemplified a 'lessening of competitive class consciousness . . . they did not allow the privileges of their class to obstruct the greater good of group progress'.[99]

A number of problems ensue. The club itself undermines her radical understanding of liberation. In Riggs' own words: 'Although the work of clubs in this regard was not radical in the sense of a socialist critique of capitalist society's labor structure, the work had at least a latent liberative intent considering the emphasis on educating (not merely training) people to just compensation and their means for advancement.'[100] This is far from the ambitious goal she had set out for her project. Her choice of tools, therefore, does not meet her needs. In addition, her whole analysis is tainted by monochromatism. By her own admission the problem of social stratification – divisions arising from the class advancement of some and not others – has plagued black communal consciousness from day one. Why then insist on its possibility? If her historical overview has a lesson, it is that class has a greater pull on blacks than race and so to rely on the existence of a black communal consciousness for liberation is futile. Indeed, the insistence on community stems from her insistence on blackness above all. Finally, like Townes, her constructive proposals lack substance. She writes that blacks must recognize that:

> Class status rather than God has become the center of value for the community . . . The black community is betraying the vision of God's justice and is thus responding out of distrust rather than trust or faith in God. With class status as the center of value, other values become disordered, and God's justice is subverted and undermined.[101]

Once this fact is recognized then 'the upper and middle classes must

---

98 Riggs, *Awake*, pp. 36 and 87.
99 Riggs, *Awake*, p. 80.
100 Riggs, *Awake*, p. 72.
101 Riggs, *Awake*, p. 89.

think about how to renounce privileges (to move from sympathy to empathy) that deny the interconnection with the lower classes. The aim is to reduce tensions and alienation, for reunion is essential to liberation.'[102] Whenever the voluntary giving up of privilege becomes a recipe for liberation you can be sure that naiveté has set in.

Womanists, of course, are not the only liberation théologians to succumb to naiveté. Remember that Townes asked 'What is the society we are trying to create?'[103] I end with Hopkins' answer to that question:

> [B]etween the cutthroat reality of the now, on the one hand, and the period of the ultimate goal, on the other hand, we envision an intermediate period. Here the preferential option for the poor becomes even more clear. During the in-between time, we envision the poor, the least sectors of society, and the marginalized people among us owning and controlling the wealth of this land. A true majority of society will govern. With this condition in place, issues of universal health care, housing, employment, vacations, recreations, education, day care, and all of the issues that ensure a positive quality of daily life for those who were suffering from poverty will become easily attainable. The sole criterion during this interim period will be how we participate in the process of eliminating the system of poverty and the host of related forms of brokenness in the human family.[104]

It is clear that naiveté at this point leaves Townes, Riggs and Hopkins with little more than poetic licence and wishful thinking. Let me

---

102 Riggs, *Awake*, p. 89.

103 Townes, 'Living in the New Jerusalem', p. 89.

104 Hopkins, *Heart and Head*, p. 73. Another example: 'Those living in poverty, therefore, should participate in the stewardship and ownership of the major economic corporations and commercial businesses and wealth – the land, everything built on it, and scientific innovation. To carry out such a new democracy requires reallocation of current political economic structures toward sharing ... To facilitate this process and spirit of liberation, major corporations and financial institutions would be used to help poor and working people to set up small and medium size businesses in their communities as another form of collective participation and healthy renewal for the common good. Economic democracy, the ethics of this stewardship, provides various ways of unleashing the creative potential of previously untapped people and ideas.' One more: 'Because the majority of the U.S. population is made up of poor and working people, the elected officials (on national, regional, and local levels) should be chosen from among that group ... The reason that this does not happen today is because now the first criterion to be elected in the United States is to own, control, and monopolize wealth or have access to resources and money.' Obviously, however, the reasons why Hopkins' vision does not happen are more complex. There are all sorts of institutional mechanisms that impede the presentation of third-party or independent candidates that would have to be addressed. Hopkins, *Heart and Head*, pp. 180 and 181.

stress that I do believe that the recovery of forgotten and suppressed histories is an important scholarly and political task. But for a liberation theology, it is also only a preliminary task. We have a right to wonder whether this rhetoric, unsubstantiated by economic and political analyses, is at all productive. James Cone once stressed: 'Love's meaning is not found in sermons or theological textbooks but rather in the creation of social structures that are not dehumanizing and oppressive.'[105] By this standard, it is not.

Liberation Theology Today

The dominant American liberation theologies and the global economy parallel each other. In both, the majority of the world's population is excluded. In some cases, resistance is deemed the only available option, in others the inclusion of voice is revealed as the goal. The bottom line is that the debilitating conditions ensure that material poverty and social liberation are never successfully placed at the forefront of theology. Properly understanding the theological context within which a liberation theologian currently works means recognizing that the material misery of the majority of the Americas is not a central concern to many theologies that dub themselves 'liberation' theologies. Today many 'liberation' theologies do not focus on the poor of the Americas. Today, many liberation theologies are in intent and/or result theologies for the middle class.

At the beginning of this chapter I wrote that Marx's eleventh thesis on Feuerbach – 'philosophers have only interpreted the world in various ways, the point however is to change it' – was not entirely fair to philosophers past. I stressed that before changing the world we had to first interpret it correctly. Now, though, I must give Marx his due. At their best all these American liberation theologies can muster is enriching our interpretation of the world with the retrieval and recovery of marginalized voices; they come to a halt after merely interpreting the world of different groups.[106] Writing on its Latin American variant,

---

105 James Cone, 'Black Theology and the Black Church', in James Cone and Gayraud Wilmore (eds), *Black Theology: A Documentary History, Volume I 1966–1979*, Maryknoll, NY: Orbis Books, 2003, p. 268. Alistair Kee also asks in reference to womanist theology: 'But what is the point of such romantic rhetoric if it is not supported by economic analyses? . . . Once again we find that womanist theologians refuse to engage in dialogue with the wider intellectual tradition, decline to use critical resources which could serve them and the poor black women they claim to represent.' Kee, *The Rise and Demise of Black Theology*, p. 127.

106 Karen Baker-Fletcher pumps up her defence of retrieval: 'The theme of coming to

Alistair Kee once reflected that 'Liberation theology has provided the poor an interpretation of their own poverty. It has given it meaning and value. It has even given the poor status. God has chosen the poor. They are the Chosen people with whom He is well pleased. Their suffering now has a place in the grand scheme of liberation.' We can apply this thought to US liberation theologies as well. By only recovering and interpreting the world of the various ethnic and racial groups, by stopping at giving their race and ethnicity theological significance, US liberation theology 'makes the intolerable tolerable'.[107] In focusing on the first part of Marx's thesis while forgetting the second, therefore, liberation theology may have unwittingly become a painkiller, in Marx's words, 'the opium of the people'.[108] If so, these liberation theologies are their own worst enemy, they have become the very thing they were intended to overcome.

---

voice is essential to womanism. Voice calls attention to pain and suffering. Voice criticizes oppression. Voice offers and demands solutions to problems. Voice cries out in passion, anger, and outrage. Voice motivates others to follow. Voice shocks and touches people to respond. Voice challenges attitudes, social customs, and practice. Voice motivates reform. Voice calls people out for radical, revolutionary action. Voice resists systems of injustice.' Karen Baker-Fletcher, 'Soprano Obligato: The Voices of Black Women and American Conflict in the Thought of Anna Julia Cooper', in Townes (ed.), *A Troubling in My Soul: Womanist Perspectives on Evil and Suffering*, Maryknoll, NY: Orbis Books, 2002, p. 184. See also Ada Maria Isasi-Diaz, *En la Lucha: Elaborating a Mujerista Theology*, Minneapolis: Fortress Press, 1993, pp. 62–80.

107 Both quotations are from Alistair Kee, 'The Conservatism of Liberation Theology: Four Questions for Jon Sobrino', *Political Theology: The Journal of Christian Socialism* 3 (Nov. 2000), p. 34.

108 Karl Marx, *On Religion*, ed. and trans. Saul Padover, New York: McGraw-Hill, 1974, vol. 5 of *The Karl Marx Library*, p. 36.

4

Beyond Liberation Theology

If one is not to be crushed by the accepted ... there seems little
choice but with violent arrogance to pit oneself as a living force
against everything learned, given.

Friedrich Hölderlin[1]

Richard Rorty once described philosophers and philosophy in the
following way:

We can pick out 'the philosophers' in the contemporary intellectual
world only by noting who is commenting on a certain sequence of
historical figures. All that 'philosophy' as a name for a sector of culture means is 'talk about Plato, Augustine, Descartes, Kant, Hegel,
Frege, Russell ... and that lot'. Philosophy is best seen as a kind
of writing. It is delimited, as is any literary genre, not by form or
matter, but by tradition – a family romance involving, e.g. Father
Parmenides, honest old uncle Kant, and bad brother Derrida.'[2]

Rorty's scepticism of philosophy's relevance outside the academy
allows him to remain satisfied with this understanding of the philoso-
pher's task. But I cannot be content with transferring his definition
of philosophy and philosophers to liberation theology and liberation theologians. Is Latin American liberation theology no more than
talk of Gutiérrez, Boff, Assmann, Bonino, Segundo 'and that lot'? Is
womanist theology nothing else than a writing that distinguishes itself
by its links to Alice Walker, black female narratives, and the cross cita-
tion among black female scholars? Are black and Latino(a) theologians
engaged in nothing more than a dialogue among a small number of
privileged minority scholars, nestled safely away in the academy? Are
liberation theologies just a kind of writing?

---

1 Cited in J. M. Coetzee, 'The Poet in the Tower', *The New York Review of
Books* LIII.16 (19 Oct. 2006), p. 72.

2 Richard Rorty, *Consequences of Pragmatism (Essays: 1972–1980)*, Minneapolis:
University of Minnesota Press, 1982, p. 92.

The easy answer to this question is, of course not. Let me take Latin American liberation theology as an example. This strand of liberation theology was born proclaiming itself a theology that would not rest with merely writing about liberation but would actually help people liberate themselves from material deprivation. As Juan Luis Segundo noted, 'the most progressive theology in Latin America is more interested in *being liberative* than in *talking about liberation*'.[3] It is for this reason that Gustavo Gutiérrez stressed the point that, 'theology *follows*; is the second step, what Hegel used to say about philosophy can be applied to theology; it rises only at sundown'.[4] Theology is a second step; that is, commitment and participation in the struggles of marginalized communities comes first. The writing emerges from and reflects upon those struggles and is literally embodied in the blood of martyred theologians, of which Ignacio Ellacuría is only the most famous. Recall that Ellacuría and his colleagues Ignacio Martin-Baro and Segundo Montes, three other Jesuits, their housekeeper and daughter, were murdered on 16 November 1989 by the Salvadoran army at the Universidad Centroamericana Simeon Cañas where Ellacuría was president of the University and chair of its philosophy department. Their murder coincided with the fall of the Berlin Wall; political freedom on one part of the globe – and the triumph of global capitalism – marched hand in hand with repression in another. In addition, while not a professional theologian himself, Oscar Romero, Archbishop of San Salvador, was assassinated for putting liberation theology's tenets into practice. Appointed by the Vatican in 1977, he took office as a conservative bishop, one who criticized any connection between religion and politics, one who believed the Church should stand aloof from the civil unrest of the time. Yet in the face of rampant poverty and human rights abuses by the Salvadoran government he became an active spokesperson for the poor. Three years after his appointment, on 23 March 1980, in the midst of great political violence, Romero proclaimed the following in a stirring Sunday homily:

> Brothers, you came from our own people. You are killing your own brothers. Any human order to kill must be subordinate to the law of God which says 'Thou shall not kill'. No soldier is obliged to obey an order contrary to the law of God. No-one has to obey an immoral law. It is high time you obeyed your consciences rather than sinful

---

3 Juan Luis Segundo, *The Liberation of Theology*, Maryknoll: Orbis Books, 1985, p. 9.

4 Gustavo Gutiérrez, *A Theology of Liberation: History, Politics and Salvation*, trans. Caridad Inda and John Eagleson, New York: Maryknoll, 1985, p. 11.

orders. The church cannot remain silent before such an abomina-
tion. In the name of God, in the name of this suffering people whose
cry rises to heaven more loudly each day, I implore you, I beg you, I
order you, stop the repression.[5]

Romero was gunned down the next evening while saying Mass by a
member of an El Salvadoran death squad. Nobody is killed by death
squads, or persecuted by the Vatican, by a writing that is just a kind
of writing.[6] In that sense liberation theology can be grouped with the
Communist Manifesto or the *Declaration of Independence*, writing
that seeks to advance political and economic freedom and thus aim at
much more than merely expounding upon Rorty's family romance.

This easy answer, however, today seems a bit too easy. As is well
known, Latin American liberation theology was born at the crossroads
of a changing Catholic and Protestant church and the revolutionary
political-economic climate of the late 1960s and early 70s.[7] Much has
changed. Back then Vatican II gave national episcopates greater freedom in applying church teaching to their particular contexts; now,
instead, the Vatican has all but eliminated supporters of liberation
theology from its ruling clique.[8] Back then the Cuban revolution gave

---

5 http://www.abc.net.au/rn/relig/enc/stories/s936657.htm   or   http://en.wikipedia.
org/wiki/%C3%93scar_Romero

6 Author of many individual works, Ellacuría was also co-editor of the work that attempted to systematize liberation theology's theological perspective. See Ignacio Ellacuría
and Jon Sobrino (eds), *Mysterium Liberationis: Fundamental Concepts of Liberation
Theology*, Maryknoll, NY: Orbis Books, 1993. For the Universidad Centroamericana
webpage that remembers the martyrs see http://www.uca.edu.sv/martires/new/indice.
htm. For the account of one liberation theologian persecuted by the Vatican see Harvey
Cox, *The Silencing of Leonardo Boff: The Vatican and the Future of World Christianity*,
Oak Park, IL: Meyer-Stone Books, 1988.

7 For an overview of Latin American liberation theology's early development in Eng-
lish see Christian Smith, *The Emergence of Liberation Theology: Radical Religion and
Social Movement Theory*, Chicago: The University of Chicago Press, 1991; for one in
Spanish see Enrique Dussel, *Teología de la Liberación: Un Panorama de su Desarrollo*,
Ciudad de Mexico: Potrerillos Editores, 1995; for one in English from a liberation theolo-
gian see José Míguez Bonino, *Doing Theology in a Revolutionary Situation*, ed. William
H. Lazareth, Confrontation Books, Philadelphia: Fortress Press, 1975.

8 The most recent example being the silencing of Jon Sobrino in 2007. Mario Aguilar
wrote a touching open letter on the topic: 'It is with great sadness that I received the news
this morning that the Latin American theologian and Jesuit Jon Sobrino SJ has been
under doctrinal investigation by the Vatican Congregation for the Doctrine of the Faith.
Further, on the 10th March several Spanish newspapers announced that he and the Jesuit
Superior General have decided not to appeal to such condemnation that will be made
public this week. The effect on a frail and ill Sobrino would be difficult to predict but he
has been forbidden from writing and speaking in public about his theology. The main accusation is that he has not stressed enough in his writing the divinity of Christ and has put

hope that an alternative to US capitalism and Soviet communism was possible; now, however, Cuba's lack of political freedom and rampant poverty makes it no model for emulation or admiration. Back then dependency theory provided a framework to understand the mechanisms of the global economy; today the social sciences are rarely incorporated into liberationist writings.[9] Back then the poor were seen as an organized force taking the reins of history; now it seems that history has passed them over. Back then liberation theology was opposed with bullets, persecution and defamation; today liberation theology operates at the margins of politics and has been co-opted into mainstream theological discourse.[10]

---

too much emphasis on the historical Jesus and the Jesus of history . . . He remains a dear friend and an example of commitment to the poor and the marginalized in El Salvador, his land of adoption. He had all his Jesuit community at the University of Central America assassinated on the 16th November 1989 and despite that he returned to El Salvador and to his theological work . . . The condemnation by the Vatican is particularly disheartening as all the Latin American Bishops prepare to gather at Aparecida, Brazil, for the 5th General Meeting of the Latin American Episcopal Conference in May. Pope Benedict XVI, previously Cardinal Ratzinger, who humiliated Gustavo Gutiérrez and Leonardo Boff in the same manner, will open the conference. I ask for your solidarity with Jon, on behalf of Gustavo and others who like me are in shock. Jon Sobrino has decided not to defend himself and he is too tired and ill to challenge those accusations while he has the full backing of the Jesuits.' On Aguilar see Mario Aguilar, *The History and Politics of Latin American Theology, Volume I*, London: SCM Press, 2007 and *The History and Politics of Latin American Theology, Volume II*, London: SCM Press, 2008.

9 For a groundbreaking critique of liberation theology's abandonment of economics as an integral part of the theological task see Jung Mo Sung, *Economía: Tema Ausente en la Teología de la Liberación*, San José, Costa Rica: DEI, 1994.

10 For a brilliant examination of the co-option of liberation theology's vocabulary see Franz Hinkelammert, 'Liberation Theology in the Economic and Social Context of Latin America: Economy and Theology, or the Irrationality of the Rationalized', in David Batstone, Eduardo Mendieta, Lois Ann Lorenzten, and Dwight N. Hopkins (eds), *Liberation Theologies, Postmodernity, and the Americas*, New York: Routledge, 1997, pp. 25–52. The original Spanish can be found in Franz Hinkelammert, *Cultura de la Esperanza y Sociedad sin Exclusion*, San José, Costa Rica: DEI, 1995. Take, for example, Jose Comblin's reaction to the Vatican's incorporation of liberation theology's terminology. He notes that in 1984 the Vatican's 'Instructions on Certain Aspects of the Theology of Liberation' denounced liberation theology in no uncertain terms. More recently, though, documents such as *Libertatis Nuntius* and *Libertatis Conscientia* take up the notions of liberation and the preferential option for the poor. This move can be seen as a tribute to liberation theology's impact, its themes being incorporated into official teaching. Comblin, however, is sceptical: 'The words are there, but always in a context that avoids all possibility of conflict: this is a poor and a liberation with which all social classes can identify themselves. No one feels denounced. In this way liberation theology's themes acquire a level of generality, abstraction and also of insignificance so that they become valid for all continents, for all peoples.' José Comblin, 'La Iglesia Latinoamericana Desde Puebla a Santo Domingo', in José Comblin, José I. Gonzalez Faus, and Jon Sobrino (eds), *Cambio Social y Pensamiento Cristiano en América Latina*, Madrid: Editorial Trotta, 1993, p. 51.

The end result of these changes is that in addition to using an increasingly domesticated vocabulary, Latin American liberation theologians also lack a viable social movement and a viable vision of an alternative society. While today they do have academic support, in itself such support is a double-edged sword – a liberation theology that comfortably exists in the academy is one that will rarely pose a threat to the status quo.[11] Given these factors, if there ever was a time when Latin American liberation theology was just a kind of writing – that time is now. Indeed, Pope Benedict XVI, as Cardinal Joseph Ratzinger, wrote off liberation theology after the fall of the Berlin Wall: 'The fall of the European governmental systems based on Marxism turned out to be a kind of twilight of the gods for that theology.'[12] Small wonder that Christopher Rowland could write of a meeting with an important liberation theologian who treated him 'to a very gloomy set of predictions about the future of the theology of liberation: "All that will be left of it in a few years' time will be our books," he said.' Rowland adds: 'In some respects, even that now looks optimistic. If book sales offered an accurate guide to its continuing influence, the situation would seem to be rather hopeless. Whereas books on the subject might have been expected to sell a decade ago, there is little market for them now.'[13] If writing is all that remains, it is writing that is not even read.

Black theology has also traced a path from revolutionary effervescence to bourgeois respectability. Two essays by Gayraud Wilmore will make this point. In 'Black Theology: Review and Assessment', he stresses black theology's radical political beginnings:

> I was converted to a different kind of Blackness on a country road between Memphis, Tennessee and Jackson, Mississippi, when the call the Black Power was first raised on what was called the James

---

11 For a powerful critique of liberation theology's move toward 'decency' see Marcella Althaus-Reid, *Indecent Theology: Theological Perversions in Sex, Gender and Politics*, New York: Routledge, 2000. An academic support, however, that varies per institution. Some of my colleagues have accused me (and tried to force me out of the department) because I work in the 'narrow' and 'limited' field of liberation theology. They would rather I publish something, which, I quote one of them, 'doesn't have "liberation theology" in the title'.

12 Joseph Ratzinger, 'Relación Sobre la Situación Actual de la Fe y la Teología', *Fe y Teología en América Latina*, Santa Fe de Bogota, Colombia: CELAM, 1997, p. 14. Unfortunately for Ellacuría, the Salvadoran army did not agree.

13 Christopher Rowland (ed.), *The Cambridge Companion to Liberation Theology*, Cambridge: Cambridge University Press, 1999, p. 249. This, however, may be changing. There is now a second edition of the *Cambridge Companion*, and the book you are reading is published in SCM Press's new *Reclaiming Liberation Theology* series.

Meredith March in July, 1966. But that was only the beginning. An irreversible confirmation of my new identity as a Black man came one year later at the first National Black Power Conference in Newark, New Jersey, while the fires were still burning in the Newark ghetto. After that meeting, which did so much to clarify the concept of Black Power . . . I knew that Christian theology would never be the same for me.[14]

This history should be well known: on 5 June 1966, James Meredith, the first black student to integrate the University of Mississippi in 1962, set out on a solo, 220-mile 'March Against fear' designed to encourage black voting in Mississippi. He was shot down the very next day by white racist Aubrey James Norvell. Upon hearing the news, Martin Luther King and a group of marchers that included soon-to-be Black Power leader Stokely Carmichael continued the march from the spot on Highway 51 where Meredith had been shot the day before. The number of marchers eventually reached several hundred. Arrested during the march, upon his release on 17 June, Stokely Carmichael addressed a mass meeting in Greenwood where the 'Black Power' slogan gained its first show of public support as he proclaimed: 'What we need is black power'. James Meredith rejoined the march on 24 June and participated in the final rally of 15,000 people at the state capitol in Jackson, Mississippi on 26 June.[15]

For those who like Wilmore lived this tumultuous time,

what we experienced during that period was not to be found in the sanctuary, but in the streets . . . I can remember the many theological debates which took place in the siren-shattered nights in Newark, Watts, Detroit, and Cairo, Illinois – and, of course, during the later sit-ins at the interchurch Center in New York . . . I will never forget a strained debate on violence and Black faith with a group of young urban guerrillas who brought their submachine guns

---

14 Gayraud S. Wilmore, 'Black Theology: Review and Assessment', *Voices From the Third World* 5.2 (1982), p. 7.

15 King and Carmichael disagreed regarding the participation of whites in the march. King emphasized the importance of unity: 'Consciences must be enlisted in our movement, not merely racial groups.' On 8 June 1966, the group held a joint press conference, confirming that the march would be non-violent and open to white participation. A manifesto was issued, calling for the President to send voting examiners into 600 Southern counties, order the FBI and US Marshals to actively enforce laws, and strengthen the Civil Rights Bill of 1966. See http://www.stanford.edu/group/King/about_king/encyclopedia/marchagainstfear.htm. Interestingly, Meredith was an active Republican and was for a number of years a domestic advisor on the staff of Senator Jesse Helms.

and other automatic weapons into my hotel and spent the night in heated conversation.[16]

Such were the radical origins of black theology and the context in which Cone's *Black Theology and Black Power* was conceived. By the 1970s, however, Wilmore laments that black theology had become institutionalized and retreated

> to a largely academic dialogue between black scholars . . . Today I see more clearly than I did ten years ago that an elitist guild was premature and a strategic error on our part. While it was inevitable that Black scholars would want to 'credentialize' a theological perspective that was misunderstood if not maligned in the predominately white seminaries, it was both unnecessary and contrary to the best interests of Black theology to turn the movement over to professional theologians who had one eye on their latest books and the other on the tenure track.[17]

The extent of Wilmore's pessimism reveals itself in the more recent 'Black Theology at the Turn of the Century: Some Unmet Needs and Challenges', his contribution to *Black Faith and Public Talk*, a volume celebrating the thirtieth anniversary of the publication of James Cone's *Black Theology and Black Power*:

> The unspoken question hovering over this conference on the thirtieth anniversary of the publication of Cone's work is whether or not black theology ought not to be pronounced dead at the Divinity School of the University of Chicago [where the conference took place] and given a decent burial back at Union Theological Seminary in New York City [where Cone teaches] and at the Interdenominational Theological Center (ITC) in Atlanta [from which Gilmore retired] where it was first acclaimed.[18]

---

16 Wilmore, 'Black Theology', p. 8.

17 Wilmore, 'Black Theology', pp. 9, 10.

18 Gayraud S. Wilmore, 'Black Theology at the Turn of the Century: Some Unmet Needs and Challenges', in Dwight H. Hopkins (ed.), *Black Faith and Public Talk: Critical Essays on James H. Cone's Black Theology and Black Power*, Maryknoll, NY: Orbis Books, 1999, p. 236. Kee cites this passage (I take the parenthetical clarifications from him) in *The Rise and Demise of Black Theology*, Aldershot, England: Ashgate, 2006, p. 196. For another ambivalent statement on the prospects of Black theology see Gayraud S. Wilmore, 'A Revolution Unfulfilled, but not Invalidated', in James Cone (ed.), *A Black Theology of Liberation: Twentieth Edition*, Maryknoll, NY: Orbis Books, 1986, pp. 145–63.

He answers his provocative question in the negative, but as Alistair Kee points out, what's significant is that the question is neither inappropriate nor absurd – it can be asked.[19] In fact, of the reasons given for black liberation theology's decline, one stands out:

> the eventually sincere though half-hearted embrace of the white academy which, while helpfully accrediting black theology for seminary and university teaching, flattered and then distracted black theologians and scholars of religion from dealing more directly with the urgent problems of the poor and disinherited black people who needed them the most.[20]

From siren-filled nights and submachine guns to tenure and academic respectability, there lies the path black liberation theology has taken.

Statements like Wilmore's have become commonplace within US liberation theologies. Emilie Townes, for example, has complained about black theology's irrelevance and seeming failure of nerve:

> We are caught in whirlpools of individualistic narcissism. Even though black theology is largely ignored by the majority of adherents and practitioners of dominant academic discourses, it appears that this weary state of affairs is even more so in the majority of black Christian churches. I do not hear, witness, or see a groundswell of calls for liberation from most black churches . . . It is as though we in the academy and we in the church are ships passing in the night and we are not even looking for one another. Our continued arrogance and hoarding of our meager privileges must stop, or we need to find another name for ourselves because we have ceased being Christian.[21]

Cone, in turn, has confessed to a sense of helplessness: 'Is God still going to call the oppressors to account? If so, when? Black suffering in America and throughout the world, however, seems to be a blatant contradiction of that faith claim. Black suffering is getting worse, not better, and we are more confused than ever about the reasons for it.'[22]

---

19 Kee, *Rise and Demise*, p. 196.

20 Wilmore, 'Black Theology at the Turn of the Century', pp. 235–6.

21 Emilie M. Townes, 'On Keeping Faith with the Center', in Linda E. Thomas (ed.), *Living Stones in the Household of God: The Legacy and Future of Black Theology*, Minneapolis: Fortress Press, 2004, pp. 189–202.

22 James Cone, 'Calling the Oppressors to Account: God and Black Suffering', in Thomas (ed.), *Living Stones in the Household of God*, p. 10.

You find the same tone and questions within Hispanic/Latino(a) theology. Manuel Mejido has asked:

> Which Latino theologian would deny that U.S. Hispanics are an oppressed people? Who would deny that those asymmetrical power structures need to be transformed? But how, I ask, does U.S. Hispanic theological discourse reflect the monstrosity of oppression? How does it contribute – albeit intellectually – to the critique of unjust structures and to the creation of a society where the Latino worker would be free from the yoke of an oppressive labor market that is held in place by the ideology of the 'minimum wage', a society where the Latino culture would no longer be colonized, instrumentalized, and reduced to, for instance, the fast-food aphorism 'Yo quiero Taco Bell'? Indeed, I fail to see how U.S. Hispanic theology speaks to the monstrosity of oppression which defines the everydayness of Latino reality in the United States.[23]

While Benjamín Valentín echoes Cone's conclusion:

> We can pretend that our current particularist, identity- and culture-based theologies of liberation will somehow produce a liberationist movement that will raise the living standards for Latino/as and members of other social groups, and will somehow bring to bear meaningful broad-based pressure on the unjust institutional structures of society, but the evidence thus far has been overwhelmingly to the contrary. After three decades of our discursive and activistic affiliation with the paradigm of identity and a cultural politics of difference, the poor have become poorer while the truly wealthy have become wealthier, racism continues to permeate institutional life, and cultural oppression and sexism continue to exist.[24]

Given the scepticism expressed by major liberationists themselves, we must ask ourselves whether Cornel West was right when he suggested that 'the high moment of liberation theology has passed'.[25] Are we back, therefore, to a view of liberation theology as just a kind of writing – the

---

23 Manuel Mejido, 'A Critique of the "Aesthetic Turn" in U.S. Hispanic Theology: A Dialogue with Roberto Goizueta and the Positing of a New Paradigm', *Journal of Hispanic/Latino Theology* 8.3 (2001), p. 37.

24 Benjamín Valentín, *Mapping Public Theology: Beyond Culture, Identity, and Difference*, Harrisburg, PA: Trinity Press International, 2002, p. 139.

25 Cornel West, 'On Liberation Theology: Segundo and Hinkelammert', in West (ed.), *The Cornel West Reader*, New York: Basic, 1999, p. 394.

elucidation of Rorty's family romance? Perhaps. But I am not interested in answering these questions; I am interested in eliminating them from the range of questions that can be asked. I want to render them mute, I want to make them disappear. Liberation theologies were born of rebellion against poverty, discrimination, imperialism, and death. Liberation theologies were born of rebellion against the blindnesses and biases of the wealthy and white theology of the North Atlantic world. To make these questions disappear liberation theology must once again rebel; this time, however, it must rebel against itself. To properly address the material poverty that is at the heart of its social and economic context – to properly address the reality of Vita – a liberation theology for the Americas must rebel against its theological context by refusing to become a theology for the middle class. To do so is to move beyond liberation theology as it currently stands.

What follows are thus signposts on the road beyond. As Tissa Balasuriya once argued, any theology must be a dialectical relation between local struggles and the global situation, between local theologies and a theology that reads the significance of global realities.[26] As in the rest of the book, I outline here what I understand as the wider parameters of self-understanding within which local struggles must be articulated, the broader context within all American liberation theologies must be developed. Allow me to add a caveat. While I consider myself a student of all the American liberation theologies, my thinking has been most strongly influenced by the Latin American variant. This emphasis is at this point unavoidable, as Franz Rosenzweig once remarked: 'We all see reality through our own eyes, but it would be foolish to think we can pluck out our eyes to see straight.'[27] I thus ask the reader, where my argument fails, to be guided by its spirit, and revise it, make it stronger. What, then, must we focus on to develop a liberation theology for the Americas? As an initial and preliminary reflection, six points, moving from the general to the specific, must suffice.

26 Tissa Balasuriya, *Planetary Theology*, Maryknoll, NY: Orbis Books, 1984, p. 14. See also Robert McAfee Brown, 'A Preface and a Conclusion', in Sergio Torres and John Eagleson (eds), *Theology in the Americas*, Maryknoll, NY: Orbis Books, 1976, p. xix.

27 Cited in John Parratt (ed.), *An Introduction to Third World Theologies*, Cambridge: Cambridge University Press, 2004, p. 9. Parratt does not give the original reference.

On Liberation Theology and Outrage

In 1948, barely three years after the liberation of Auschwitz, 'Little Boy', 'Fat Man', and over 60 million dead marked the end of the twentieth-century's second great intracolonial war, otherwise known as World War Two, Karl Barth noted our ability to become accustomed to the unimaginable:

> According the present trend, we may suppose that even on the morning after the Day of Judgment – if such a thing were possible – every cabaret, every night club, every newspaper firm eager for advertisements and subscribers, every nest of political fanatics, every pagan discussion group, indeed, every Christian tea-party and Church synod would resume business to the best of its ability, and with a new sense of opportunity, completely unmoved, quite uninstructed, and in no serious sense different from what it was before. Fire, drought, earthquake, war, pestilence, the darkening of the sun and similar phenomena are not the things to plunge us into real anguish, and therefore to give us real peace. The Lord was not in the storm, the earthquake, or the fire (1 Kings 19.11–12). He really was not.[28]

In his *Remnants of Auschwitz*, Giorgio Agamben draws from Primo Levi to present a dramatic example of that ability. In Auschwitz there was a special group of prisoners, the *Sonderkommando*, who were responsible for managing the gas chambers and the crematoria:

> Their task was to lead naked prisoners to their death in the gas chambers and maintain order among them; they then had to drag out the corpses, stained pink and green by the cyanotic acid, and wash them with water; make sure that no valuable objects were hidden in the orifices of the bodies; extract gold teeth from the corpses' jaws; cut the women's hair and wash it with ammonia chloride; bring the corpses into the crematoria to oversee their incineration; and, finally, empty out the ovens of the ash that remained.[29]

---

28 Karl Barth, *Church Dogmatics, Volume III, Part 2; The Doctrine of Creation*, Edinburgh: T. & T. Clark, 1986, p. 115. I first read this passage in Giorgio Agamben, *Remnants of Auschwitz: The Witness and the Archive*, New York: Zone Books, 2002, p. 49. Auschwitz, of course, was the largest of Nazi German concentration camps. At least 1.1 million people were killed in there, of which 90% were Jews. 'Little Boy' and 'Fat Man' were the code names for the atomic bombs dropped on Japan. Little Boy was dropped on Hiroshima on 6 August 1945; three days later, Fat Man was dropped over Nagasaki.

29 Agamben, *Remnants of Auschwitz*, pp. 24–5.

For Levi, 'the intrinsic horror of this human condition has imposed a sort of reserve on all the testimony, so that even today it is difficult to conjure up an image of "what it meant" to be forced to exercise this trade for months'.[30]

One witness, however, stands out. Miklos Nyszli remembers that during a break from his terrible task he played in a soccer game between the Nazi SS and members of the *Sonderkommando*: 'Other men of the SS and the rest of the squad are present at the game; they take sides, bet, applaud, urge the players on as if, rather than at the gates of hell, the game were taking place on the village green.'[31] Agamben's conclusion is relevant to liberation theology today:

This match might strike someone as a brief pause of humanity in the middle of an infinite horror. I, like the witnesses, instead view this match, this moment of normalcy, as the true horror of the camp . . . hence our shame, the shame of those who did not know the camps and yet, without knowing how, are spectators of that match in our stadiums, in every television broadcast, in the normalcy of everyday life. If we do not succeed in understanding that match, in stopping it, there will never be hope.[32]

The horror is that the normalcy of everyday life is itself horrendous; the shame is forgetting that horror is not exception but rule. Most of us, however, fail to understand the reality of the vast majority of humankind – the world that is satisfying to us is the same world that is utterly devastating to them.[33] Agamben must have had Walter Benjamin's eighth thesis on the philosophy of history, which reads as if it had been penned by a liberation theologian, in mind: 'The tradition of the oppressed teaches us that the "state of emergency" in which we live is not the exception but the rule.'[34] For liberation theology, theology is a second step, commitment comes first, but before commitment must come outrage at things as they are. It strikes me that underlying Wilmore's complaint, and that of everyone else, is the sense that the outrage has been lost, that liberation theology has become an academic exercise, that while liberation theologians are active and committed in

---

30 Primo Levi, *The Drowned and the Saved*, New York: Random House, 1989, pp. 52–3; cited in Agamben, *Remnants of Auschwitz*, p. 25.

31 Levi, *The Drowned and the Saved*, p. 55.

32 Agamben, *Remnants of Auschwitz*, p. 26.

33 This sentence is appropriated from Juan Luis Segundo as cited in Robert McAfee Brown, *Liberation Theology: An Introductory Guide*, Louisville: Westminster/John Knox Press, 1993, p. 44.

34 Walter Benjamin, 'Theses on the Philosophy of History', 8.

their personal practice, the intellectual production has lost its radical edge and succumbed to complacency. To begin, therefore, we must echo the question thundered by Cone in *Black Theology and Black Power*, 'Is it not time for theologians to get upset?'[35]

On the Scope of Liberation Theology

In 'The Critique of Religion in the Name of Christianity: Dietrich Bonhoeffer', Franz Hinkelammert uses the German theologian to highlight a key difference between North Atlantic theology and Latin American liberation theology. Bonhoeffer, a German Lutheran pastor and theologian, a founding member of the Confessing Church, and active participant in the German resistance movement against Nazism, was imprisoned and hanged in the concentration camp at Flossenburg just weeks before the city's liberation. While in prison, Bonhoeffer wrote a series of letters where he develops an understanding of Christianity in a 'religionless world' that led Gustavo Gutiérrez to place him at the cusp of liberation theology.[36]

Indeed, Bonhoeffer anticipates the liberationist understanding of Christianity in several ways. For him, true Christianity is this-worldly,

> the difference between the Christian hope of resurrection and the mythological hope is that the former sends a man back to his life on earth ... This world must not be prematurely written off ... Redemption myths arise from human boundary-experiences, but Christ takes hold of a man at the centre of his life.[37]

Overcoming the false divide into two worlds, one religious and one secular, leads to full participation in this world with all its problems: 'it is not the religious act that makes the Christian, but participation in the sufferings of God in the secular life ... Jesus calls men [and women], not to a new religion, but to life.'[38] Bonhoeffer, like liberation theologians, believes that Jesus' call to life has an irreducible physical component. He asks: 'But is it an accident that sickness and death are

---

35 James Cone, *Black Theology and Black Power*, Maryknoll, NY: Orbis Books, 1997, p. 3.

36 See Gustavo Gutiérrez, 'Los Limites de la Teología Moderna: Un Texto de Bonhoeffer', *La Fuerza Histórica de los Pobres*, Lima: Centro de Estudios y Publicaciones, 1979, pp. 397–415.

37 Dietrich Bonhoeffer, *Letter and Papers from Prison*, ed. Eberhard Bethge, New York: Macmillan, 1972, pp. 336–7.

38 Bonhoeffer, *Letters and Papers*, pp. 361–2.

mentioned in connection with the misuse of the Lord's Supper, that Jesus restored people's health, and that while disciples were with him they "lacked nothing".[39] All this leads Bonhoeffer to see Christian life and practice as directed toward living within God's suffering in the world, a suffering that is found in that of our neighbours: 'our relation to God is a new life in "existence for others", through participation in the being of Jesus. The transcendental is not infinite and unattainable tasks, but the neighbor who is within reach in any given situation.'[40] In a text written before his famous prison letters he even comes close to the liberationist premise that theology must be done from the perspective of the poor and the oppressed: 'We have for once learnt to see the great events of world history from below, from the perspective of the outcast, the suspects, the maltreated, the powerless, the oppressed, the reviled – in short, from the perspective of those who suffer.'[41]

These similarities make the central difference Hinkelammert uncovers striking.[42] In his writings, Bonhoeffer questions whether the notion of idolatry remains an important category in a religion-less world. Idols, he writes, 'are worshipped, and idolatry implies that people still worship something. But we don't worship anything now, not even idols.'[43] Idolatry, however, remains a central category within liberation theology. Bonhoeffer, Hinkelammert stresses, fails to see that a world that has emancipated itself from God

produces its own religion and its own idols. Bonhoeffer's belief that this world lacks religion and believes in nothing is striking . . . He himself lies before an enormous idol that under which he will be sacrificed. But he doesn't see it as such, because he understands idol-

---

39 Bonhoeffer, *Letters and Papers*, p. 374.

40 Bonhoeffer, *Letters and Papers*, p. 381.

41 Bonhoeffer, *Letters and Papers*, p. 17.

42 The difference I draw from Hinkelammert is ignored by Gutiérrez in his far bet-ter-known essay. For Gutiérrez, Bonhoeffer lacks the incorporation of social theories and social sciences that would allow him to develop his musing on seeing from the perspective of the powerless. Gutiérrez's critique is essentially the critique that Marx levels toward Feuerbach in his 'Contribution to the Critique of Hegel's *Philosophy of Right*: Introduc-tion'. Marx writes, 'The basis of irreligious criticism is: *Man makes religion*, religion does not make man . . . But man is not an abstract being, crouching outside the world. Man is the *world of men*, the state, society.' Robert Tucker (ed.), *The Marx-Engels Reader*, New York, NY: W. W. Norton & Company, 1978, p. 53. For Marx, Feuerbach failed to place human beings within their social context and thus failed to grasp the cause of our alienation. Similarly, the lack of a social scientific mediation in Bonhoeffer keeps him from properly contextualizing the 'oppressed'. His understanding of the 'powerless' and the 'oppressed' remains at too high a level of abstraction. See Gutiérrez, 'Los Limites de la Teología Moderna', pp. 414–15.

43 Bonhoeffer, *Letters and Papers*, p. 336.

atry as falling exclusively within the ecclesial sphere, and not in the wider world.[44]

Here a central difference with liberation theology is revealed. Bonhoeffer is blind to the idolatry under which he is about to be executed because it falls within the realm of political ideology and so lies outside theology's traditional areas of concern. Liberation theology, instead, takes Bonhoeffer's critique of religion a step further to the critique of idolatry in the world; it thus does not speak of an irreligious world but of idolatries found in the world that are masked by an understanding of modernity as secular. A by now classic example of the unmasking of idolatry within a supposedly secular discourse is the liberationist critique of neoliberalism best articulated by Jung Mo Sung. Neoliberalism has its own vision of paradise; Francis Fukuyama stresses that technological developments make possible the unlimited accumulation of wealth and thus the satisfaction of ever more desires; neoliberalism demands faith; for Milton Friedman critics of the market lack faith in market liberty; neoliberalism has its own version of original sin; for Friedrich Hayek the greatest of economic sins is the pretension of knowledge that lies behind market intervention, the belief that government knows how to allocate resources better than the free market; neoliberalism demands sacrifice; insofar as the market is the one and only path toward the development of humankind then the suffering of those excluded from the market are but the necessary sacrifices required for the progress of humanity as a whole.[45] Neoliberalism is theology disguised as social science.

Marx once wrote that the critique of religion is the premise of all criticism. For liberation theology Marx's statement remains true, with a twist. Marx was drawing from Feuerbach, who limited himself to a critique of Christian theology. Today, however, the most dangerous religions and theologies, those that affect the life chances of the greatest number of people, are not found in churches or the traditionally

44 Franz Hinkelammert, 'La Critica de la Religión en Nombre del Cristianismo: Dietrich Bonhoeffer', *Teología Alemana y Teología Latinoamericana de la Liberación: Un Esfuerzo de Dialogo*, San José: DEI, 1990, p. 64.

45 See Jung Mo Sung, *Deseo, Mercado y Religión*, Santander: Editorial Sal Terrae, 1999, pp. 24–34, English translation: *Desire, Market and Religion*, London: SCM Press, 2007. For more on the theological critique of economics see Jung Mo Sung, *Neoliberalismo y Pobreza*, San José, Costa Rica: DEI, 1993 and *La Idolatría del Capital y la Muerte de los Pobres*, San José, Costa Rica: DEI, 1991. For a similar move within black theology see Dwight N. Hopkins, 'The Religion of Globalization', in Dwight N. Hopkins, Lois Ann Lorentzen, Eduardo Mendieta, and David Batstone (eds), *Religions/Globalizations: Theories and Cases*, Durham, NC: Duke University Press, 2001, pp. 7–32.

religious sphere, but outside of it, in what is usually mistakenly understood as the secular world. The critique of religion is thus still the premise of all criticism, but that critique is now directed toward the uncovering of the idolatrous theologies that lurk within the social sciences. If modernity is idolatrous rather than secular, there is no longer a traditional theological realm that theology should be concerned with or traditionally theological disciplines that must necessarily be included within the theological endeavour. The scope of liberation theology expands beyond theology into the secular/idolatrous world and the monochromatism of guild is overcome.

On Liberation Theology and the Third/Two-Thirds World

If US liberation theologies are to ally themselves with liberation theologies produced beyond their own geographical boundaries they will need to begin to understand themselves as Third/Two-Thirds World theologies. The term 'Third World' itself was coined by Alfred Sauvy in the anti-colonial Parisian paper *L'Observateur* where he presented a three-part division of the planet into the First, Second and Third World. The First was composed of the United States and Western Europe, those nations committed to capitalism and the North Atlantic Treaty Organization (NATO), while the Second included the Soviet Union and the wider communist bloc. What of the Third? The Third World, Sauvy wrote, 'ignored, exploited, scorned . . . like the Third Estate, demands to be something as well'.[46] Notice that for Sauvy, the Third World is more than a place; it is, like the Third Estate, a political movement – the Third World is a project.[47] As Frantz Fanon once wrote: 'The Third World today faces Europe like a colossal mass whose project should be to try to resolve the problems to which Europe has been unable to find the answers.'[48] In our time, when exclusion from the global economy is best understood not as a geographic divide but rather as a social rich–poor divide that cuts across geography and territorial boundaries, this is precisely the understanding of Third/Two-Thirds World that needs to be recovered

---

46 Alfred Sauvy, 'Trois Mondes, Une Planété', *L'Observateur* 118 (14 Aug. 1952), cited in Vijay Prashad, *The Darker Nations: A People's History of the Third World*, New York: The New Press, 2007, p. 11.

47 For a history of the Third World as project see Prashad, *The Darker Nations*.

48 Frantz Fanon, *The Wretched of the Earth*, pref. by Jean-Paul Sartre, trans. Constance Farrington, New York: Grove Press, 1963, p. 314; as Prashad points out, the English mistranslates the French *projet* into the English 'aim' rather than the English 'project'. Prashad, *The Darker Nations*, p. 283.

and placed at the basis of a theology for the Americas, an American liberation theology.[49]

In the United States no one understood this better than the early James Cone. From the outset of his irruption into the theological scene, black theology was to identify itself 'with the religionists of the Third World'.[50] Looking back upon years of black and Third World theological dialogue he remembers the misgivings as to whether US blacks and other minorities were really part of the Third World. In those conversations Paulo Freire stressed that when 'I look at my friend James Cone, whom I admire, as a Third World man – it does not matter that he was born in the United States – it's an accident. He is a Third World man because he was born in the world of dependence – of exploitation – within the First World'; while Hugo Assmann also noted that 'In the United States and Europe, there are people of the Third World – the poor and oppressed world'.[51] 'It was finally agreed by all,' Cone recalls, 'that "Third World" referred to a condition of poverty *and* the struggle to overcome it, and thus was not primarily or exclusively a geographic concept.'[52] Black theology was part of a wider movement that included the rest of the impoverished populations of the world in a

---

49 Maria Pilar Aquino nods in this direction when she writes: 'The economic and sociocultural processes of neoliberal globalization increasingly demonstrate the similarities of situations lived across the world: the violence and impunity with which the "powerful" of the world perpetrate crimes and injustices (with concomitant increases in fear and poverty among the "weak") are well documented facts. On the other hand, there is also a growing similarity in the response of peoples and cultures who, grounded, on a religious vision of justice and human dignity, fight for an alternative civilization, for greater humanization, and for the end of violence.' Maria Pilar Aquino, 'Theological Method in U.S. Latino/a Theology: Toward an Intercultural Theology for the Third Millennium', in Orlando O. Espin and Miguel H. Diaz (eds), *From the Heart of Our People*, Maryknoll, NY: Orbis Books, 1999, p. 40.

50 Cone, *Black Theology and Black Power*, p. 135.

51 'Black Theology and Latin American Liberation Theology: Excerpts from a Symposium of the World Council of Churches', in James Cone and Gayraud Wilmore (eds), *Black Theology: A Documentary History, Volume I 1966–1979*, Maryknoll, NY: Orbis Books, 1993, Freire on pp. 404–5, Assmann on p. 407. Freire also remembers the experience of reading *A Black Theology of Liberation*: 'I remember perfectly that I received my copy the day before a trip to Rome. At home that night after dinner, I began reading the book, carefully. I was spellbound page after page, not putting it down until the early morning and finishing it some hours later, en route from Geneva to Rome. When I returned to Geneva, I read it for a second time and then wrote to Cone, giving him my impressions and stressing the importance of its immediate publication in Latin America, because black theology, of which Cone was the foremost proponent in the United States, is unquestionably linked with the theology of liberation flourishing today in Latin America.' Paulo Freire, 'Foreword to the 1986 Edition', James Cone, *A Black Theology of Liberation: Twentieth Anniversary Edition*, Maryknoll, NY: Orbis Books, 1986, p. vii.

52 James Cone, *For My People: Black Theology and the Black Church*, Maryknoll, NY: Orbis Books, 1984, p. 145.

project geared toward changing not just the United States' racial order but the global order as a whole. That's why Cone stressed that for any revolutionary changes to take place 'in the international structures of oppression, poor people in the First World must make a coalition with each other and also with the poor in the Third World'.[53] Indeed, it was Cone who, following this line of reasoning, issued the strongest challenge ever posed to US liberation theologies:

> If we do not place our claims for justice in a global context, then we will appear to Asians, Africans, and Latin Americans to be black capitalists who are upset only because we have not been given a larger piece of the American pie. What does the black church have to say about the fact that more than two-thirds of the world's population exists in poverty and that such material conditions are directly trace- able to the exploitation of poor countries by rich ones? The United States represents six per cent of the world's population but consumes forty per cent of the world's resources. When we black people speak of justice, do we mean that we want an equal share of the forty per cent? If that is what we mean, then there is very little difference between black people and white people in the United States when they are evaluated from the viewpoint of global justice.[54]

In a letter to one of Johannes Baptist Metz's doctoral students, Freire once wrote that the '"primary concern" of Third World theologians is to be men [and women] of the Third World; to soak themselves in the Third World so that they could become hopeful, prophetic and utopian men [and women] of that World'.[55] I read Cone's challenge in the light of this statement. Cone demands from black theology that it become a Third/Two-Thirds World theology. For him:

> The new black perspective must be a global vision that includes the struggles of the poor in the Third World. African Americans are linked in countless ways with their brothers and sisters in Africa, the Caribbean, Latin America, Asia, and the Pacific ... We must create a 'rainbow coalition' that includes all the disadvantaged in

53 James H. Cone, 'International Versus National Oppression', in Cornel West, Caridad Guidote, and Margaret Coakly (eds), *Theology in the Americas: Detroit II, Conference Papers*, Maryknoll, NY: Orbis Books, 1982, p. 41.

54 James Cone, *Speaking the Truth: Ecumenism, Liberation, and Black Theology*, Michigan, Grand Rapids: William B. Eerdmans, 1986, p. 153.

55 Paulo Freire, 'Tercer Mundo y Teología', *Perspectivas de Dialogo* 5 (1970), p. 305.

the U.S.A. and throughout the globe. There will be no freedom for anybody until all are set free.[56]

As the previous chapter makes clear, the challenge issued has been forgotten, as has his call to 'enlarge our vision by connecting it with that of other oppressed peoples so that together all of the victims of the world might take charge of their history for the creation of a new humanity'.[57] The end result is that Cone's fear has come true. From the wider viewpoint of the Third/Two-Thirds World and the Americas, there is little difference between US liberation theologies and non-liberationist US theologies. Both are First World theologies.[58]

On Liberation Theology and Contextual Theologies

It is common today to speak of liberation theologies as contextual theologies. One reader in theology, *The Practice of Theology*, includes Latin American, black, womanist and feminist theologies under the heading of 'Local Theologies'. Another, *The Modern Theologians*, lists them under 'Particularizing Theologies'.[59] I see the point. As David Ford notes:

---

56 Cone, *For My People*, p. 204.

57 James Cone, 'Black Theology and the Black Church', in Cone and Wilmore (eds), *Black Theology: A Documentary History, Volume I*, pp. 271–2.

58 As far as I know, Cornel West was the only black liberationist to understand the implications of Cone's challenge. He writes: 'Except for the latest writings of James Cone, Black theologians remain uncritical of America's imperialist presence in Third World countries, its capitalist system of production, and its grossly unequal distribution of wealth. Therefore we may assume that they find this acceptable. If this is so, then the political and socioeconomic components of Black liberation amount to racial equality before the law; equal opportunities in employment, education, and business; and economic parity with Whites in median income. Surely this situation would be better than the current dismal one. But it hardly can be viewed as Black liberation. It roughly equates liberation with American middle-class status, leaving the unequal distribution of wealth relatively untouched and the capitalist system of production, along with its capitalist ventures, intact. Liberation would consist of including Black people within the mainstream of liberal capitalist America. If this is the social vision of Black theologians, they should drop the meretricious and flamboyant term "liberation" and adopt the more accurate and sober word "inclusion".' Cornel West, 'Black Theology and Marxist Thought', in Cone and Wilmore (eds), *Black Theology: A Documentary History, Vol. I*, p. 413. See also James Cone, 'Theologies of Liberation Among U.S. Racial-Ethnic Minorities', *Convergences and Differences* 5.199 (1988), pp. 54–64. For the best overview and analysis of theologies geared toward development or liberation see Thia Cooper, *Controversies in Political Theology: Development or Liberation?*, London: SCM Press, 2007.

59 See Colin E. Gunton, Stephen R. Holmes, and Murray A. Rae (eds), *The Practice of Theology: A Reader*, London: SCM Press, 2001 and David F. Ford and Rachel Muers (eds), *The Modern Theologians: An Introduction to Christian Theology Since 1918* (Malden, MA: Blackwell Publishing, 2005. As a teaching assistant for the 'Introduction

All theology is partial and particular, arising in and speaking to historical, social, and political contexts in which theologians are interested parties. The twentieth century, however, saw the development of *self-consciously* partial and particular theologies, deliberately adopting standpoints previously marginalized or excluded in 'mainstream' theology, and hence drawing attention to the limitations of the mainstream itself.[60]

Gutiérrez similarly states:

People today often talk about contextual theologies but, in point of fact, theology has always been contextual. Some theologies, it is true, may be more conscious of and explicit about their contextuality, but all theological investigation is necessarily carried out within a specific historical context. When Augustine wrote *The City of God*, he was reflecting on what it meant for him and for his contemporaries to live the Gospel within a specific context of serious historical transformations.[61]

There is, however, something fundamentally wrong with the designation of liberation theology as a contextual, particular, or local theology. Robert McAfee Brown has highlighted the different ways the academy has tried to downplay the radical nature of liberation theology's critique of modern theology: liberation theologies have been called a fad and its adherents naive, its terminology has been co-opted, 'until the word "liberation" has no more political content left than simply changing-things-a-little-bit-but-not-too-much'. It has been kept at a safe distance, 'we can examine oppression far away – the denial of civil rights to Spanish-speaking people in Santiago, Chile, for example – and never have to confront the denial of civil rights to Spanish-speaking poor in the central valley of California,' and it has been discredited by associating it with 'emotionally discrediting terms' such as Marxism or communism.[62] The designation of liberation theologies as contextual is the new way to take the edge off their critique. Most recently, Manuel Mejido warned liberation theologians to be wary of

---

to Christian Theology' class while in graduate school I was asked by the professor to give a lecture on liberation theology, or, as the professor put it, 'advocacy theology'.

60 Ford and Muers, *Modern Theologians*, p. 429.

61 'Remembering the Poor: An Interview with Gustavo Gutiérrez', by Daniel Hartnett in *America: The National Catholic Weekly*, Vol. 188, No 3 (3 February 2003). Consulted online at http://www.americamagazine.org/gettext.cfm?textID=2755&articleTypeID=1&issueID=420

62 See Robert McAfee Brown, 'A Preface and a Conclusion', pp. xv–xvii.

calls for dialogue between different theological perspectives. For him, 'yesterday's detractors have become today's "conversation partners". These days the theologies of liberation are no longer explicitly critiqued and pushed to the periphery. They are instead assimilated into the community of "particular" theologies.'[63] To label a liberation theology as contextual is to reduce it to the category of a particular theology in dialogue with other strands of modern theology. Insofar as this occurs, the fact that liberation theology, whatever the strand, is a fundamentally different discourse from the bulk of theology is missed. Modern theologies, to use Mejido's phrasing, understand themselves within the rubric of the historical-hermeneutic sciences, while liberation theologies understand themselves as critically oriented sciences. The former are interested in the '*interpretation* of the meaning of transcendence' and constitute the bulk of the theology produced from positions of privilege, while the latter, liberation theologies, are 'interested in the *making* of transcendence . . . understood as the making of "better" history'.[64] They are fundamentally different projects. He succinctly concludes his warning about dialogue: 'But not all religious traditions want to communicate. Some, for example, want to transform.'[65]

Of course, current liberation theologies themselves are also responsible for their designation as a contextual theology. Mejido is right to assert that liberation theologies, when confronted with 'the tension between the universality of the idea of liberation and the plurality of particular liberationist perspectives' have opted to downplay the former in favour of the latter.[66] The proliferation of liberation theologies, that nonetheless remain mute to each other, can be seen as a sign of health in the academic marketplace, but it is also a sign of disarray in the struggle for liberation. The interests of all the liberation theologies are one. As Leonardo and Clodovis Boff state of liberation theology as a whole: 'There is one, and only one theology of liberation. There is only one point of departure – a reality of social misery – and one goal – the liberation of the oppressed.'[67] Hugo Assmann once asked:

My question is about this point of particularity in theology today. It's not so particular that more than thirty million people die every

---

63 Manuel Mejido, 'Beyond the Postmodern Condition, or the Turn Toward Psychoanalysis', in Ivan Petrella (ed.), *Latin American Liberation Theology: The Next Generation*, p. 134.

64 Mejido, 'Beyond the Postmodern Condition', p. 119.

65 Mejido, 'Beyond the Postmodern Condition', p. 135.

66 See Mejido, 'Beyond the Postmodern Condition', 127.

67 Clodovis Boff and Leonardo Boff, *Salvation and Liberation: In Search of a Balance Between Faith and Politics*, Maryknoll, NY: Orbis Books, 1984, p. 24.

year of starvation, hunger, and other oppressive means. It's not so particular that two-thirds of humankind today are oppressed people. Are we not falling into a new ideological control when we speak always from our particular or contextual point of departure . . . We are representatives of two-thirds of humankind today. What kind of particular theologies do we need? Do we not need to come together for a common struggle against the oppressor?[68]

Liberation theologies are born from the struggles of the poor and the oppressed, struggles that were translated into an epistemological break with the whole of the Western, wealthy, white, and male theological tradition; they are not one theological school among others in the canon. Frederick Herzog was thus right when he wrote, 'Some say that liberation theology is merely a thematic theology. Not so: it is one of the few unrelenting efforts to think hard about the theological task as a whole.'[69] They sought and seek a new understanding of theology itself. The basis of that new understanding is the attempt to do theology from the perspective of the oppressed majority of humankind. Here lies the famous epistemological break: liberation theologies – whether Latin American, black, womanist, African, feminist, queer etc. – realize that theology has traditionally been done from a standpoint of privilege. Western theology, like the distribution of global resources, is slanted toward the affluent, the male, the white and the heterosexual; it is the product of a minority of humankind living in a state of affluent exception and enjoying gender, sexual, and racial dominance. Oppression and poverty remain the norm for the majority of the world's population. The Latin American critique of modern theology's focus on the sceptic as the object of theology sought to highlight the narrowness of the 'mainstream' focus; to focus on the sceptic as the object of theology is to organize theology around the material context of a small percentage of humankind.[70] By grounding themselves in the perspective of the

---

68 Sergio Torres and John Eagleson (eds), *Theology in the Americas*, Maryknoll, NY: Orbis Books, 1976, pp. 353–4.

69 Frederick Herzog, 'Birth Pangs: Liberation Theology in North America', in Gerald H. Anderson and Thomas F. Stransky (eds), *Liberation Theologies in North America and Europe*, New York: Paulist Press, 1979, p. 26.

70 For a classic comparison of modern theology and liberation theology see Gustavo Gutiérrez, 'Two Theological Perspectives: Liberation Theology and Progressivist Theology', in Sergio Torres and Virginia Fabella (eds), *The Emergent Gospel: Theology from the Underside of History*, Maryknoll, NY: Orbis Books, 1978, pp. 227–58. A few examples of the focus of the bulk of modern religious thought: Friedrich Schleiermacher's *On Religion: Speeches to its Cultured Despisers*; the title itself points to the theologian's main interlocutor, the sceptic, the person who thinks that Christian faith is anachronistic or even dangerous; Karl Rahner's *Foundations of the Christian Faith*, which is directed

oppressed, therefore, liberation theologies are grounded in the broadest context available today and so come as close as possible to being the first truly global theologies. All theologies are particular and local, but liberation theologies, in their particularity, are as universal as theology can today ever be.

On Liberation Theology and the Social Sciences

There are at least three reasons why the social sciences must become an integral part of all the American liberation theologies.[71] The first reason stems from the scope of liberation theology and the notion of idolatry previously touched upon; simply put, the social sciences are the place where God's promise of life is realized. Whether people live or die is most directly related not to theology, but to disciplines such as economics, political science, medical anthropology, sociology development studies. As the place where God's promise of life is most concretely played out, the social sciences themselves are theological spaces in possession of idolatries that must be unmasked or deposits of tools to be grasped for the cause of liberation. When in 'Black Theology at the Turn of the Century' Gayraud Wilmore recounted the most important challenges black theology must face at the cusp of the twenty-first century he listed issues such as hunger and homelessness, attempts to dismantle the Civil Rights Act, high incarceration rates for black men, the spread of guns and crack in black neighbourhoods, the unequal treatment of blacks by the police and the legal system, the poor condition of public schools, the reduction of black voting power through Congressional redistricting, the spread of white supremacy groups, and attacks on affirmative action and the welfare system.[72] These are the issues that determine the concrete physical existence of

toward a person who 'is living in an intellectual and spiritual situation today . . . which does not allow Christianity to appear as something indisputable and to be taken for granted'; and Gordon Kaufman's *In Face of Mystery*, which remarks that 'many in our time have become especially sensitive to how implausible, indeed unacceptable or even intolerable, is the understanding of God which we have inherited'. Quotations from Karl Rahner, *Foundations of Christian Faith: An Introduction to the Idea of Christianity*, trans. William V. Dych, New York: Crossroads-Seabury Press, 1978, p. 5 and Gordon Kaufman, *In Face of Mystery: A Constructive Theology*, Cambridge: Harvard University Press, 1993, p. 3.

71 See Ivan Petrella, *The Future of Liberation Theology: An Argument and Manifesto*, London: SCM Press, 2006, for my take on the role of the social sciences within Latin American liberation theology. See chapter 2 for my view of how the social sciences should be integrated as an intrinsic part of liberation theology's methodology.

72 Wilmore, 'Black Theology at the Turn of the Century', p. 239.

African Americans, their *lives*, yet they are not traditional theological issues. To tackle them you must first widen the scope of theology and then arm yourself with the best possible tools to deal with such issues. How are they to be effectively dealt with otherwise?

I am not highlighting anything that has gone unnoticed by black theologians themselves. The second reason the social sciences must be integrated into liberation theology can be found in Cone's complaint that 'the response of black theologians to white racism was based too much upon moral suasion and too little upon the tools of social analysis . . . it seems that we thought that change would occur through rhetoric alone. There is no analysis of the depth of racism or capitalism.'[73] Here the social sciences function as a critical tool that would allow liberation theologians better to understand the causes of oppression. In addition to this critical function, however, the social sciences also serve the constructive function of outlining, with as much content as possible, the concrete social, political and economic forms that could help people attain better living conditions. The critical and constructive functions, moreover, are interrelated. As Cornel West noted, 'the lack of a clear-cut social theory prevents the emergence of any substantive political program or vision.' He is right to stress that without a 'clear-cut social theory about what *is*, it is difficult to say anything significant about what *can* be'.[74]

The third reason the social sciences are essential to liberation theology lies in that they are the means to unmask the false neutrality of theological concepts by working out their political, economic, and social implications. Say you and I both embrace the liberationist claim that the body is the locus of salvation and that food, water, shelter are part of God's plan for all. We would still need, however, to work out what these ideas mean in practice; we need to develop the implications of that understanding for the way we relate to ourselves, to others and to the way society is organized. For some this could mean supporting a higher minimum wage and greater welfare benefits, perhaps even socialized health care. For others it might mean radical structural change such as the replacing of capitalism for a system not based on profit and competition. For still others this could mean that Christians should cease trying to change society and organize their own communities where any of these options may be worked out.[75] Others still

---

73 Cone, *For My People*, p. 88.

74 West, 'Black Theology and Marxist Thought', p. 413.

75 This is the 'radical orthodoxy' option. For my views on radical orthodoxy see chapter 6 of my *The Future of Liberation Theology*. For an excellent critique of radical orthodoxy from a different angle see Nelson Maldonado-Torres, 'Liberation Theology

might argue that neoliberal structural adjustment policies are the way to go.[76]

Concepts, once developed, lose their neutrality. To be stated neutrally, a term must be made too abstract to be a useful tool. It must be rid of content – if we don't work out our concept of 'God' then we would never know that underneath it lay all these possibilities. As each possibility gets developed further, moreover, different institutional futures emerge. Thus Latin American liberation theology's belief that developing 'historical projects', models of political and economic organization that might replace an unjust status quo, was necessary to truly work through and understand theological terms. As José Míguez Bonino once wrote, 'expressions and symbols as "justice", "peace", "redemption", . . . cannot be operative except in terms of historical projects which must incorporate, and indeed, always do incorporate, an analytical and ideological human, secular, verifiable dimension.'[77] By incorporating the development of historical projects as an integral part of theology, Latin American liberation theologians were highlighting the emptiness of theological talk that did not work out its implications for society. Theological talk that refuses to do so, moreover, by default falls into the hands of the status quo by leaving things the same.[78]

Liberation theology, however, must choose among different social

---

and the Search for the Lost Paradigm: From Radical Orthodoxy to Radical Diversality', in Ivan Petrella (ed.), *Latin American Liberation Theology: The Next Generation*, Maryknoll, NY: Orbis Books, 2005, pp. 39–61.

76 This is the World Bank's position. See Hinkelammert, 'Liberation Theology in the Economic and Social Context of Latin America.'

77 Bonino, *Doing Theology*, p. 151.

78 In its early stages, the notion of 'historical projects' was a central way that Latin American liberation theology differentiated itself from German political theology. See, for example, Bonino's critique of Moltmann in *Doing Theology* as well Moltmann's open letter in reply: Jürgen Moltmann, 'An Open Letter to José Míguez Bonino', in Alfred Hennelly (ed.), *Liberation Theology: A Documentary History*, Maryknoll, NY: Orbis Books, 1990, pp. 195–204. For more on this see chapter 1 of Petrella, *Future*. Outside of Latin American liberation theology Ada María Isasi-Diaz has most made use of the notion of a 'historical project'. See Ada Maria Isasi-Diaz, *La Lucha Continues: Mujerista Theology*, Maryknoll, NY: Orbis Books, 2004, especially chapter 9 and *MujeristaTheology: A Theology for the Twenty-First Century*, Maryknoll, NY: Orbis Books, 2002, especially chapters 4–6 and pp. 153–8. I find that her use of the concept lacks sufficient rigour and so borders on naiveté. Where she displays greater insight than many Hispanic/Latino(a) theologians is in the recognition that historical projects must be developed because ultimately they are about the transformation of daily life and thus fall squarely within her mujerista focus on *lo cotidiano*. See also her comments on the need for a 'sociological mediation' in 'Preoccupations, Themes, and Proposals of Mujerista Theology', in Anthony B. Pinn and Benjamín Valentín (eds), *The Ties That Bind: African American and Hispanic/American/Latino/a Theologies in Dialogue*, New York: Continuum, 2001, pp. 135–44.

science approaches carefully because the adoption of a social theory, the selection of metaphors one chooses to use as a roadmap to our environment, is inevitably a political act in that they are constitutive of the worlds we inhabit.[79] What really matters, therefore, is how different theories make sense of the world and move people to act in different ways and in different directions. A liberation theology for the Americas must avoid totalizing social theories such as dependency theory or world systems theory that present economic and political systems as monolithic wholes.[80] The adoption of these theories is the cause of the paralysing gigantism and demonization that plagues Latin American liberation theology. To my mind, the most useful resource available is critical legal theory.

For example, critical legal theory would allow liberationists to move beyond a blanket condemnation of 'capitalism' or 'globalization' and instead examine the way the legal minutiae of the variety of actually existing capitalisms affects the distribution of resources in society. When specifically examined, a market economy is a particular legal regime and so law, in the form of the regime choice, influences the distribution of income achieved.[81] Social interactions – say, for example, the bargaining between labour and capital over wages – can be analogized to a game played under a set of rules.[82] Even if the rules are stated in a way that applies equally to all, they can be examined for their impact on each player's chances for success. The rules of basketball, for instance, could be changed to affect the advantage tall players have over short players; lowering the height of the hoop would affect the relative ability of each player. Similarly, the legal rules that set the terms by which capital and labour negotiate are generally deemed as

---

79 For a brilliant examination of how leftist political and economic narratives contribute to creating a world where radical change is deemed impossible see J. K. Gibson-Graham, *The End of Capitalism (as we Knew It): A Feminist Critique of Political Economy*, Cambridge: Blackwell Publishers, 1996.

80 See chapter 3 of Petrella, *Future*, for the extended argument backing up this claim.

81 Duncan Kennedy, *Sexy Dressing Etc.: Essays on the Power and Politics of Cultural Identity*, Cambridge, MA: Harvard University Press, 1993, p. 97. For a sampling of books within or about critical legal studies see Roberto Mangabeira Unger, *What Should Legal Analysis Become?*, New York: Verso, 1996; Roberto Mangabeira Unger, *The Critical Legal Studies Movement*, Cambridge: Harvard University Press, 1983; and Mark Kelman, *A Guide to Critical Legal Studies*, Cambridge, MA: Harvard University Press, 1987. For some representative articles see Mark Tushnet, 'Critical Legal Studies: A Political History', *Yale Law Journal* 100.1515 (1991) and Joseph William Singer, 'Legal Realism Now', *California Law Review* 76 (1988), pp. 465–544. For my take on critical legal studies and liberation theology see chapter 5 of Petrella, *Future*.

82 The basketball example is taken from Kennedy, *Sexy Dressing Etc.*, pp. 84–5.

'background' and thus part of the neutral rules of the game. In this perspective, law only plays a role in distributing power and privilege when it actively intervenes in society to resolve a conflict. Intervention is the exception rather than the rule; the rule being that the law merely sets the apolitical ground rules within which conflict and cooperation can take place. Yet, if one imagines alternative rules, then the background rules are brought forward as far from neutral. Rules are only 'background' rules from the point of view of analyses that operate under the assumption of *ceteris paribus* – other things being equal – that is, the assumption that those rules remain constant. When the background conditions change, however, they undermine analyses that assume them constant.[83] Laws pertaining to collective bargaining, unionization, duration of strikes, the nature and scope of picketing, and many other details necessarily tilt the scale of power in one direction or another. To change these rules is to change the bargaining power of the groups involved which, in turn, affects the distributional consequences of the capitalism in question. Critical legal theory lets liberation theologians see that the legal ground rules that make particular societies, as well as the global order itself as I showed in Chapter 1, can take many different forms – the goal, therefore, is not to replace an abstract 'capitalism' for an equally abstract 'socialism', but instead to examine the rules behind a social order concretely and then to find the steps that would democratize access to economic and political opportunity by tilting the rules of the game toward the less fortunate.[84]

Gutiérrez once warned against the dangers of naiveté: 'the lyrical and vague calls for the defense of human dignity that do not take into account the real causes of the present social order and the concrete conditions for the construction of a just society are totally useless, and

---

83 Fred Block, *Postindustrial Possibilities: A Critique of Economic Discourse*, Berkeley: University of California Press, 1990, p. 30.

84 For an example of what this would look like see chapter 5 of Petrella, *Future*. Outside of early Latin American liberation theology, Cornel West had the clearest sense of the importance of social analyses for both the critical and the constructive moves I've outlined: 'For instance, all Christians today seem to be for freedom, equality, and democracy. Yes, but the question is how do you interpret these claims; what is the analytical content and substance of these assertions? The analytical content and substance are supplied by one's social analysis. As Christians, we wish to employ social analysis from the vantage point of society's victims, from the vantage point of the Cross, the christocentric perspective. Therefore the types of social analyses we would deploy not only attempt to interpret the world but also attempt to isolate potentialities for ultimate realization in struggle.' Cornel West, 'Present Socio-Political-Economic Movements for Change', in Simon S. Maimela and Dwight H. Hopkins (eds), *We Are One Voice*, Cape Town: Skotaville Publishers, 1989, pp. 75–6.

in the long run subtle ways to delude and be deluded.'[85] These are the moves that show we heeded his warning.

On Liberation Theology and Identity

I agree with Benjamín Valentín's claim that 'our theological discourses must somehow navigate across racial, cultural, gender, and religious lines to cultivate holistic social arrangements that may harmonize the interests of diverse constituencies and, in this way, facilitate the possibilities for social change.'[86] I have also argued, however, that US theologies, as currently constituted, are incapable of doing so. The first step in building coalitions lies in getting black and Hispanic/Latino(a) liberation theologies to overcome their obsession with legitimizing themselves through racial and ethnic categories. Take Virgilio Elizondo's foundational *Galilean Journey* as an example. He tells us that 'the Catholic conquest of the Americas brought with it a new people, a new ethnos – *la raza mestiza* ('mixed clan, family', or 'race').[87] Mexican-Americans are thus neither Mexican nor American, rather they are the product of a 'unique historical process that includes aspects of both but with an originality of its own – the uniqueness of a newborn ethnic strain'.[88] The outsider and marginal position of the mestizo, moreover, parallels the marginal position of Jesus. As Jesus breaks the exclusiveness of ancient thought and religion by pointing toward a universal salvation, mestizo mixed blood harbours a new humanity where racial and ethnic divides are overcome. While this approach should undermine the focus on limited sources of identity, the focus on *mestizaje* has paradoxically led to a theology obsessed with the purity of mestizo sources. Indeed, Elizondo's theology ends up providing a divine sanction to race by making mestizos the chosen people who will be the carriers of God's promised future: 'God has chosen them (mestizos) to be his historical agents of a new unity.'[89] But if *mestizaje* really is about mixed blood, then it should herald the irrelevance of race and ethnicity as a foundation for theology and humanity. *Mestizaje*, therefore, means that the only races that matter are the future races emerging from further mixing – to thus focus on a ghettoed theological/racial

85 Gustavo Gutiérrez, *Praxis de Liberación y Fe Cristiana*, Madrid: Zero, 1974, p. 21; translation my own.

86 Valentín, *Mapping Public Theology*, p. 109.

87 Virgilio Elizondo, *Galilean Journey: The Mexican-American Promise*, Maryknoll, NY: Orbis Books, 2003, p. 10.

88 Elizondo, *Galilean Journey*, p. 19.

89 Elizondo, *Galilean Journey*, p. 102.

project betrays the central insight. In the end, the right question is not 'what makes theology Hispanic/Latino(a)?' in the same way that the right question is not 'what makes theology black?'. The right question is 'what makes theology liberative to the materially poor?' It is precisely this question that these racial and ethnic liberation theologies fail to address. Still, I think there is a way to retrieve Elizondo's vision from the clutches of monochromatism by moving beyond the multicultural idea of racial harmony toward anti-racism understood as abolishing the lure of racial thinking itself. Doing so, however, requires rethinking our understanding of race, recognizing the failure of legality based on colourblindness, rejecting the black/white binary that dominates US racial thinking, and rethinking identity around politics.

Racial differences among people in fact do not exist.[90] What matters are the existence of racialized individuals and groups. It is for this reason that black and Latino(a) critical race theorists have noted that the meaning of race is never static nor fixed; some groups use the concept of race to further the subordination of people of colour, others use the concept as a tool of resistance. Race, as Angela Harris stresses, 'is an unstable and "decentered" complex of social meanings constantly being transformed by political struggle'.[91] It is neither biological fact nor an illusion, it is a system of power that works at both the material and the symbolic levels. Race refers to group differences in power, wealth, social status and health, but is ideological, rather than physical, in origin. Rather than speak of race as a thing, it is more

---

90 A large body of literature in the sciences, the humanities, and the social sciences criticizes the concept of race as a natural and fixed division among humankind. In 1997, for example, the American Anthropological Association drafted the following statement: 'The species is not divided into exclusive, genetically distinct, homogeneous groupings similar to subspecies, as the concept of "race" implies. All human groups share many features with other groups, and it is impossible to draw rigid boundaries around them. Genetically there are greater differences between individuals within a group defined popularly as a race than there are between two "races". There are no pure "races", and no groups are physically, intellectually or morally superior, or inferior, to others.' Cited in Antonia Darder and Rodolfo D. Torres, *After Race: Racism After Multiculturalism*, New York: New York University Press, 2004, pp. 145–6, note 4.

91 Angela P. Harris, 'Foreword: The Jurisprudence of Reconstruction', *California Law Review* 82.4 (July 1994), p. 774. She is citing from Michael Omi and Howard Winant, *Racial Formation in the United States: From the 1960s to the 1980s*, New York: Routledge, 1986, p. 68. There is an immense body of literature produced by critical race theorists and about critical race theory. For two comprehensive anthologies see Kimberle Crenshaw *et al.*, *Critical Race Theory: The Key Writings That Formed the Movement*, New York: The New Press, 1995 and Richard Delgado (ed.), *Critical Race Theory: The Cutting Edge*, Philadelphia: Temple University Press, 1995. For an examination of the different ways race has been constructed see Neil Gotanda, 'A Critique of "Our Constitution is Colorblind"', in Crenshaw *et al.*, *Critical Race Theory*, pp. 257–75.

accurate and useful to speak of race as a 'concept which signifies and symbolizes social conflicts and interests by referring to different types of human bodies'.[92] Notice that to think of race in this way opens up a space to question the status of whiteness as a normative and thus neutral and uninterrogated category. Whiteness hides its privileged status in two ways. First, by remaining in the background as the invisible norm by which other categories are judged. As bell hooks puts it: 'racial categories are not only black, Latino, Asian, Native American, and so on; they are also white. To ignore white ethnicity is to redouble its hegemony by naturalizing it.'[93] Second, by promoting the image of multiracial America in which whites are recast as just another group competing with many others. Here all racialized groups stand on an equal footing, none is more privileged than the other.[94] To unmask uninterrogated whiteness is to engage in what Laura Nader calls 'studying up'. As she puts it:

Studying 'up' as well as 'down' would lead us to ask many 'common sense' questions in reverse. Instead of asking why some people are poor, we would ask why other people are so affluent. How on earth would a social scientist explain the hoarding patterns of the American rich and middle class? How can we explain the fantastic resistance to change among those whose options 'appear to be many'?[95]

Among liberation theologians, Emilie Townes has made the first move in this direction. More work needs to be done.[96]

---

92 I'm drawing from Leslie Espinoza and Angela P. Harris, 'Afterword: Embracing the Tar-Baby – LatCrit Theory and the Sticky Mess of Race', *California Law Review* 85 (Oct. 1997), p. 1620. They cite Omi and Winant, *Racial Formation*, p. 55.

93 Cited in Cheryl I. Harris, 'Whiteness as Property', *Harvard Law Review* 106.8 (June 1993), p. 1761, note 230. This piece is a brilliant assault on the neutral, and thus silent, hegemony of whiteness.

94 See Alexandra Natapoff, 'Trouble in Paradise: Equal Protection and the Dilemma of Interminority Group Conflict', *Stanford Law Review* 47.5 (May 1995), pp. 1059–96.

95 See Laura Nader, 'Up the Anthropologist – Perspectives Gained in Studying Up', in Dell Hymes (ed.), *Reinventing Anthropology*, New York: Pantheon Books, 1972, pp. 284–311; cited in Paul Farmer, *Pathologies of Power: Health, Human Rights, and the New War on the Poor*, Berkeley: University of California Press, 2003, p. 269.

96 See chapter three of Emilie M. Townes, *Womanist Ethics and the Cultural Production of Evil*, New York: Palgrave Macmillan, 2006. See also scholars within 'Whiteness Studies'. For one example see the essays collected in Ashley Doane and Eduardo Bonilla-Silva (eds), *White Out: The Continuing Significance of Racism*, New York: Routledge, 2003. Chapter 2, Margaret Anderson's 'Whitewashing Race: A Critical Perspective on Whiteness', is an excellent overview and critique of the field. My presentation of data in Chapter 2 reinforces the normativity of whiteness. Ideally, I would have presented data under a general category, then white, then African-American, Latino(a) and women. The

California's passing of Proposition 209 in 1996 should have marked the death of black liberation theology's monochromatism. Indeed, the logic behind Proposition 209 is eerily similar to black theology's understanding of identity. Let me explain. At the heart of the roll back of affirmative action lie the ideas of colourblindness and equal treatment. Of course, open white supremacy enshrined in law came to an end with *Brown v. Board of Education*. White supremacy, however, was preserved by defining racial discrimination as intentional malice; differences between racialized groups are beyond the reach of the law unless there is evidence that they were intentionally and maliciously produced. Within this framework, race consciousness was racism, and race-conscious mediations were deemed as exceptional interventions within an otherwise neutral legal frame. This is the understanding of law that in *Adarand v. Peña* lets Justice Scalia write that 'to pursue the concept of racial entitlement – even for the most admirable and benign of purposes – is to reinforce and preserve for future mischief the way of thinking that produced race slavery, race privilege and race hatred. In the eyes of government, we are just one race here. It is American.'[97] Now affirmative action is reread as discrimination against whites. Such an understanding of colourblindness and equal treatment, however, narrows affirmative action to corrective and compensatory measures to the exclusion of distributive issues.[98] As Cheryl Harris notes, the fact that Proposition 209 eliminated official preferences based on race does not mean that racial preferences have been eliminated. They persist in the form of housing segregation, educational inequality, access to health care and employment. Colourblindness 'does not in fact ignore race; it rests upon and reflects an investment in a *particular* conception of race in which race is divested of its historical, societal, or experiential meaning. Under colorblindness race is reduced to color, a biological attribute like height or eye color, and is therefore presumptively normatively irrelevant.'[99] Remember that Cone once advocated an understanding of blackness which had little to do with skin colour. For him, to be black meant 'that your heart, your soul, your mind, and your body are where the dispossessed are . . . being reconciled to God does not mean that one's skin is physically black. It essentially depends

---

fact that is it very difficult (I don't say impossible, but I don't know of a source) to get data exclusively on white poverty highlights its status as normative; white is not a colour with characteristics warranting examination.

97 *Adarand Constructors, Inc. v. Peña*, 63 U.S.L.W. 4523 (U.S. 12 June 1995).

98 Cheryl I. Harris, 'Whiteness as Property', p. 1780.

99 Cheryl I. Harris, 'Critical Race Studies: An Introduction', *UCLA Law Review* 49.5 (2002), p. 1229.

on the color of your heart, soul and mind.'[100] Recall that Wilmore countered by asking whether black theology finds 'in the experience of the oppression of blacks in the Western world, *as black*, a singular religious meaning?'[101] For him, 'Simply being oppressed, or psychologically and politically in empathy with the dispossessed, does not deliver one into the experience of blackness any more than putting on a blindfold delivers one into the experience of being blind.'[102] The dominant understanding of race within black and womanist theology focuses on race as colour, just as in Proposition 209. Small wonder, then, that they fail to make inroads toward changing a racialized order.

To do so, the black/white binary that dominates US racial thinking must be overcome.[103] Latino(a) legal scholars have taken the lead in this regard. Rachel Moran points out that Latino(a) activists remain ambivalent about *Brown*'s elevation of race and ethnicity to a position of centrality when defining equality of opportunity, since Latino(as)

---

100 Cone, *Black Theology and Black Power*, p. 151.

101 Gayraud S. Wilmore, *Black Religion and Black Radicalism: An Interpretation of the Religious History of Afro-American People*, Maryknoll, NY: Orbis Books, 1983, pp. 217–18.

102 Wilmore, *Black Religion and Black Radicalism*, p. 218.

103 I recognize that it isn't easy to give up race as the default foundation for community. Harris notes that 'one of the comforts of belonging to a racially subordinated community has often been the sense of being "home", the sense that everyone in the community shares a unified perspective on the world. Modernist narratives that speak of 'people of color' or subgroups thereof as a unified force draw on this powerful yearning for home. In a postmodern world, however, it is clear that no such unity exists. Angela P. Harris, 'Foreword: The Jurisprudence of Reconstruction', p. 783. Paul Gilroy also writes: 'people who have been subordinated by race-thinking and its distinctive social structures (not all of which come tidily color-coded) have for centuries employed the concepts and categories of their rulers, owners, and persecutors to resist the destiny "race" has allocated to them and to dissent from the lowly value it places upon their lives. Under the most difficult of conditions and from imperfect materials that they surely would not have selected if they had been able to choose, these oppressed groups have built complex traditions of politics, ethics, identity, and culture. They have involved elaborate, improvised constructions that have the primary function of absorbing and deflecting abuse. But they have gone far beyond merely affording protection and reversed the polarities of insult, brutality, and contempt, which are unexpectedly turned into important sources of solidarity, joy, and collective strength. When ideas or racial particularity are inverted in this defensive manner so that they provide sources of pride rather than shame and humiliation, they become difficult to relinquish. For many racialized populations, "race" and the hard-won, oppositional identities it supports are not to be lightly or prematurely given up. These groups will have to be persuaded very carefully that there is something worthwhile to be gained from a deliberate renunciation of "race" as the basis for belonging to one another and acting in concert.' Read my analysis as an initial attempt at persuasion. Paul Gilroy, *Against Race: Imagining Political Culture Beyond the Color Line*, Cambridge, MA: Harvard University Press, 2000, p. 12. For an indication that this sentiment may be ripening see Monica A. Coleman, 'Must I Be Womanist?', *Journal of Feminist Studies in Religion* 221.1 (2006), pp. 85–134.

come from different racial origins and countries and the racial/ethnic paradigm is not an easy fit. For this reason, Latino(as) have been more focused on issues of class when formulating an agenda for reform. In *San Antonio Independent School District v. Rodriguez* the Mexican American Legal Defense Fund (MALDEF) argued since education was a fundamental right schools could not offer markedly different levels of education based on the wealth of districts. In essence, MALDEF argued that class differences deserve scrutiny from the courts just as much as racial ones; it sought class-based affirmative action. While ultimately defeated, the legal system's increasing unwillingness to deal with issues of racial desegregation means that the *Brown* paradigm is becoming anachronistic for blacks as well, making this alternative approach a tantalizing avenue for change.[104]

Brown's decline also means that differences in the reform agendas of blacks and Latino(as) may be shrinking. Alliances that existed in the past, yet were rendered invisible by the black/white binary, can resurface. The paradigmatic story of civil rights is the story of an exclusively black struggle and white concession to that struggle. The Latino(a) contribution to civil rights is thus excised from the historical record. In *Mendez v. Westminster School District of Orange County*, for example, Gonzalo Mendez and other Mexican-American parents successfully challenged the segregation of Mexican-American children in Orange County, California. This is a defining, monumental moment in the history of civil rights in the United States. In his decision, Judge McCormick rejected the entire basis for *Plessy v. Ferguson* and anticipates the logic behind the *Brown* decision.[105] Thurgood Marshall, Robert

---

104 I draw from Rachel F. Moran, 'Foreword – Demography and Distrust: The Latino Challenge to Civil Rights and Immigration Policy in the 1990s and Beyond', *La Raza Law Journal* 8.1 (1995), pp. 10–11. LatCrit theory is an immense body of literature. For starters, see Richard Delgado and Jean Stefancic (eds), *The Latino Condition: A Critical Reader*, New York: NYU Press, 1998. Scholars in LatCrit often draw from Stuart Hall's work on race, ethnicity, and identity. In particular, see Stuart Hall, 'New Ethnicities', in David Morley and Kuan-Hsing Chen (eds), *Stuart Hall: Critical Dialogues in Cultural Studies*, New York: Routledge, 1996, pp. 441–9.

105 The judge wrote: '"The equal protection of the laws" pertaining to the public school system in California is not provided by furnishing in separate schools the same technical facilities, text books and courses of instruction to children of Mexican ancestry that are available to other public school children regardless of their ancestry. *A paramount requisite in the American system of public education is social equality. It must be open to all children by unified school association regardless of lineage.*' Cited in Juan F. Perea, 'The Black/White Binary Paradigm of Race: The "Normal Science" of American Racial Thought', *La Raza Law Journal* 10 (Spring 1998), p. 158. Italics added by Perea. The revolutionary implications of this decision were highlighted by *The Yale Law Journal*: 'a recent district Court decision [*Mendez*] . . . has questioned the basic assumption of the *Plessy* case and may portent a complete reversal of the doctrine . . . A

L. Carter, Assistant Special Counsel of the NAACP and Loren Miller worked with the litigants *Mendez* and Carter used this case as a basis for his oral argument in *Brown*. The NAACP's involvement in the case is an example of an early coalition between blacks and Latino(as) in the struggle for equal rights. There are many more, but you would be hard pressed to find them in textbooks relating the history of the Civil Rights Movement.[106]

Recovering the history of common struggles is the basis for envisioning a future where struggles for emancipation not only bring identities together, but forge new ones as well.[107] Racial identities, which are imposed by a racialized society, need to be transformed into political identities that are then turned against the racial status quo. I amend what Albert Cleage once wrote: 'Being Black [or Latino(a)] is a condition, not a program, and we can't make a program out of being Black [or Latino(a)].'[108] That is, we must see identity positions as political acts rather than as an essential position, in which case the progressive nature of a struggle does not depend on its place of origin, it depends on its links with other struggles. The colour line itself is created by human subjects and is a sight of conflict and contestation. What can unite different groups in struggle is not biology but a common oppositional relation to racist, sexist, and classist structures which are inhabited, and suffered, in various ways.[109] The task,

---

dual school system, even if "equal facilities" were ever in fact provided, does imply social inferiority.' Cited by Perea on pp. 159–60. My discussion of *Mendez* is taken from this article; see the entire piece for many more examples.

106 See Perea 'Black/White Binary Paradigm'.

107 For a notable attempt to write history by drawing forgotten links between struggles for emancipation see Vijay Prashad, *Everybody Was Kung Fu Fighting: Afro-Asian Connections and the Myth of Cultural Purity*, Boston: Beacon Press, 2001 and Vijay Prashad, *The Karma of Brown Folk*, Minneapolis: University of Minnesota Press, 2000.

108 Albert Cleage, *Black Christian Nationalism: New Directions for the Black Church*, New York: William Morrow, 1972, p. 197.

109 For three expressions of this sentiment see Darder and Torres, *After Race*, Paul Gilroy, 'The End of Antiracism', in James Donald and Ali Rattansi (eds), *'Race', Culture and Difference*, London: Sage, 1992, pp. 49–61, Chandra Talpade Mohanty, 'Cartographies of Struggle', in Chandra Talpade Mohanty, Anna Russo, and Lourdes Torres (eds), *Third World Women and the Politics of Feminism*, Indiana: Indiana University Press, 1991, pp. 3–5; Ernesto Laclau and Chantal Mouffe, *Hegemony and Socialist Strategy: Towards a Radical Democratic Politics*, New York: Verso, 1985. Angela Harris puts it well: 'There are no "people of color" waiting to be found, we must give up our romance of racial community. Abandoning romance, however, does not mean ending commitment. If any lesson of the politics of difference can yet be identified, it is that solidarity is the product of struggle, not wishful thinking; and struggle means not only political struggle, but moral and ethical struggle as well.' Angela P. Harris, 'Foreword: The Jurisprudence of Reconstruction', p. 784. I see Gutiérrez making the same point as he voices frustration:

therefore, is to redraw the colour line and reconstitute identity around politics.

I like the way Robert Chang frames the issue around Spike Lee's *Do the Right Thing*: at the end of the movie, after Sal's pizzeria is set on fire, the crowd of blacks and Latinos turn toward the Korean grocery store across the street: 'One member of the crowd, ML, tells the Korean immigrant grocer that he's next. The grocer responds, "I Black." ML explodes, telling him to open his eyes, saying "*I'm* Black." The grocer repeats, "I Black. You, me, same. We same." The crowd is incredulous and laughs.' The reason why the Korean's statement fails to resonate with the crowd in the movie and movie goers themselves stems from the lack of a chain of equivalences between the experiences of Korean immigrants and African Americans; that is, understanding is impeded by the way the colour line has been drawn. Fortunately for the grocer, violence is avoided by Coconut Sid, who tells his friend, 'the Korean is all right, he's all right.' For Chang, 'we need more moments such as this.'[110] More moments of unity, a common front. This is not the way black theology has understood race and it is not the way Hispanic/Latino(a) theology has understood *mestizaje*. But it is a way pregnant with untapped possibility. And in conjunction with the other signposts here presented the way that Vita, one day, might be better resisted.

'You are Black, you have your point of view; you are Hispanic, you have your point of view; you are a woman, you have your point of view; you are White, nice White people, you have your point of view. But enough is enough! With this tool, it is impossible to struggle for liberation.' Gustavo Gutiérrez, 'The Historical Project of the Poor', in Cornel West, Caridad Guidote, and Margaret Coakley (eds), *Theology in the Americas: Detroit II Conference Papers*, Maryknoll, NY: Orbis Books, 1982, p. 83.

110 I'm drawing liberally from Robert S. Chang, 'The End of Innocence or Politics After the Fall of the Essential Subject', *American University Law Review* 45 (1996), pp. 687–94.

Coda

Perhaps the future of liberation theology lies beyond theology. At the heart of liberation theology lie two elements: the first is epistemological, the liberationist attempt to do theology from the standpoint of the oppressed. The second is practical/moral, liberation theology's commitment to thinking about ideals by thinking about institutions. Indeed, Latin American liberation theology's attempt to think Christianity in relation to socialism is best understood as a response to a vexing problem in social and political thought – the gap between our ideals and the institutions that are meant to realize them. The epistemological has priority over the practical/moral: before changing the world you need to be converted to the need for such change.

Economics, law, medical anthropology, political science, sociology and a host of other disciplines could engage in the same epistemological shift and be fuelled with the same practical/moral drive with revolutionary consequences for each field. No discipline possesses a neutral framework of analysis, and these usually encounter the world with a set of preconceptions that are biased, much like modern religious thought, toward the wealthy. They too ignore the reality of Vita. Yet these, rather than theology, are the disciplines that set the intellectual frameworks through which the world is most influentially analysed. The above elements thus need urgent elucidation in disciplines with a wider impact than theology or religious studies.

Here the liberation theologian must operate undercover as an economist or legal theorist and work from within to transform the discipline's presuppositions.[1] As far as I know there is no liberation

---

1 Gayraud Wilmore has called for 'the development of think-tanks, policy institutes, and publication outlets. In other words, black theology needs to establish a strategic presence at the places where political and economic decisions are made and – perhaps even more important – to indicate to blacks, whites, and other ethnic minorities, the points at which theological and spiritual questions intersect with public issues.' My argument takes his logic of interaction between theology and disciplinary power a step further. Gayraud S. Wilmore, 'Black Theology at the Turn of the Century: Some Unmet Needs and Challenges', in Dwight H. Hopkins (ed.), *Black Faith and Public Talk: Critical*

theologian involved in this task (perhaps s/he is too well disguised, too far undercover, perhaps our education is too faulty) so my example comes from the work of Paul Farmer, who rethinks medical anthropology from the perspective of liberation theology. Farmer, a medical anthropologist at Harvard Medical School, is founder of Partners in Health, an organization that provides health care to poor communities around the world. His intellectual production, grounded in the reality of caring for tuberculosis victims in Russian prisons and AIDS victims in Haiti, focuses on health and human rights.

Farmer notes that 'diseases themselves make a preferential option for the poor'.[2] Yet the focus of medical research operates oblivious to the needs of the communities that are most threatened by disease. For example, for the well off, the minority of humankind, tuberculosis is barely a threat, with a cure rate of 95%. From the perspective of the majority of humankind, however, 'tuberculosis deaths *now* – which each year number in the millions – occur almost exclusively among the poor, whether they reside in the inner cities of the United States or in the poor countries of the Southern hemisphere'.[3] The organizational paradigm upon which the medical profession is based renders this fact invisible. Medicine, Farmer shows, is based upon a health transition model according to which, as societies develop, 'death will no longer be caused by infections such as tuberculosis but will occur much later and be caused by heart disease and cancer'.[4] A different standpoint reveals that:

> For the poor, wherever, they live, there is, often enough, no health transition. In other words, wealthy citizens of 'underdeveloped' nations (those countries that have not yet experienced their health transition) do not die young from infectious diseases; they die later and from the same diseases that claim similar populations in wealthy countries. In parts of Harlem, in contrast, death rates of certain age groups are as high as those in Bangladesh; in both places, the leading causes of death in young adults are infections and violence.[5]

This model makes the present sufferings of the poor unimportant

Essays on James H. Cone's Black Theology and Black Power, Maryknoll, NY: Orbis Books, 1999, p. 238.

2 Paul Farmer, *Pathologies of Power: Health, Human Rights, and the New War on the Poor*, Berkeley: University of California Press, 2003, p. 140.

3 Farmer, *Pathologies of Power*, p. 147.

4 Farmer, *Pathologies of Power*, p. 156.

5 Farmer, *Pathologies of Power*, pp. 156–7.

– they are in fact sacrificed for the development of remedies for diseases that afflict the wealthy.

Medical ethics, from the standpoint of the poor majority of humankind, fares no better. Farmer notes:

> What is defined, these days, as an ethical issue? End-of-life decisions, medicolegal questions of brain death and organ transplantation, and medical disclosure issues dominate the published literature. In the hospital, the quandary ethics of the individual constitute most of the discussion of medial ethics. The question 'When is life worth preserving?' is asked largely of lives one click of the switch away from extinction, lives wholly at the mercy of the technology that works to preserve some. The countless people whose life course is shortened by unequal access to health care are not topics of discussion.[6]

This is an ethics for the few and the wealthy. Farmer's work as a doctor and medical anthropologist parallels the work of a liberation theologian within theology. Both struggle to reshape their disciplines around the concerns and issues that affect the majority of humankind.

Perhaps the task is that of disentangling the 'liberation' from the 'theology' in liberation theology. To work in liberation theology today could mean to work outside of it, by finding ways the epistemological and practical-moral elements can infiltrate, subvert, and transform other bodies of knowledge. Here the liberation theologian need not carry the label of 'theologian' and works best under a different disciplinary guise. Could the future of liberation call for the dissolution of liberation theology as an identifiable field of production?

---

6 Farmer, *Pathologies of Power*, p. 174.

Afterword

The work that adorns the cover of this book, Karina and Marcelo Chechik's *The Promised Land*, depicts a lonely figure plodding across a bridge from South America to the United States. Perhaps because the piece was composed scarcely a few months after the greatest economic meltdown in modern history – Argentina's economic debacle at the end of 2001 – neither the journey nor the destination seem joyous. The colours are bleak and the World Trade Center looming in the distance speaks of tragic history recently gone. To me the bridge seems like a apocalyptic scene, suspended precariously over empty space while the angle itself gives the impression of a heavy wind rocking its suspension back and forth. Writing this book, at times I felt like the figure on the bridge. As an almost white or only slightly brown (my great uncle's nickname for me was Arafat) Argentine national living in the United States who nonetheless feels himself fully Argentine, I share in none of the advantages – funding, specially marked awards, guaranteed readership, acknowledgment and citations – of those who have a liberationist cultural or racial home. Critiques of the guild from within the guild have gone largely ignored – think of Victor Anderson – so it rests to see how this work is received, or whether it is acknowledged at all.

As I write this book's final sentences, however, a recently arrived copy of the American Academy of Religion's *Religious Studies News* gives me hope that my attempt to think liberation theology across the Americas will not remain a lonely venture for long. Inside, in a piece titled 'Theological Education in the New Global Reality', Dwight Hopkins outlines what he calls a 'global theological strategy' for this century.[1] If you read it, it will strike you that the elements Hopkins calls for are already developed in my argument throughout this book. He states that 'to do theology as if the United States is the only or most dominant social location of theological education is an incomplete strategy' and that the Third World must be added to the publics

---

[1] See Dwight N. Hopkins, 'Theological Education in the New Global Reality', *Religious Studies News* 22.2 (Mar. 2007), p. xii. All the citations are from this page.

to which US theology must be accountable. He stresses the need for an interdisciplinary methodology and exclaims that 'one needs a host of nontheological disciplines to help unravel how religion operates in a complex, particular, and messy environment. Political economy as well as psychology can aid the theological field'. Finally, he stresses that 'when the First World United States develops ongoing ties with the majority of the world, one might discover that the global issue for theological education is not terrorism but poverty. This in turn might even help refocus our eyes domestically on the pressing issue of poverty with the 50 states of the U.S. itself.' Enacting this strategy, however, requires recognizing both the global and national socio-economic contexts, as well as the theological context, within which liberation theologians work, and following the signposts outlined here. It essentially requires deep-seated changes of which liberation theologians have yet to even become aware. Little, if any, liberationist work fulfils the requirements he desires. I hope more do in the future.

Select Bibliography

Agamben, Giorgio, *Homo Sacer: Sovereign Power and Bare Life*, Stanford, CA: Stanford University Press, 1998.
—— *Remnants of Auschwitz: The Witness and the Archive*, New York: Zone Books, 2002.
Aguilar, Mario, *The History and Politics of Latin American Theology, Volume I*, London: SCM Press, 2007.
—— *The History and Politics of Latin American Theology, Volume II*, London: SCM Press, 2008.
Althaus-Reid, Marcella, 'From Liberation Theology to Indecent Theology: The Trouble with Normality in Theology', in Ivan Petrella (ed.), *Latin American Liberation Theology: The Next Generation*, Maryknoll, NY: Orbis Books, 2005, pp. 20–38.
—— *Indecent Theology: Theological Perversions in Sex, Gender and Politics*, New York: Routledge, 2000.
—— *The Queer God*, New York: Routledge, 2003.
Amsden, Alice, *The Rise of the 'Rest': Challenges to the West from Late-Industrializing Economies*, Oxford: Oxford University Press, 2001.
Anderson, Victor, *Beyond Ontological Blackness: An Essay on African American Religious and Cultural Criticism*, New York: Continuum, 1995.
—— 'Critical Reflection on the Problems of History and Narrative in a Recent African-American Research Program', in Eleazar Fernandez and Fernando Segovia (eds), *A Dream Unfinished: Theological Reflections on America from the Margins*, Maryknoll, NY: Orbis Books, 2001, pp. 37–51.
—— '"We See Through a Glass Darkly": Black Narrative Theology and the Opacity of African American Religious Thought', in Anthony B. Pinn and Benjamín Valentín (eds), *The Ties That Bind: African American and Hispanic American/Latino/a Theologies in Dialogue*, New York: Continuum, 2001, pp. 78–93.
Apel, Karl-Otto, *Selected Essays: Ethics and the Theory of Rationality*, New Jersey: Humanities Press, 1996.
—— *Selected Essays: Towards a Transcendental Semiotics*, New Jersey: Humanities Press, 1994.
—— *Towards a Transformation of Philosophy*, trans. Glyn Adey and David Frisby, The International Library of Phenomenology and Moral Sciences, London: Routledge & Kegan Paul, 1980.
—— *Understanding and Explanation: A Transcendental-Pragmatic Perspective*, trans. Georgia Warnke, Studies in Contemporary German Social

Thought, Cambridge, MA: MIT Press, 1984.

Aponte, Edwin David and Miguel A. De La Torre (eds), *Handbook of Latina/o Theologies*, St Louis: Chalice Press, 2006.

Aquino, Maria Pilar, 'The Collective "Dis-Covery" of Our Own Power: Latin American Feminist Theology', in Ada Maria Isasi-Diaz and Fernando F. Segovia (eds), *Hispanic/Latino Theology: Challenge and Promise*, Minneapolis: Fortress Press, 1996, pp. 240–60.

—— 'Directions and Foundations of Hispanic/Latino Theology: Toward a Mestiza Theology of Liberation', *Journal of Hispanic/Latino Theology* 1, no. 1 (1993): 5–21.

—— 'Latin American Feminist Theology', *Journal of Feminist Studies in Religion* 14, no. 1 (Spring 1998): 87–107.

—— 'Latina Feminist Theology: Central Features', in Maria Pilar Aquino, Daisy Machado, and Jeanette Rodriguez (eds), *A Reader in Latina Feminist Theology: Religion and Justice*, Austin, TX: University of Texas Press, 2002, pp. 133–60.

—— *Nuestro Clamor por la Vida: Teología Latinoamericana Desde la Mujer*, San José, Costa Rica: Departamento Ecuménico de Investigaciones (DEI), 1992.

—— *Our Cry for Life: Feminist Theology from Latin America*, Maryknoll, NY: Orbis Books, 1993.

—— *La Teología, la Iglesia y la Mujer en America Latina*, Chapinero, Santa fe de Bogota, Colombia: Indo-American Press Service, 1994.

—— 'Theological Method in U.S. Latino/a Theology: Toward an Intercultural Theology for the Third Millennium', in Orlando O. Espin and Miguel H. Diaz (eds), *From the Heart of Our People*, Maryknoll, NY: Orbis Books, 1999, pp. 6–48.

Aquino, Maria Pilar, Daisy Machado and Jeanette Rodriquez, *A Reader in Latina Feminist Theology: Religion and Justice*, Austin, TX: University of Texas Press, 2002.

Aquino, Maria Pilar and Roberto Goizueta (eds), *Theology: Expanding the Borders*, Mystic, CT: Twenty-Third Century Publications, 1998.

Aquino, Maria Pilar and Mieth Dietmar (eds), *The Return of the Just War*, London: SCM Press, 2001.

Assmann, Hugo, *Economía y Religión*, San José, Costa Rica: DEI, 1994.

—— *La Idolatría del Mercado*, San José, Costa Rica: DEI, 1997.

—— *Teología Desde la Praxis de la Liberación*, Salamanca: Ediciones Sígueme, 1973.

—— *Theology for a Nomad Church*, trans. Paul Burns, Maryknoll, NY: Orbis Books, 1975.

Aurelius, Marcus, *Meditations*, New York: Walter J. Black, 1945.

Bairoch, Paul, *Economics and World History: Myths and Paradoxes*, Chicago, IL: University of Chicago Press, 1993.

Baker-Fletcher, Karen, 'Soprano Obligato: The Voices of Black Women and American Conflict in the Thought of Anna Julia Cooper', in Emilie M. Townes (ed.), *A Troubling in My Soul: Womanist Perspectives on Evil and Suffering*, Maryknoll, NY: Orbis Books, 2002, pp. 172–85.

Balasuriya, Tissa, *Planetary Theology*, Maryknoll, NY: Orbis Books, 1984.

Bales, Kevin, *Disposable People: New Slavery in the Global Economy*, Berkeley: University of California Press, 1999.

Barth, Karl, *Church Dogmatics, Volume III, Part 2; The Doctrine of Creation*, Edinburgh: T. & T. Clark, 1986.

—— *The Epistle to the Romans*, trans. Edwyn C. Hoskyns, Oxford: Oxford University Press, 1968.

Bataille, Georges, *The Accursed Share, Vol. 1*, New York: Zone Books, 1991.

Bauman, Zygmunt, *Wasted Lives: Modernity and Its Outcasts*, Cambridge: Polity Press, 2004.

Bell Jr, Daniel M., *Liberation Theology After the End of History: The Refusal to Cease Suffering*, London: Routledge, 2001.

Bellamy Foster, John, 'Aspects of Class in the United States: An Introduction', *Monthly Review* 58, no. 3 (July–August 2006): http://www.monthlyreview.org/0706jbf.htm.

Bernstein, Richard, *The New Constellation: The Ethical-Political Horizons of Modernity/Postmodernity*, Cambridge, MA: MIT Press, 1992.

Bethel, James, 'Sometimes the Word is "Weed"', *Forest Management*, no. 1984 (June 1984), pp. 17–22.

Bezruchka, Stephen and Mary Anne Mercer, 'The Lethal Divide: How Economic Inequality Affects Health', in Meredith Fort, Mary Anne Mercer, and Oscar Gish (eds), *Sickness and Wealth: The Corporate Assault on Global Health*, Cambridge, MA: South End Press, 2004, pp. 11–18.

Biehl, João, 'Vita: Life in a Zone of Social Abandonment', *Social Text* 19, no. 3 (Fall 2001), pp. 131–48.

—— *Vita: Life in a Zone of Social Abandonment*, Berkeley: University of California Press, 2005.

'Black Theology and Latin American Liberation Theology: Excerpts from a Symposium of the World Council of Churches', in James Cone and Gayraud Wilmore (eds), *Black Theology: A Documentary History, Volume I 1966–1979*, Maryknoll, NY: Orbis Books, 1993, pp. 404–8.

Block, Fred, *Postindustrial Possibilities: A Critique of Economic Discourse*, Berkeley: University of California Press, 1990.

Boff, Clodovis and Leonardo Boff, *Salvation and Liberation: In Search of a Balance Between Faith and Politics*, Maryknoll, NY: Orbis Books, 1984.

Boff, Leonardo, *Ecology and Liberation: A New Paradigm*, New York: Orbis Books, 1995.

Bonhoeffer, Dietrich, *Letter and Papers from Prison*, ed. Eberhard Bethge, New York: Macmillan, 1972.

Bonino, José Míguez, *Doing Theology in a Revolutionary Situation*, ed. William H. Lazareth, Confrontation Books, Philadelphia: Fortress Press, 1975.

Bourgeois, Jacques H. J., *Trade Law Experienced: Pottering About in the GATT and WTO*, London: Cameron May, 2005.

Bowen, William G., Martin A. Kurzweil, Eugene M. Tobin and Susanne C. Pichler, *Equity and Excellence in American Higher Education*, Charlottesville, VA: University of Virginia Press, 2005.

Burrows, Beth, 'Patents, Ethics and Spin', in Brian Tokar (ed.), *Redesigning Life? The Worldwide Challenge to Genetic Engineering*, New York, NY: Zed Books, 2001, pp. 238–51.

Byrd, W. Michael and Linda A. Clayton, *An American Health Dilemma: Race, Medicine, and Health Care in the United States, 1990–2000*, New York: Routledge, 2002.

Cannon, Katie Geneva, *Katie's Canon: Womanism and the Soul of the Black Community*, New York: Continuum, 1995.

Carrithers, Michael, *The Buddha: A Very Short Introduction*, Oxford: Oxford University Press, 2001.

Carter, Kameron J., 'Contemporary Black Theology: A Review Essay', *Modern Theology* 19, no. 1 (January 2003), pp. 117–38.

Carwardine, Richard, *Lincoln: A Life of Purpose and Power*, New York: Knopf, 2006.

Cervantes Saavedra, Miguel de, *El Ingenioso Hidalgo Don Quijote de la Mancha*, Madrid: Aguilar S.A., 1993.

Chakrabarty, A. M., 'Patenting of Life-Forms: From a Concept to Reality', in David Magnus, Arthur Caplan, and Glenn McGee (eds), *Who Owns Life?*, Amherst, NY: Prometheus Books, 2002, pp. 17–24.

Chang, Ha-Joon, *Kicking Away the Ladder: Development Strategy in Historical Perspective*, London: Anthem Press, 2002.

——'Kicking Away the Ladder: "Good Policies" and "Good Institutions" in Historical Perspective', in Kevin P. Gallagher (ed.), *Putting Development First: The Importance of Policy Space in the WTO and International Financial Institutions*, New York, NY: Zed Books, 2005, pp. 102–25.

Chang, Ha-Joon and Duncan Green, *The Northern WTO Agenda on Investment: Do As We Say, Not As We Did*, Geneva: South Center and CAFOD, 2003.

Chang, Robert S., 'The End of Innocence or Politics After the Fall of the Essential Subject', *American University Law Review* 45 (1996), pp. 687–94.

Cleage, Albert, *Black Christian Nationalism: New Directions for the Black Church*, New York: William Morrow, 1972.

Coetzee, J. M., 'The Poet in the Tower', *The New York Review of Books* LIII, no. 16 (19 October 2006), pp. 69–76.

Coleman, Monica A., 'Must I Be Womanist?', *Journal of Feminist Studies in Religion* 221, no. 1 (2006), pp. 85–134.

Coleman, Will, 'Introduction', in Dwight N. Hopkins and George C. L. Cummings (eds), *Cut Loose Your Stammering Tongue: Black Theology in the Slave Narratives*, Louisville: Westminster John Knox Press, 2003, pp. ix–xvi.

Comblin, José, 'La Iglesia Latinoamericana Desde Puebla a Santo Domingo', in José Comblin, José I. Gonzalez Faus, and Jon Sobrino (eds), *Cambio Social y Pensamiento Cristiano en America Latina*, Madrid: Editorial Trotta, 1993, pp. 29–56.

Cone, Cecil, *The Identity Crisis in Black Theology*, Nashville: AMEC, 1975.

Cone, James H., *A Black Theology of Liberation*, C. Eric Lincoln Series in Black Religion, Philadelphia: J. B. Lippincott Company, 1970.

——'International Versus National Oppression', in Cornel West, Caridad Guidote, and Margaret Coakly (eds), *Theology in the Americas: Detroit II, Conference Papers*, Maryknoll, NY: Orbis Books, 1982, pp. 39–43.

——*Black Theology and Black Power*, Maryknoll, NY: Orbis Books, 1997.

—— 'Black Theology and the Black Church', in James Cone and Gayraud Wilmore (eds), *Black Theology: A Documentary History, Volume I 1966–1979*, Maryknoll, NY: Orbis Books, 2003, pp. 266–75.

—— 'Calling the Oppressors to Account: God and Black Suffering', in Linda E. Thomas (ed.), *Living Stones in the Household of God: The Legacy and Future of Black Theology*, Minneapolis: Fortress Press, 2004, pp. 3–12.

—— *For My People: Black Theology and the Black Church*, Maryknoll, NY: Orbis Books, 1984.

—— *Speaking the Truth: Ecumenism, Liberation, and Black Theology*, Michigan, Gran Rapids: William B. Eerdmans, 1986.

—— 'Theologies of Liberation Among U.S. Racial-Ethnic Minorities', *Convergences and Differences* 5, no. 199 (1988), pp. 54–64.

—— 'The Vocation of a Theologian', in Linda E. Thomas (ed.), *Living Stones in the Household of God: The Legacy and Future of Black Theology*, Minneapolis: Fortress Press, 2004, pp. 203–12.

Conley, Dalton, *Being Black, Living in the Red: Race, Wealth, and Social Policy in America*, Berkeley: University of California Press, 1999.

—— *Honky*, New York: Vintage, 2001.

Cooper, Thia, *Controversies in Political Theology: Development or Liberation*, London: SCM Press, 2007.

Cox, Harvey, *The Silencing of Leonardo Boff: The Vatican and the Future of World Christianity*, Oak Park, IL: Meyer-Stone Books, 1988.

Crenshaw, Kimberle, Neil Gotanda, Gary Peller and Kendall Thomas (eds), *Critical Race Theory: The Key Writings That Formed the Movement*, New York: The New Press, 1995.

Crouch, Martha L., 'From Golden Rice to Terminator Technology: Agricultural Biotechnology Will Not Feed the World or Save the Environment', in Brian Tokar (ed.), *Redesigning Life? The Worldwide Challenge to Genetic Engineering*, New York, NY: Zed Books, 2001, pp. 22–39.

Cummings, George, 'Slave Narratives, Black Theology of Liberation (USA), and the Future', in Dwight Hopkins and George Cummings (eds), *Cut Loose Your Stammering Tongue: Black Theology in the Slave Narratives*, Maryknoll, NY: Orbis Books, 1991, pp. 137–48.

Darder, Antonia, and Rodolfo D. Torres, *After Race: Racism After Multiculturalism*, New York: New York University Press, 2004.

Davis, Paul and Meredith Fort, 'The Battle Against Global Aids', in Meredith Fort, Mary Anne Mercer and Oscar Gish (eds), *Sickness and Wealth: The Corporate Assault on Global Health*, Sickness and Wealth, Cambridge, MA: South End Press, 2004, pp. 145–58.

De La Torre, Miguel A. and Edwin David Aponte, *Introducing Latino/a Theologies*, Maryknoll, NY: Orbis Books, 2001.

De Reuck, Anthony and Julie Knight (eds), *Caste and Race: Comparative Approaches*, Boston: Little, Brown, 1967.

Delbanco, Andrew, 'Scandals of Higher Education', *The New York Review of Books* LIV, Number 5 (29 March 2007), pp. 42–46.

Delgado, Richard (ed.), *Critical Race Theory: The Cutting Edge*, Philadelphia: Temple University Press, 1995.

Delgado, Richard and Jean Stefancic (eds), *The Latino Condition: A Critical Reader*, New York: NYU Press, 1998.

Doane, Ashley and Eduardo Bonilla-Silva (eds), *White Out: The Continuing Significance of Racism*, New York: Routledge, 2003.

Duberman, Lucile, *Social Inequality: Class and Caste in America*, Philadelphia: J. B. Lippincott, 1976.

Duque, José and German Gutiérrez, *Itinerarios de la Razón Critica: Homenaje a Franz Hinkelammert en Sus 70 Años*, San José: DEI, 2001.

Dussel, Enrique, *Etica de la Liberación en la Edad de la Globalización y de la Exclusión*, Madrid: Editorial Trotta, 1998.

—— *Historia de la Filosofía y la Filosofía de la Liberación*, Bogota, Colombia: Editorial Nueva America, 1994.

—— *El Humanismo Semita*, Buenos Aires: Eudeba, 1969.

—— *The Invention of the Americas: Eclipse of the 'Other' and the Myth of Modernity*, New York: Continuum, 1995.

—— *Teología de la Liberación: Un Panorama de su Desarrollo*, Ciudad de Mexico: Potrerillos Editores, 1995.

—— *The Underside of Modernity: Apel, Ricoeur, Rorty, Taylor and the Philosophy of Liberation*, ed. and trans. Eduard Mendieta. New York: Humanity Books, 1998.

Ehrenreich, Barbara. *Bait and Switch: The (Futile) Pursuit of the American Dream*, New York: Metropolitan Books, 2005.

—— *Nickel and Dimed: On (Not) Getting By in America*, New York: Owl Books, 2002.

Elizondo, Virgilio, *Galilean Journey: The Mexican-American Promise*, Maryknoll, NY: Orbis Books, 2003.

Ellacuria, Ignacio and Jon Sobrino (eds), *Mysterium Liberationis: Fundamental Concepts of Liberation Theology*, Maryknoll, NY: Orbis Books, 1993.

Ellwood, Wayne, *The No-Nonsense Guide to Globalization*, New York, NY: Verso, 2003.

Escobar, Arturo, *Encountering Development: The Making and Unmaking of the Third World*, Princeton, NJ: Princeton University Press, 1995.

Espin, Orlando O. and Miguel H. Diaz (eds), *From the Heart of Our People*, Maryknoll, NY: Orbis Books, 1999.

Espinoza, Leslie and Angela P. Harris, 'Afterword: Embracing the Tar-Baby – LatCrit Theory and the Sticky Mess of Race', *California Law Review* 85 (October 1997), pp. 1585–645.

Fanon, Frantz, *The Wretched of the Earth*, with a preface by Jean-Paul Sartre, translated by Constance Farrington, New York: Grove Press, 1963.

Farmer, Paul, *Pathologies of Power: Health, Human Rights, and the New War on the Poor*, Berkeley: University of California Press, 2003.

Flusty, Steven, *De-Coca-Colonization: Making the Globe from the Inside Out*, New York: Routledge, 2004.

Ford, David F., and Rachel Muers (eds), *The Modern Theologians: An Introduction to Christian Theology Since 1918*, Malden, MA: Blackwell Publishing, 2005.

Ford, John, 'Hispanic/Latino Theology – En Marcha!', *Religious Studies Review* 29, no. 1 (2003), pp. 35–42.

Fort, Meredith, Mary Anne Mercer and Oscar Gish (eds), *Sickness and Wealth: The Corporate Assault on Global Health*, Cambridge, MA: South End Press, 2004.

Foucault, Michel, *Discipline and Punishment: The Birth of the Prison*, trans. Alan Sheridan, New York: Random House, Vintage, 1979.

Frank, Andre Gunder, *Capitalism and Underdevelopment in Latin America: Historical Studies of Chile and Brazil*, New York: Monthly Review Press, 1967.

Freire, Paulo, 'Foreword to the 1986 Edition', in James Cone, *A Black Theology of Liberation: Twentieth Anniversary Edition*, Maryknoll, NY: Orbis Books, 1986, pp. vii–ix.

—— 'Tercer Mundo y Teología', *Perspectivas de Dialogo* 5 (1970), pp. 304–5.

Fukuyama, Francis, *The End of History and the Last Man*, New York: Free Press, 1992.

—— 'The End of History', *The National Interest*, no. Summer (1989), pp. 3–18.

Galbraith, John Kenneth, *The Affluent Society*, Boston: Houghton Mifflin, 1984.

Gallagher, Kevin P. (ed.), *Putting Development First: The Importance of Policy Space in the WTO and International Financial Institutions*, New York, NY: Zed Books, 2005.

—— 'Globalization and the Nation-State: Reasserting Policy Autonomy for Development', in Kevin P. Gallagher (ed.), *Putting Development First: The Importance of Policy Space in the WTO and International Financial Institutions*, New York, NY: Zed Books, 2005, pp. 1–14.

George, Susan and Fabrizio Sabelli, *Faith and Credit: The World Bank's Secular Empire*, Boulder, CO: Westview Press, 1994.

Gerth, H. H. and C. Wright Mills (eds & trans.), *From Max Weber: Essays in Sociology*, New York: Oxford University Press, 1958.

Gibson-Graham, J. K., *The End of Capitalism (as we Knew It): A Feminist Critique of Political Economy*, Cambridge: Blackwell Publishers, 1996.

Gilroy, Paul, *Against Race: Imagining Political Culture Beyond the Color Line*, Cambridge, MA: Harvard University Press, 2000.

—— 'The End of Antiracism', in James Donald and Ali Rattansi (eds), *'Race,' Culture and Difference*, London: Sage Publications, 1992, pp. 49–61.

Glasmeier, Amy K., *An Atlas of Poverty in America: One Nation, Pulling Apart, 1960–2003*, New York: Routledge, 2006.

Goizueta, Roberto, *Caminemos con Jesus: Toward a Hispanic/Latino Theology of Accompaniment*, Maryknoll, NY: Orbis Books, 1995.

Gonzalez, Justo L., 'Latino/a Theology', in Miguel A. De La Torre (ed.), *Handbook of U.S. Theologies of Liberation*, St Louis: Chalice Press, 2004, pp. 204–17.

—— *Mañana: Christian Theology from a Hispanic Perspective*, Nashville: Abingdon Press, 1990.

Gonzalez, Michelle A., *Afro-Cuban Theology: Religion, Race, Culture, and Identity*, Gainesville: University Press of Florida, 2006.

—— 'Latino/a Theology: Doing Theology Latinamente', *Dialog: A Journal of Theology* 41, no. 1 (Spring 2002), pp. 63–72.

Goodwin, Doris Kearns, *Team of Rivals: The Political Genius of Abraham Lincoln*, New York: Simon & Schuster, 2006.

Gotanda, Neil, 'A Critique of "Our Constitution is Colorblind"', in Kimberle Crenshaw, Neil Gotanda, Gary Peller, and Kendall Thomas (eds), *Critical Race Theory: The Key Writings That Formed the Movement*, New York: The New Press, 1995, pp. 257–75.

Grant, Jacquelyn, *White Women's Christ and Black Women's Jesus: Feminist Christology and Womanist Response*, Atlanta, GA: Scholars Press, 1989.

Greenfeld, Liah, *The Spirit of Capitalism: Nationalism and Economic Growth*, Cambridge, MA: Harvard University Press, 2001.

Gunton, Colin E., Stephen R. Holmes and Murray A. Rae (eds), *The Practice of Theology: A Reader*, London: SCM Press, 2001.

Gutierrez, Gustavo, 'The Historical Project of the Poor', in Cornel West, Caridad Guidote and Margaret Coakley (eds), *Theology in the Americas: Detroit II Conference Papers*, Maryknoll, NY: Orbis Books, 1982, pp. 80–4.

—— 'Los Limites de la Teología Moderna: Un Texto de Bonhoeffer', in *La Fuerza Historica de los Pobres*, Lima: Centro de Estudios y Publicaciones, 1979, pp. 397–415.

—— *Praxis de Liberación y Fe Cristiana*, Madrid: Zero, 1974.

—— *Teología Desde el Reverso de la Historia*, Lima, Peru: Ed. CEP, 1977.

—— *A Theology of Liberation: History, Politics and Salvation*, Caridad Inda and John Eagleson, New York: Maryknoll, 1985.

—— 'Two Theological Perspectives: Liberation Theology and Progressivist Theology', in Sergio Torres and Virginia Fabella (eds), *The Emergent Gospel: Theology from the Underside of History*, Maryknoll, NY: Orbis Books, 1978, pp. 227–58.

Habermas, Jürgen, *Between Facts and Norms*, Cambridge, MA: Massachusetts Institute of Technology Press, 1996.

—— *Lifeworld and System: A Critique of Functionalist Reason*, Vol. 2 of *The Theory of Communicative Action*, trans. Thomas McCarthy, Boston: Beacon Press, 1987.

—— *The Philosophical Discourse of Modernity: Twelve Lectures*, trans. Frederick Lawrence, Studies in Contemporary German Social Thought, Cambridge, Massachusetts: MIT Press, 1987.

—— *Reason and the Rationalization of Society*, Vol. 1 of *The Theory of Communicative Action*, trans. Thomas McCarthy, Boston: Beacon Press, 1984.

Hall, Stuart, 'New Ethnicities', in David Morley and Kuan-Hsing Chen (eds), *Stuart Hall: Critical Dialogues in Cultural Studies*, New York: Routledge, 1996, pp. 441–9.

Harris, Angela P., 'Foreword: The Jurisprudence of Reconstruction', *California Law Review* 82, no. 4 (July 1994), pp. 741–85.

Harris, Cheryl I., 'Critical Race Studies: An Introduction', *UCLA Law Review* 49, no. 5 (2002), pp. 1215–40.

—— 'Whiteness as Property', *Harvard Law Review* 106, no. 8 (June 1993), pp. 1707–91.

Hays, Sharon, *Flat Broke with Children: Women in the Age of Welfare Reform*, New York: Oxford University Press, 2003.

Herzog, Frederick, 'Birth Pangs: Liberation Theology in North America', in Gerald H. Anderson and Thomas F. Stransky (eds), *Liberation Theologies in North America and Europe*, New York: Paulist Press, 1979, pp. 25–36.

Hinkelammert, Franz, *Las Armas Ideológicas de la Muerte; el Discernimiento de los Fetiches: Capitalismo y Cristianismo*, Centroamerica: EDUCA, 1977.

—— 'Changes in the Relationships Between Third World and First World Countries', in K. C. Abraham and Bernadette Mbuy-Beya (eds), *Spirituality of the Third World*, Maryknoll, NY: Orbis, 1994.

—— *Critica a la Razón Utópica*, San José: DEI, 1990.

—— 'La Critica de la Religión en Nombre del Cristianismo: Dietrich Bonhoeffer', in *Teología Alemana y Teología Latinoamericana de la Liberación: Un Esfuerzo de Dialogo*, San José: DEI, 1990, pp. 45–66.

—— *Cultura de la Esperanza y Sociedad sin Exclusión*, San José, Costa Rica: DEI, 1995.

—— 'Determinación y Auto constitución del Sujeto: Las Leyes Que Se Imponen a Espaldas de los Actores y el Orden por el Desorden', *Pasos* 64 (March–April 1993), pp. 18–31.

—— *El Grito del Sujeto*, San José, Costa Rica: DEI, 1998.

—— *The Ideological Weapons of Death: A Theological Critique of Capitalism*, Maryknoll, NY: Orbis Books, 1986.

—— 'Liberation Theology in the Economic and Social Context of Latin America: Economy and Theology, or the Irrationality of the Rationalized', in David Batstone, Eduardo Mendieta, Lois Ann Lorenzten, and Dwight N. Hopkins (eds), *Liberation Theologies, Postmodernity, and the Americas*, New York: Routledge, 1997, pp. 25–52.

Hochschild, Jennifer L., *Facing Up to the American Dream: Race, Class, and the Soul of the Nation*, Princeton, NJ: Princeton University Press, 1995.

Hoogvelt, Ankie, *Globalization and the Postcolonial World: The New Political Economy of Development*, Baltimore: Johns Hopkins University Press, 1997.

Hopkins, Dwight N., 'Introduction', in Dwight N. Hopkins and George Cummings (eds), *Cut Loose Your Stammering Tongue: Black Theology in the Slave Narratives*, Maryknoll, NY: Orbis Books, 1991, pp. ix–xxiii.

—— 'The Religion of Globalization', in Dwight N. Hopkins, Lois Ann Lorentzen, Eduardo Mendieta, and David Batstone (eds), *Religions/Globalizations: Theories and Cases*, Durham, NC: Duke University Press, 2001, pp. 7–32.

—— (ed.), *Black Faith and Public Talk: Critical Essays on Jame's Cone's Black Theology and Black Power*, Maryknoll, NY: Orbis Books, 1999.

—— *Being Human: Race, Culture, and Religion*, Minneapolis: Fortress Press, 2005.

—— 'Black Theology and a Second Generation: New Scholarship and New Challenges', in James Cone and Gayraud Wilmore (eds), *Black Theology, A Documentary History: Volume II 1980–1992*, Maryknoll, NY: Orbis Books, 1993, pp. 61–75.

—— *Black Theology in the U.S.A. and South Africa: Politics, Culture, and Liberation*, Maryknoll, NY: Orbis Books, 1989.

—— *Down, Up, and Over: Slave Religion and Black Theology*, Minneapolis: Fortress Press, 2000.

—— *Heart and Head: Black Theology – Past, Present and Future*, New York: Palgrave, 2002.

—— *Introducing Black Theology of Liberation*, Maryknoll, NY: Orbis Books, 1999.

—— 'Postmodernity, Black Theology of Liberation and the USA: Michel Foucault and James H. Cone', in David Batstone, Eduardo Mendieta, Lois Ann Lorentzen, and Dwight Hopkins (eds), *Liberation Theologies, Postmodernity, and the Americas*, New York: Routledge, 1997, pp. 205–21.

—— *Shoes That Fit Our Feet: Sources for a Constructive Black Theology*, Maryknoll, NY: Orbis Books, 1993.

Hopkins, Dwight N. and George Cummings (eds), *Cut Loose Your Stammering Tongue: Black Theology in the Slave Narratives*, Maryknoll, NY: Orbis Books, 1991.

Hopkins, Dwight N. and Linda Thomas, 'Womanist Theology and Black Theology: Conversational Envisioning of an Unfinished Dream', in Eleazar Fernandez and Fernando Segovia (eds), *A Dream Unfinished: Theological Reflections on America from the Margins*, Maryknoll, NY: Orbis Books, 2001, pp. 72–86.

Human Development Report 1998, United Nations Development Programme, 1998.

Hutchinson, William R., and Hartmut Lehmann (eds), *Many Are Chosen: Divine Election and Western Nationalism*, Minneapolis: Fortress Press, 1994.

Iceland, John, *Poverty in America: A Handbook*, Berkeley: University of California Press, 2003.

Iriart, Celia, Howard Waitzkin and Emerson Merhy, 'HMO's Abroad: Managed Care in Latin America', in Meredith Fort, Mary Anne Mercer, and Oscar Gish (eds), *Sickness and Wealth: The Corporate Assault on Global Health*, Cambridge, MA: South End Press, 2004, pp. 69–78.

Isaak, Robert, *The Globalization Gap: How the Rich Get Richer and the Poor Get Left Further Behind*, New York: Prentice Hall, 2005.

Isasi-Diaz, Ada Maria, *En la Lucha: Elaborating a Mujerista Theology*, Minneapolis: Fortress Press, 1993.

—— *La Lucha Contiues: Mujerista Theology*, Maryknoll, NY: Orbis Books, 2004.

—— *Mujerista Theology: A Theology for the Twenty-First Century*, Maryknoll, NY: Orbis Books, 2002.

—— 'Preoccupations, Themes, and Proposals of Mujerista Theology', in Anthony B. Pinn and Benjamín Valentín (eds), *The Ties That Bind: African American and Hispanic/American/Latino/a Theologies in Dialogue*, New York: Continuum, 2001, pp. 135–44.

Isasi-Diaz, Ada Maria and Fernando F. Segovia (ed.), *Hispanic/Latino Theology: Challenge and Promise*, Minneapolis: Fortress Press, 1996.

Jawara, Fatoumata and Aileen Kwa, *Behind the Scenes at the WTO: The Real World of International Trade Negotiations*, New York, NY: Zed Books, 2003.

Jones, Kent, *Who's Afraid of the WTO?*, New York, NY: Oxford University Press, 2004.

Kapstein, Ethan, 'The New Global Slave Trade', *Foreign Affairs* 85, no. 6 (November/December 2006), pp. 103–16.

Katrak, Homi and Roger Strange (eds), *The WTO and Developing Countries*, New York, NY: Palgrave Macmillan, 2004.

Kaufman, Gordon, *In Face of Mystery: A Constructive Theology*, Cambridge: Harvard University Press, 1993.

Kee, Alistair, 'The Conservatism of Liberation Theology: Four Questions for Jon Sobrino', *Political Theology: The Journal of Christian Socialism* 3 (November 2000), pp. 30–43.

—— *The Rise and Demise of Black Theology*, Aldershot, England: Ashgate, 2006.

Kelman, Mark, *A Guide to Critical Legal Studies*, Cambridge, MA: Harvard University Press, 1987.

Kennedy, Duncan, *Sexy Dressing Etc.: Essays on the Power and Politics of Cultural Identity*, Cambridge, MA: Harvard University Press, 1993.

Keown, Damien, *Buddhism: A Very Short Introduction*, Oxford: Oxford University Press, 1996.

Kiely, Ray, *Sociology and Development: The Impasse and Beyond*, London: UCL Press Limited, 1995.

Kilty, Keith M. and Elizabeth A. Segal (eds), *Rediscovering the Other America: The Continuing Crisis of Poverty and Inequality in the United States*, New York: The Hawthorn Press, 2003.

Kim, Jim Yong, Joyce Millen, Alec Irwin and John Gershman (eds), *Dying for Growth: Global Inequality and the Health of the Poor*, Boston, MA: Common Courage Press, 2000.

Klein, Naomi, *Fences and Windows: Dispatches From the Front Lines of the Globalization Debate*, New York, NY: Picador USA, 2002.

—— *No Logo*, New York, NY: Picador USA, 2000.

Kloppenburg, Jack Ralph, *First the Seed: The Political Economy of Plant Biotechnology, 1492–2000*, New York, NY: Cambridge University Press, 1988.

Kornbluh, Felicia, *The Battle for Welfare Rights: Politics and Poverty in Modern America*, Philadelphia: University of Pennsylvania Press, 2007.

Korten, David C., *When Corporations Rule the World*, San Francisco, CA and Bloomfield, CO: Berrett-Koehler Publishers, Inc. and Kumarian Press, 2001.

Laclau, Ernesto and Chantal Mouffe, *Hegemony and Socialist Strategy: Towards a Radical Democratic Politics*, New York: Verso, 1985.

Lareau, Annette, *Unequal Childhoods: Class, Race, and Family Life*, Berkeley: University of California Press, 2003.

Levi, Primo, *The Drowned and the Saved*, New York: Random House, 1989.

List, Friedrich, *The National System of Political Economy*, New York, NY: Augustus Kelley, 1966.

Lorde, Audre, *Sister Outsider*, New York: Crossing Press, 1984.

Lui, Meizhu, Bárbara Robles, Betsy Leondar-Wright, Rose Brewer and Rebecca Adamson (eds), *The Color of Wealth: The Story Behind the U.S. Racial Wealth Divide*, New York: The New Press, 2006.

MacIntyre, Alasdair, *After Virtue: A Study in Moral Theory*, Notre Dame, Indiana: University of Notre Dame Press, 1981.
—— *Whose Justice? Whose Rationality?*, Notre Dame, Indiana: University of Notre Dame Press, 1988.
Maclean, Iain, *Opting for Democracy: Liberation Theology and the Struggle for Democracy in Brazil*, New York: Peter Lang, 1999.
Magnus, David, 'Intellectual Property and Agricultural Biotechnology: Bioprospecting or Biopiracy?', in David Magnus, Arthur Caplan, and Glenn McGee (eds), *Who Owns Life?*, Amherst, NY: Prometheus Books, 2002, pp. 265–76.
Maimela, Simon and Dwight Hopkins (eds), *We Are One Voice*, Cape Town: Skotaville Publishers, 1989.
Maldonado-Torres, Nelson, 'Liberation Theology and the Search for the Lost Paradigm: From Radical Orthodoxy to Radical Diversality', in Ivan Petrella (ed.), *Latin American Liberation Theology: The Next Generation*, Maryknoll, NY: Orbis Books, 2005, pp. 39–61.
Mangum, Garth L., Stephen L. Mangum and Andrew M. Sum, *The Persistence of Poverty in the United States*, Baltimore: The Johns Hopkins University Press, 2003.
Marx, Karl, *Capital*, Vol. 1, with an introduction by Ernest Mandel, trans. Ben Fowkes, The Marx Library, New York: Random House, Vintage, 1977.
—— *On Religion*, Vol. 5 of *The Karl Marx Library*, ed. and trans. Saul Padover, New York: McGraw-Hill, 1974.
—— *The Poverty of Philosophy*, New York: International Publishers, 1974.
Massey, Douglas S. and Nancy A. Denton, *American Apartheid: Segregation and the Making of the Underclass*, Cambridge, MA: Harvard University Press, 1993.
Mbembe, Achille, *On the Postcolony*, Berkeley: University of California Press, 2001.
McAfee Brown, Robert, 'A Preface and a Conclusion', in Sergio Torres and John Eagleson (eds), *Theology in the Americas*, Maryknoll, NY: Orbis Books, 1976, pp. ix–xxviii.
Mejido, Manuel, 'Beyond the Postmodern Condition, or the Turn Toward Psychoanalysis', in Ivan Petrella (ed.), *Latin American Liberation Theology: The Next Generation*, Maryknoll, NY: Orbis Books, 2005, pp. 119–46.
—— 'A Critique of the "Aesthetic Turn" in U.S. Hispanic Theology: A Dialogue with Roberto Goizueta and the Positing of a New Paradigm', *Journal of Hispanic/Latino Theology* 8, no. 3 (2001), pp. 18–48.
—— 'The Fundamental Problematic of U.S. Hispanic Theology', in Benjamín Valentín (ed.), *New Horizons in Hispanic/Latino(a) Theology*, Cleveland, OH: The Pilgrim Press, 2003, pp. 163–80.
—— 'Propaedeutic to the Critique of the Study of U.S. Hispanic Religion: A Polemic Against Intellectual Assimilation', *Journal of Hispanic/Latino Theology* 10, no. 2 (2002), pp. 31–63.

Michaels, Walter Benn, *The Trouble with Diversity: How We Learned to Love Identity and Ignore Inequality*, New York: Metropolitan Books, 2006.

Mitchem, Stephanie Y., *Introducing Womanist Theology*, Maryknoll, NY: Orbis Books, 2002.

Mohanty, Chandra Talpade, 'Cartographies of Struggle', in Chandra Talpade Mohanty, Anna Russo, and Lourdes Torres (eds), *Third World Women and the Politics of Feminism*, Indiana: Indiana University Press, 1991, pp. 3–5.

Moltmann, Jürgen, 'An Open Letter to Jose Miguez Bonino', in Alfred Hennelly (ed.), *Liberation Theology: A Documentary History*, Maryknoll, NY: Orbis Books, 1990, pp. 195–204.

Moran, Rachel F., 'Foreword – Demography and Distrust: The Latino Challenge to Civil Rights and Immigration Policy in the 1990s and Beyond', *La Raza Law Journal* 8, no. 1 (1995), pp. 1–24.

Morita, Akio, 'Toward a New World Economic Order', *Atlantic Monthly*, June 1993.

Nader, Laura, 'Up the Anthropologist – Perspectives Gained in Studying Up', in Dell Hymes (ed.), *Reinventing Anthropology*, New York: Pantheon Books, 1972, pp. 284–311.

Narlikar, Amrita, *The World Trade Organization: A Very Short Introduction*, New York, NY: Oxford University Press, 2005.

Natapoff, Alexandra, 'Trouble in Paradise: Equal Protection and the Dilemma of Interminority Group Conflict', *Stanford Law Review* 47, no. 5 (May 1995), pp. 1059–96.

Oliver, Melvin and Thomas Shapiro, *Black Wealth/White Wealth: A New Perspective on Racial Inequality*, New York: Routledge, 1995.

Omi, Michael and Howard Winant, *Racial Formation in the United States: From the 1960s to the 1980s*, New York: Routledge, 1986.

Padilla, Alvin, Roberto Goizueta and Eldin Villafane (eds), *Hispanic Christian Thought at the Dawn of the 21st Century: Apuntes in Honor of Justo L. Gonzalez*, Nashville: Abingdon Press, 2005.

Pedraja, Luis G., *Teología: An Introduction to Hispanic Theology*, Nashville, TN: Abingdon Press, 2003.

Peet, Richard and Elaine Hartwick, *Theories of Development*, New York: The Guilford Press, 1999.

Perea, Juan F., 'The Black/White Binary Paradigm of Race: The "Normal Science" of American Racial Thought', *La Raza Law Journal* 10 (Spring 1998), pp. 127–72.

Perkins, John, *Confessions of an Economic Hit Man*, San Francisco, CA: Berrett-Koehler Publishers, Inc., 2004.

Petrella, Ivan (ed.), *Latin American Liberation Theology: The Next Generation*, Maryknoll, NY: Orbis Books, 2005.

—— *The Future of Liberation Theology: An Argument and Manifesto*, London: SCM Press, 2006.

Pinn, Anthony and Benjamín Valentín (ed.), *The Ties That Bind: African American and Hispanic American/Latino/a Theologies in Dialogue*, New York: Continuum, 2001.

Prashad, Vijay, *The Darker Nations: A People's History of the Third World*, New York: The New Press, 2007.

―― *Everybody Was Kung Fu Fighting: Afro-Asian Connections and the Myth of Cultural Purity*, Boston: Beacon Press, 2001.

―― *The Karma of Brown Folk*, Minneapolis: University of Minnesota Press, 2000.

Quadagno, Jill, *One Nation Uninsured: Why the U.S. Has No National Health Insurance*, Oxford: Oxford University Press, 2005.

Rahner, Karl, *Foundations of Christian Faith: An Introduction to the Idea of Christianity*, trans. William V. Dych, New York: Seabury Press, Crossroads, 1978.

Rank, Mark Robert, *One Nation, Underprivileged: Why American Poverty Affects Us All*, Oxford: Oxford University Press, 2004.

Ratzinger, Joseph, 'Relación Sobre la Situación Actual de la Fe y la Teología', in *Fe y Teología en America Latina*, Santa Fe de Bogota, Colombia: CELAM, 1997, pp. 13–36.

Rawls, John, *Political Liberalism*, New York, NY: Columbia University Press, 2005.

―― *A Theory of Justice*, Cambridge, MA: Harvard University Press, 1971.

Richard, Pablo, 'Teología de la Solidaridad en el Contexto Actual de Economía Neoliberal de Mercado', in Franz Hinkelammert (ed.), *El Huracán de la Globalización*, San José, Costa Rica: DEI, 1999, pp. 223–38.

Richard, Pablo *et al.*, *The Idols of Death and the God of Life*, Maryknoll, New York: Orbis Books, 1983.

Riggs, Marcia Y., *Awake, Arise and Act: A Womanist Call for Black Liberation*, Cleveland, OH: The Pilgrim Press, 1994.

Roffe, Pedro, Geoff Tansey and David Vivas-Egui (eds), *Negotiating Health: Intellectual Property and Access to Medicines*, London: Earthscan, 2006.

Rorty, Richard, *Consequences of Pragmatism (Essays: 1972–1980)*, Minneapolis: University of Minnesota Press, 1982.

Rowland, Christopher (ed.), *The Cambridge Companion to Liberation Theology*, Cambridge: Cambridge University Press, 1999.

Sampson, Gary P., *The WTO and Sustainable Development*, New York, NY: United Nations University Press, 2005.

Sauvy, Alfred, 'Trois Mondes, Une Planété', *L'Observateur* 118 (14 August 1952).

Schweitzer, Albert, *The Quest of the Historical Jesus: A Critical Study of Its Progress from Reimarus to Wrede*, ed. James M. Robinson, trans. W. B. D. Montgomery, New York: Macmillan, 1968.

Seabrook, Jeremy, *The No-Nonsense Guide to World Poverty*, New York, NY: Verso, 2003.

Segundo, Juan Luis, *The Liberation of Theology*, Maryknoll: Orbis Books, 1985.

Sen, Amartya, *Development as Freedom*, New York: Knopf, 1999.

Sered, Susan Starr and Rushika Fernandopulle, *Uninsured in America: Life and Death in the Land of Opportunity*, Berkeley: University of California Press, 2005.

Shaffer, Ellen and Joseph Brenner, 'Trade and Health Care: Corporatizing Vital Human Services', in Meredith Fort, Mary Anne Mercer, and Oscar Gish (eds), *Sickness and Wealth: The Corporate Assault on Global Health*, Cambridge, MA: South End Press, 2004, pp. 79–94.

Shand, Hope, 'Gene Giants: Understanding the "Life Industry"', in Brian Tokar (ed.), *Redesigning Life? The Worldwide Challenge to Genetic Engineering*, New York, NY: Zed Books, 2001, pp. 222–37.

Sharma, Ursala, *Caste*, Philadelphia: Open University Press, 1999.

Shiva, Vandana, 'Biopiracy: The Theft of Knowledge and Resources', in Brian Tokar (ed.), *Redesigning Life? The Worldwide Challenge to Genetic Engineering*, New York, NY: Zed Books, 2001, pp. 40–4.

—— *Monocultures of the Mind: Perspectives on Biodiversity and Biotechnology*, New York: Zed Books, 1993.

—— *Protect or Plunder? Understanding Intellectual Property Rights*, New York: Zed Books, 2001.

—— *Tomorrow's Biodiversity*, New York, NY: Thames & Hudson, 2000.

—— *Water Wars: Privatization, Pollution, and Profit*, Cambridge, MA: South End Press, 2002.

Sidel, Ruth, *Keeping Women and Children Last: America's War on the Poor*, New York: Penguin, 1996.

Singer, Joseph William, 'Legal Realism Now', *California Law Review* 76 (1988), pp. 465–544.

Smith, Adam, *An Inquiry Into the Nature and Causes of the Wealth of Nations*, ed. and notes by Edwin Cannan, with an introduction by Edwin Cannan and Max Lerner, New York: Modern Library, 1937.

Smith, Christian, *The Emergence of Liberation Theology: Radical Religion and Social Movement Theory*, Chicago: The University of Chicago Press, 1991.

Steger, Manfred, *Globalism: The New Market Ideology*, Lanham, MD: Rowman & Littlefield, Inc., 2002.

Sung, Jung Mo, *Deseo, Mercado y Religión*, Santander: Editorial Sal Terrae, 1999.

—— *Economía: Tema Ausente en la Teología de la Liberación*, San José, Costa Rica: DEI, 1994.

—— *La Idolatría del Capital y la Muerte de los Pobres*, San José, Costa Rica: DEI, 1991.

—— *Neoliberalismo y Pobreza*, San José, Costa Rica: DEI, 1993.

Susin, Luiz Carlos and Maria Pilar Aquino (ed.), *Reconciliation in a World of Conflicts*, London: SCM Press, 2003.

Sutcliffe, Bob, *100 Ways of Seeing an Unequal World*, New York: Zed Books, 2001.

Sweezy, Paul M., *Post-Revolutionary Society*, New York: Monthly Review Press, 1980.

Tabb, William, *Unequal Partners: A Primer on Globalization*, New York: The New Press, 2002.

Taylor, Charles, *The Ethics of Authenticity*, Cambridge, MA: Harvard University Press, 1992.

——*Sources of the Self: The Making of Modern Identity*, Cambridge, MA: Harvard University Press, 1989.

Thomas, Linda E., 'Womanist Theology, Epistemology, and a New Anthropological Paradigm', in Linda E. Thomas (ed.), *Living Stones in the Household of God: The Legacy and Future of Black Theology*, Minneapolis: Fortress Press, 2004, pp. 37–48.

Tirres, Christopher D., '"Liberation" in the Latino(a) Context: Retrospect and Prospect', in Benjamín Valentín (ed.), *New Horizons in Hispanic/Latino(a) Theology*, Cleveland, OH: The Pilgrim Press, 2003, pp. 138–62.

Tokar, Brian (ed.), *Redesigning Life? The Worldwide Challenge to Genetic Engineering*, New York, NY: Zed Books, 2001.

Torres, Sergio and John Eagleson (eds), *Theology in the Americas*, Maryknoll, NY: Orbis Books, 1976.

Townes, Emilie M. (ed.), *A Troubling in My Soul: Womanist Perspectives on Evil and Suffering*, Maryknoll, NY: Orbis Books, 2002.

——*In a Blaze of Glory: Womanist Spirituality as Social Witness*, Nashville: Abingdon Press, 1995.

——'Living in the New Jerusalem: The Rhetoric and Movement of Liberation in the House of Evil', in Emilie M. Townes (ed.), *A Troubling in My Soul: Womanist Perspectives on Evil and Suffering*, Maryknoll, NY: Orbis Books, 2002, pp. 78–91.

——'On Keeping Faith with the Center', in Linda E. Thomas (ed.), *Living Stones in the Household of God: The Legacy and Future of Black Theology*, Minneapolis: Fortress Press, 2004, pp. 189–202.

——*Womanist Ethics and the Cultural Production of Evil*, New York: Palgrave Macmillan, 2006.

——'Womanist Theology', *Union Seminary Quarterly Review* 57, no. 3–4 (2003), pp. 159–75.

Tucker, Robert (ed.), *The Marx-Engels Reader*, New York, NY: W.W. Norton & Company, 1978.

Tushnet, Mark, 'Critical Legal Studies: A Political History', *Yale Law Journal* 100, no. 1515 (1991).

Tuveson, Ernest Lee, *Redeemer Nation: The Idea of America's Millennial Role*, Chicago: University of Chicago Press, 1968.

Unger, Roberto Mangabeira, *The Critical Legal Studies Movement*, Cambridge: Harvard University Press, 1983.

——*What Should Legal Analysis Become?* New York: Verso, 1996.

Valentín, Benjamín (ed.), *New Horizons in Hispanic/Latino(a) Theology*, Cleveland, OH: The Pilgrim Press, 2003.

——*Mapping Public Theology: Beyond Culture, Identity, and Difference*, Harrisburg, PA: Trinity Press International, 2002.

——'Nuevos Odres para el Vino: A Critical Contribution to Latino/a Theological Construction', *Journal of Hispanic/Latino Theology* 5, no. 4 (1998), pp. 30–47.

—— '¿Oye, Y Ahora Que?/Say, Now What? Prospective Lines of Development for U.S. Hispanic/Latino(a) Theology', in Benjamín Valentín (ed.), *New Horizons in Hispanic/Latino(a) Theology*, Cleveland, OH: The Pilgrim Press, 2003, pp. 101–18.

Wade, Robert, *Governing the Market: Economic Theory and the Role of Government in East Asian Industrialization*, Princeton, NJ: Princeton University Press, 1990.

—— 'What Strategies Are Viable for Developing Countries Today? The World Trade Organization and the Shrinking of "Development Space"', in Kevin P. Gallagher (ed.), *Putting Development First: The Importance of Policy Space in the WTO and International Financial Institutions*, New York, NY: Zed Books, 2005, pp. 80–101.

Walzer, Michael, *Spheres of Justice: A Defense of Pluralism and Equality*, New York, NY: Basic Books, 1983.

Weber, Max, *The Protestant Ethic and the Spirit of Capitalism*, trans. Talcott Parsons, with a foreword by R. H. Tawney, New York: Scribner's, 1958.

West, Cornel, 'Black Theology and Marxist Thought', in James Cone and Gayraud Wilmore (eds), *Black Theology: A Documentary History, Vol. I 1966–1979*, Maryknoll, NY: Orbis Books, 1993, pp. 409–24.

—— 'On Liberation Theology: Segundo and Hinkelammert', in Cornel West (ed.), *The Cornel West Reader*, New York: Basic Books, 1999, pp. 393–400.

—— 'Present Socio-Political-Economic Movements for Change', in Simon S. Maimela and Dwight H. Hopkins (eds), *We Are One Voice*, Cape Town: Skotaville Publishers, 1989, pp. 73–86.

—— *Race Matters*, New York: Vintage, 1994.

West, Cornel, Caridad Guidote and Margaret Coakley (eds), *Theology in the Americas: Detroit II Conference Papers*, Maryknoll, NY: Orbis Books, 1982.

West, Traci C., *Disruptive Christian Ethics: When Racism and Women's Lives Matter*, Louisville: Westminster John Knox Press, 2006.

Wilkinson, Richard, *Unhealthy Societies: The Afflictions of Inequality*, New York: Routledge, 1996.

Williams, Delores, *Sisters in the Wilderness: The Challenge of Womanist God-Talk*, Maryknoll, NY: Orbis Books, 1993.

—— 'Womanist/Feminist Dialogue', *Journal of Feminist Studies in Religion* 9, no. 2 (Spring–Fall 1993), pp. 67–73.

Wilmore, Gayraud S., 'Black Consciousness: Stumbling Block or Battering Ram?', in Joerg Rieger (ed.), *Liberating the Future: God, Mammon and Theology*, Minneapolis: Fortress Press, 1998, pp. 81–95.

—— *Black Religion and Black Radicalism: An Interpretation of the Religious History of Afro-American People*, Maryknoll, NY: Orbis Books, 1983.

—— 'Black Theology at the Turn of the Century: Some Unmet Needs and Challenges', in Dwight H. Hopkins (ed.), *Black Faith and Public Talk: Critical Essays on James H. Cone's Black Theology and Black Power*, Maryknoll, NY: Orbis Books, 1999, pp. 232–45.

—— 'Black Theology: Review and Assessment', *Voices From the Third World* 5, no. 2 (1982), pp. 3–16.

—— 'A Revolution Unfulfilled, but not Invalidated', in James Cone, *A Black Theology of Liberation: Twentieth Edition*, Maryknoll, NY: Orbis Books, 1986, pp. 145–63.

—— 'Black Theology: Its Significance for Christian Mission Today', *International Review of Mission* 63 (April 1974), pp. 211–31.

—— 'Reinterpretation in Black Church History', *The Chicago Theological Seminary Register* LXXIII, no. 1 (Winter 1983), pp. 25–37.

—— 'The Vocation of the Black Church', in William K. Tabb (ed.), *Churches in Struggle: Liberation Theologies and Social Change in North America*, New York: Monthly Review Press, 1986, pp. 240–53.

Wilson, Kimberly A., 'Exclusive Patents, Enclosure and the Patenting of Life', in Brian Tokar (ed.), *Redesigning Life? The Worldwide Challenge to Genetic Engineering*, New York, NY: Zed Books, 2001, pp. 290–96.

Wilson, William Julius, *The Bridge Over the Racial Divide: Rising Inequality and Coalitional Politics*, Berkeley: University of California Press, 1999.

—— *The Declining Significance of Race: Blacks and Changing American Institutions*, Chicago: University of Chicago Press, 1979.

—— *The Truly Disadvantaged: The Inner City, the Underclass, and Public Policy*, Chicago: University of Chicago Press, 1987.

—— *When Work Disappears: The World of the New Urban Poor*, New York: Vintage, 1997.

Wolff, Edward N., *Top Heavy: The Increasing Inequality of Wealth in America and What Can Be Done About It*, New York: The New Press, 2002.

Wood, Ellen M., *Democracy Against Capitalism: Renewing Historical Materialism*, New York: Cambridge University Press, 1995.

World Bank, *The Burden of Disease Among the Global Poor: Current Situation, Future Trends, and Implications for Strategy*, Washington, DC: World Bank, 2000.

Index of Names and Subjects